GREAT JOBS
IN THE PRESIDENT'S STIMULUS PLAN

LAURENCE SHATKIN, PH.D.

America's Career Publisher

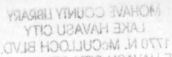

Great Jobs in the President's Stimulus Plan

© 2009 by JIST Publishing

Published by JIST Works, an imprint of JIST Publishing

7321 Shadeland Station, Suite 200

Indianapolis, IN 46256-3923

Phone: 800-648-JIST   Fax: 877-454-7839

E-mail: info@jist.com   Web site: www.jist.com

Some Other Books by the Author

150 Best Recession-Proof Jobs

10 Best College Majors for Your Personality

50 Best Jobs for Your Personality

90-Minute College Major Matcher

Visit www.jist.com for information on JIST, free job search information, tables of contents and sample pages, and ordering information on our many products.

Quantity discounts are available for JIST products. Have future editions of JIST books automatically delivered to you on publication through our convenient standing order program. Please call 800-648-JIST or visit www.jist.com for a free catalog and more information.

Acquisitions Editor: Susan Pines

Development Editor: Stephanie Koutek

Cover Designer: Honeymoon Image & Design, Inc.

Interior Designer: Toi Davis

Cover Image: © Brooks Kraft/Corbis

Interior Layout: Toi Davis

Proofreader: Jeanne Clark

Indexer: Jeanne Clark

Printed in the United States of America

14 13 12 11 10 09   9 8 7 6 5 4 3 2 1

Library of Congress Cataloging-in-Publication data is on file with the Library of Congress.

ISBN 978-1-59357-728-5

LEARN WHAT THE RECOVERY PLAN MEANS FOR YOUR CAREER

President Obama and his transition team have designed a stimulus package to boost the U.S. economy and create many job opportunities for a recession-weary nation. Why not a great job for you?

This book analyzes the initiatives that Obama developed during his presidential campaign and put into his recovery plan to help five key sectors of the economy: energy, infrastructure, health care, education, and manufacturing. You'll read about 11 major industries and more than 100 occupations that are most likely to benefit from the Obama plan.

For each sector of the economy in the stimulus package, you'll see the problems it currently faces, the policies and programs that Obama has been championing, the industries that the plan targets, and the jobs linked to the industry. You'll find descriptions of promising jobs in the mainstream of the industry, including facts about their work tasks, earnings, and long-term employment outlook. You'll also see the names of supporting jobs in the industry.

Finally, you'll learn job-finding techniques that are much more productive than help-wanted ads or Web-based job-matching sites. These are tips you can use no matter whether the economy is still trending downward or has begun bouncing back.

Some Things You Can Do with This Book

- Identify jobs that are more likely to offer hiring opportunities as the recovery package takes effect.

- Understand the connections between Obama's large economic goals and the specific industries that his plan will impact—and that may hold a job for you.

- Decide on a specific focus within a job that will take advantage of the long-term trends being shaped by the Obama plan (for example, toward clean energy or expanded early-childhood education).

- Learn how to find jobs when the want-ad listings are slim, using proven techniques developed by the experts.

Credits and Acknowledgments: While the author created this book, it is based on the work of many others. The occupational information is based on data obtained from the U.S. Department of Labor and the U.S. Census Bureau. These sources provide the most authoritative occupational information available. Some of the noneconomic job-related information is derived from the *Occupational Outlook Handbook,* 2008–2009 Edition, and the *Career Guide to Industries,* 2008–2009 Edition, both published by the U.S. Department of Labor. Other noneconomic job-related information is derived from the O*NET database, which was developed by researchers and developers under the direction of the U.S. Department of Labor. They, in turn, were assisted by thousands of employers who provided details on the nature of work in the many thousands of job samplings used in the database's development. The version of the O*NET database used for this book was the most recent, release 13. The staff of the U.S. Department of Labor deserve thanks and praise for their efforts and expertise in providing such rich sources of data. The details of the Obama recovery package were obtained from "The Job Impact of the American Recovery and Reinvestment Plan," by Christina Romer and Jared Bernstein, advisors to the Obama transition team, published January 9, 2009.

TABLE OF CONTENTS

INTRODUCTION

When Barack Obama was sworn in on January 20, 2009, he became president in the midst of America's worst economic crisis since the Great Depression. Every month of the previous year saw more jobs lost than created, for a net loss of more than 2.5 million jobs. In December of 2008, 11.1 million Americans were out of work and looking for jobs. Probably another 10 million had given up looking for work or were working part-time, either because they couldn't find full-time jobs or because their work hours had been cut. Even worse, the economy was showing no signs that it had yet hit bottom.

In response to these alarming trends, the Obama transition team put together a package of policies and priorities called the American Recovery and Reinvestment Plan—often referred to as the Obama economic stimulus plan. The plan is intended to create 3 to 4 million jobs by the end of 2010.

This book is about many of the industries and jobs that are expected to get the greatest boost from the Obama stimulus package.

Why You Need This Book

Every president comes into office with his own priorities: intended policies and programs that reflect his vision of what America can be and should do now. Barack Obama's priorities break from the past with particular force and are expected to have great impact on career options over the next several years. You need to know about these priorities and their expected effects, and that goes beyond just being informed about current events.

In the long run, the Obama initiatives are likely to make some occupations obsolete and cause new occupations to emerge. But even in the short run, we can expect Obama's priorities to boost the demand for workers in existing jobs in **energy, infrastructure, health care, education, manufacturing,** and several other industries. You need to know about Obama's plans for these high-priority fields so you can identify possible job opportunities.

One of the most important tasks that Obama has taken on is leading the nation out of a recession. Ten days before his swearing-in, he remarked, "Our first job is to put people back to work and get our economy working again." The economic slowdown that began in early 2008 has caused job losses in nearly every industry and region of the United States, but Obama's

economic advisors hope that the economy can start to trend upward again
before 2009 is over.

It's important to understand that the Obama team wants the coming upswing
to be different from the "jobless recovery" that followed the 2001 recession,
in which businesses increased their profits without taking on many additional
workers. Instead, as our country emerges from our current recession, we are
expected to experience an era with many opportunities for employment. You
need to be aware of the fields and jobs that are likely to grow and create a
rewarding career for you.

Many people like the idea of working in a dynamic field—one that is growing, that will improve the lives of Americans and maybe the health of the
planet, and where new ideas and technologies are emerging. That's another
reason why you need to understand the Obama priorities and what parts of
the economy they will affect. This book can inform you about occupations—
some fairly new, some that have been around for decades or even centuries—
that will be at the center of exciting developments in the coming years.

How to Use This Book

Different readers will use this book in different ways. Maybe one of these
ways fits your needs:

- If you're interested in a specific field targeted for economic stimulus
  (for example, energy), you may want to read about the promising jobs
  related to that field. Turn to the chapter for the field and browse the
  industries and jobs listed there. Because the initiatives in the stimulus
  package sometimes target multiple fields, you may note suggestions to
  read other chapters.

- If you have a particular job in mind for your career, see whether it's
  listed in the index. If so, find the chapter that describes the job and
  read about the Obama initiative that is expected to affect the job
  and the industry to which the job is linked. Also read chapter 1 to
  see how Obama's policies regarding the industry have developed and
  taken shape. You may get ideas for specializations within the occupation that are likely to produce job openings.

- If you're interested in a job that's *not* described in depth in this book,
  the job title still may be listed in one of the chapters about industries.
  Many of these listed jobs offer opportunities to play a supporting
  role within the industry. For example, you might want to work as an
  accountant in the infrastructure industry or as a receptionist in the
  energy industry. Read the chapters about the industries that appeal

most to you. Perhaps you can imagine a supporting role for yourself in still another occupation that is not listed in the book.

- You may be completely undecided about your career-related interests. In that case, you'll find it useful to browse through the book, reading about the Obama initiatives and their related industries and jobs. Some industries and jobs may intrigue you and lead you to explore them further.

Where the Information Comes From

The U.S. Department of Labor provided the information for describing the jobs in this book. Its O*NET database includes information on 950 occupations and is now the primary source of detailed information on occupations. This source provided the facts for the definitions, work tasks, and work conditions. The Labor Department updates the O*NET on a regular basis, and this book uses the most recent one available: release 13.

Information about earnings, growth, and number of openings is not included in the O*NET, but it is obtainable from sources at the U.S. Department of Labor's Bureau of Labor Statistics (BLS). The Occupational Employment Statistics survey provided the most reliable available figures on earnings, and the Employment Projections program provided the nation's best figures on job growth and openings. These two BLS programs use a slightly different system of job titles than the O*NET does, but the BLS data can readily be linked to the equivalent O*NET job titles used in this book.

A third source of information obtained from the U.S. Department of Labor was the *Occupational Outlook Handbook*, 2008–2009 edition. For each occupation described in this book, the *OOH* provided the short statement that precedes the definition of the occupation. Usually this statement concerns the outlook for the job or the best way to prepare for it.

One more Labor Department source was the *Career Guide to Industries*, 2008–2009 edition, which supplied the descriptions of industries that you'll find in chapters 2 through 7. It also suggested which occupations should be linked to each industry.

As you read chapter 1, you'll find many references to the transition team's plan, including numerical figures on how many jobs are intended to be created by each stimulus initiative and within each targeted industry. The source of these figures is a document called "The Job Impact of the American Recovery and Reinvestment Plan," by Christina Romer and Jared Bernstein, economic advisors to the Obama transition team, published January 9, 2009.

You'll also find many quotes from documents released by the Obama presidential campaign, policy statements published by the transition team, and news stories covering the campaign and transition. You won't find references to any news stories or documents released after Obama was sworn in, because this book was completed hours before that historic moment.

Obama's Plans versus Congress's Implementations

As president, Obama almost certainly will not be able to implement his plan exactly as he and the transition team have designed it. The expenditures that the plan requires must first be approved by Congress, and that will probably involve compromises to gain the support of senators and representatives with diverse ideological and regional interests.

Nevertheless, President Obama has many advantages that will help him to enact a stimulus package reasonably similar to what he and his transition team have proposed. His party has a majority of seats in both houses of Congress. In the Senate, the Democrats hold enough seats to avoid procedural delays to a vote, provided they can rally a handful of Republicans to their side. In the House (which tends to be more ideologically polarized), Republicans have already expressed unhappiness with some aspects of the plan. However, in that legislative body, the minority party has fewer procedural tools for thwarting the will of the majority. Obama is enjoying the "honeymoon" season that all new presidents experience, and in his case the public's approval is unusually high. On the eve of his inauguration, around 8 in 10 Americans approved of him, a much higher rating than Bill Clinton or George W. Bush received at the same time in their transitions. Finally, polls and anecdotal evidence show that Americans now have great anxiety about the economy, a sense of urgency, and a willingness for change. In a *Wall Street Journal*/NBC News poll published on January 15, 2009, 43 percent of people surveyed called the Obama stimulus plan a "good idea," while 27 percent said it is a "bad idea." One question asked whether Republicans in Congress should do everything to stand firm for their party's principles and oppose the legislation or look to compromise with the Obama administration. In response, 68 percent of the Republicans and independents chose compromise, while only 20 percent advocated standing firm.

Therefore, we can expect that the general outlines of the Obama plan will become actual policy, and this book is based on that expectation. As you read the book, keep in mind that some unforeseen political crisis, such as a terrorist attack on the scale of 9/11, could change national priorities and result in different outcomes from those planned by the Obama transition team.

How the Jobs Were Selected

The Department of Labor's *Career Guide to Industries* lists the most important occupations for each industry, and this source guided decisions about which jobs are named and described in chapters 2 through 7. Jobs that are in the mainstream of an industry's business and that have a reasonably good outlook are described in detail. For many of the industries, so many occupations met this standard that it was necessary to highlight only a subset, chosen to represent several different levels of education. The jobs for which there was no room are named in the listing of other related jobs for the industry, along with jobs that serve an administrative role (for example, general and operations managers in several industries) or a supportive role (for example, cooks and bus drivers in the education industries). In some cases, an occupation that is merely named in the section about one industry is described in the section about another industry. Notes alert you to such instances and tell you which chapter has the full description.

Facts for Each Job

The job descriptions in chapters 2 through 7 feature these topics of information:

- **Title:** This is the name used in the O*NET database.

- **Level of Education/Training:** This tells you the most common education, training, or work experience requirement for entering the job. Keep in mind that employers differ in what kind of preparation they expect, and sometimes a combination of less-than-typical education and more-than-typical work experience (or vice versa) is acceptable.

- **Annual Earnings:** This figure is the median earnings for May 2007. See the explanation in the following section.

- **Growth** and **Annual Job Openings:** These figures are averages that apply to the period between 2006 and 2016. During a recession, opportunities are likely to be lower than average.

- **Personality Type:** The O*NET database assigns each job to its most closely related type in the Holland (RIASEC) classification of work-related personality types. The terms, which may be unfamiliar to you, are explained in the following section.

- **Introductory Statement:** This brief highlighted statement gives you an idea of what to expect if you seek this job. Usually it concerns the best employment prospects or the type of educational background that is expected.

- **Definition** and **Work Tasks:** The definition (in boldface) is followed by the most important work tasks according to current workers. Where necessary, the list of tasks is edited to keep it from exceeding 2,200 characters.

- **Work Conditions:** The list includes any work condition with a rating that exceeds the midpoint of the rating scale in the O*NET database. The order does not indicate any condition's frequency on the job. Consider whether you like these conditions and whether any of these conditions would make you uncomfortable. Keep in mind that when hazards are present (for example, contaminants), protective equipment and procedures are provided to keep you safe.

Understanding the Data

Information in a database format can be boring or even confusing, so this book attempts to make the facts about jobs easy to digest. Nevertheless, some of the formats for the facts may be unfamiliar to you or you may wonder how they were derived. If so, read on.

The earnings and outlook data came from the U.S. Department of Labor's Bureau of Labor Statistics (BLS). As you look at the figures, keep in mind that they are estimates. They give you a general idea about the annual earnings, rate of job growth, and annual job openings. The yearly earnings information in this book is based on highly reliable data obtained from a very large U.S. working population sample by the BLS. It tells us the average annual pay received as of May 2007 by people in various job titles (actually, it is the median annual pay, which means that half earned more and half less). Earnings may vary because of the educational or training background of the worker, number of years in the job, region of the country, size of employer, presence or absence of a union, and many other factors. The recession may also affect wages.

The figures for job growth and number of openings are 10-year projections by BLS economists—their best guesses about what we can expect between 2006 and 2016. These estimates are not meant to project what will happen in just one or two years. Use these projections when thinking about the *longer*-term outlook for an occupation. For example, if an occupation is projected to have 10 percent growth, remember that the figure is a 10-year average. The occupation may grow at only 5 percent during the slow year of 2009 but come roaring back at 15 percent growth in 2011. The BLS economists assume that any recessions that occur during the decade covered by these projections will be reasonably similar to those we have experienced in recent decades—and the Obama team is doing all they can to obtain that outcome. If, despite their best efforts, this downturn becomes another Great Depression, the BLS projections will not be valid.

Perhaps you're wondering why the book presents figures on both job growth *and* number of openings. Aren't these two ways of saying the same thing? Actually, you need to know both. Consider the occupation Environmental Engineering Technicians, which is projected to grow at the impressive rate of 24.8 percent. There should be lots of opportunities in such a fast-growing job, right? Not exactly. This is a small occupation, with only about 21,100 people currently employed. So, even though it is growing rapidly, it will not create many new jobs (about 2,100 per year). Now consider Team Assemblers. At the rate of 0.1 percent, this occupation is hardly growing at all. Nevertheless, this is a huge occupation that employs almost 1.3 million workers. So, even though its growth rate is unimpressive, it is expected to take on about 260,000 new workers each year as existing workers retire, die, or move on to other jobs. That's why this book reports both of these economic indicators for each job and why you should pay attention to both.

Finally, don't forget that the job market consists of both job openings and job *seekers*. The figures on job growth and openings don't tell you how many people will be competing with you to be hired. Unfortunately, the BLS does not publish figures on the supply of job candidates, so this book can't tell you exactly what level of competition you can expect. However, for many jobs you will find a brief statement that indicates where job opportunities will be best, based partly on what competition is likely. You can research this issue further by consulting the *Occupational Outlook Handbook*. You also should speak to people who educate or train tomorrow's workers; they probably have a good idea of how many graduates find rewarding employment and how quickly. People in the workforce can provide insights into this issue as well. Use your critical thinking skills to evaluate what people tell you. For example, educators or trainers may be trying to recruit you, whereas people in the workforce may be trying to discourage you from competing. Get a variety of opinions to balance out possible biases.

The personality types used in the job descriptions are based on an system of classifying interests that was developed by John L. Holland and is used in the *Self-Directed Search (SDS)* and other career assessments and information systems. If you have used one of these career inventories or systems, the lists will help you identify jobs that most closely match these personality types. Even if you haven't used one of these systems, the concept of personality types and the jobs related to them can help you identify jobs that suit the type of person you are.

Following are brief descriptions for each of the six personality types.

- **Realistic:** These occupations frequently involve work activities that include practical, hands-on problems and solutions. They often deal with plants; animals; and real-world materials such as wood, tools, and machinery. Many of the occupations require working outside and don't involve a lot of paperwork or working closely with others.

- **Investigative:** These occupations frequently involve working with ideas and require an extensive amount of thinking. These occupations can involve searching for facts and figuring out problems mentally.

- **Artistic:** These occupations frequently involve working with forms, designs, and patterns. They often require self-expression, and the work can be done without following a clear set of rules.

- **Social:** These occupations frequently involve working with, communicating with, and teaching people. These occupations often involve helping or providing service to others.

- **Enterprising:** These occupations frequently involve starting up and carrying out projects. These occupations can involve leading people and making many decisions. They sometimes require risk taking and often deal with business.

- **Conventional:** These occupations frequently involve following set procedures and routines. These occupations can include working with data and details more than with ideas. Usually there is a clear line of authority to follow.

As you can see, the job descriptions show you what the work is like from several different angles. Keep in mind, however, that no description on the printed page is complete enough to serve as the sole basis for a career decision. Be sure to explore occupations in greater depth, especially by getting firsthand experiences, and note the suggestions in chapter 8 about focusing on your career goal.

CHAPTER 1

THE OBAMA PLAN FOR RECOVERY

T his chapter outlines the Obama stimulus plan and identifies the particular sectors of the economy that the plan targets. As you read the following description of the stimulus package, keep in mind what this book's introduction said about how the plan needs to be approved by Congress and therefore may not be implemented exactly as designed.

The Outlines of the Plan

The Obama plan has these main purposes related to jobs:

- To save or create at least 3 million jobs by the end of 2010

- To move many part-time workers to full-time employment

- To create jobs paying a range of wages, not just low- or high-paying jobs

- To encourage growth in sectors of the economy that serve long-range national goals important to Obama, such as security, health, and competitiveness

The Obama plan does not try to accomplish these goals by hiring a large number of people to work for the federal government. In fact, of the jobs to be created or saved by the Obama plan, more than 90 percent are expected to be in the private sector. And of the remaining 10 percent, a large number will probably be jobs in state and local governments that will be saved from budget cuts.

As noted in the last bullet point, the plan is designed to boost certain national priorities: the same priorities that Obama emphasized in his presidential campaign. The next sections of this chapter each discuss one sector of the economy—a field that will benefit from the stimulus package and thus support Obama's priorities. You'll see why each field needs support, how many jobs the Obama team intends to create or save, and what it's like to work in the field. The following chapters discuss the jobs within each field.

Energy

The field of energy is critical for America's economic future. Reliable and affordable sources of energy are needed to heat and cool our homes, workplaces, and commercial buildings; power our manufacturing plants; and propel our vehicles.

Current State of the Field

We are the world's largest energy consumer, but we do not produce enough energy to meet our needs. The shortfall of oil is especially noteworthy, with domestic consumption of about 21 million barrels per day (and increasing 2 percent per year) but production of only about 6 million barrels per day. Oil accounts for 40 percent of our energy consumption and for some uses, especially for fueling automobiles, we are heavily committed to technologies that depend on oil and that are not easily convertible to other energy sources.

Our need for massive imports of oil not only drains dollars out of our economy, it requires us to send those dollars to countries that don't share our values and are opposed to our national interests. Some of these dollars are thought to be finding their way to militant groups that are actively plotting to harm us. Our security is also threatened by the possibility of an oil embargo, as happened in 1967 and again in 1973. Our experience in the summer of 2008 with $4-per-gallon gasoline shows that, even without an embargo, our economy can suffer from price fluctuations on the world oil market. Finally, our dependence on Middle Eastern oil requires us to pay still another price, the cost of maintaining a large military presence in that part of the world and even getting entangled in wars.

It is possible for the U.S. to increase domestic oil production to a certain extent, and this course of action was championed by John McCain and his presidential campaign. (You may remember the slogan "Drill, baby, drill!") Democrats countered that new domestic oil and gas fields would take many years to come online and at best would serve only a tiny fraction of our energy needs while exacting a high price in environmental degradation of Alaska's wilderness and our coastal waters.

Another problem with oil, no matter where it comes from, is that burning it produces carbon dioxide, which contributes to global climate change. Although it is theoretically possible to inject carbon dioxide fumes deep into the earth or encourage deep-water algae blooms that will soak up the gas from the air, these technologies have not yet been demonstrated, and many scientists and engineers doubt that they will ever be feasible. Carbon dioxide release is also a problem (though less so) with natural gas, some of which is imported and which accounts for 23 percent of our energy consumption, and especially with coal, which also provides 23 percent of our energy. We have ample domestic coal reserves, but coal mining is hazardous to workers and often to the environment. Besides carbon dioxide, coal burning releases mercury into the air, and the ash left over contains toxic heavy metals that can pollute the water supply, as happened recently in the Tennessee ash spill.

Hydroelectric power produces no carbon dioxide and has comparatively few bad effects on the environment, all of them local rather than global, but it accounts for less than 3 percent of our energy and offers few opportunities for increased production. Nuclear power provides 8 percent of our energy and also does not contribute to global climate change, but no new nuclear plants have come online for many years because of public anxiety about reactor safety and because of political difficulties in creating a permanent nuclear waste storage facility.

Corn ethanol has achieved some support as an alternative form of automobile fuel, mostly because it requires only minor changes to automobile and gas-pump technology, can be produced in the U.S., and (perhaps most important) has great political support from the powerful agriculture industry and the states where that industry is clustered. But as a fuel it does not reduce carbon emissions. Growing and processing the corn requires expensive and environmentally destructive inputs of fertilizer, pesticides, and energy, and diversion of a food crop into fuel production probably raises the price of food. So its benefits overall are questionable at best.

One more factor in the energy equation is conservation. If we use energy more efficiently, we do not need to produce or import as much. Although Dick Cheney was right in saying in 2001 that conservation "is not a sufficient basis for a sound, comprehensive energy policy," it certainly is a crucial component of such a policy and was greatly neglected during the Bush years.

Plans for Energy-Related Jobs in the Obama Campaign and Stimulus Package

Our energy crisis is not a recent development. As the candidate Obama observed in a speech he gave in Portsmouth, New Hampshire, in October of 2007, "We have heard promises about energy independence from every single U.S. president since Richard Nixon—Republicans and Democrats. We've heard proposals to curb our use of fossil fuels in nearly every State of the Union address since the oil embargo of 1973." But now, he argued, it's time to make good on these promises, and he proposed a 35 percent cut in oil imports (10 million barrels per day) by 2030. He said he planned "to invest $150 billion over the next decade to ensure the development and deployment of clean, affordable energy."

It's important to remember that as a senator for Illinois, Obama represented a state with a large output of corn. In October 2007, he was also only a few months away from the caucuses in Iowa, one of the most important stepping-stones to the White House and a bastion of support for corn ethanol. Therefore, it is not surprising that the energy plan he proposed included ethanol and (in a later policy statement) a tax credit for gas stations that upgrade their pumps to handle ethanol fuel. However, he noted that corn ethanol "is neither the perfect nor the permanent answer to our energy challenge" and advocated developing biofuels from nonfood sources such as wood chips and switchgrass.

Illinois also produces a significant amount of coal, and Obama said there's no use "pretending that our nation's most abundant energy source will just go away. It won't." Nevertheless, he said, "We must invest in clean coal technologies that we can use at home and share with the world" so that other coal-burning countries, especially China, will cut back on their emissions. In the short run, he committed to imposing a cap on carbon emissions. But his long-range plan was a "Clean Technologies Venture Capital Fund that will provide $10 billion a year for five years to get the most promising clean energy technologies off the ground." He also intended to expand the cap on carbon to reduce greenhouse gas emissions by 80 percent by 2050.

Part of Obama's message was the need for energy conservation. He set the goal of making America 50 percent more energy efficient by 2030, and to achieve that end, he mentioned "dramatically improving the efficiency of our buildings, which currently account for nearly half of all carbon emissions in America today." His target was to make all new buildings in America carbon neutral by 2030.

His October 2007 speech promised exploration of safer nuclear technologies, but it did not commit to building new nuclear power plants. He also mentioned wind and solar power and committed to generating 25 percent of the nation's electricity from renewable sources by 2025. (A month later, his campaign Web site listed an interim goal of 10 percent by 2012.) Presently, only about 7 percent of our energy comes from such sources, including hydroelectric.

A campaign statement also released in October 2007 noted, "Our energy grid is outdated and inefficient, resulting in $50–100 billion losses to the U.S.

economy each year. The 2003 East Coast blackout alone resulted in a $10 billion economic loss. As President Eisenhower did with the interstate highway system, Barack Obama will pursue a major investment in our national utility grid to enable a tremendous increase in renewable generation and accommodate 21st-century energy requirements, such as reliability, smart metering, and distributed storage. Obama will invest federal money to leverage additional state and private-sector funds to help create a digitally connected power grid. Creating a smart grid will also help insulate against terrorism concerns because our grid today is virtually unprotected from terrorists. Installing a smart grid will help consumers produce electricity at home through solar panels or wind turbines...sell electricity back through the grid for other consumers, and...reduce their energy use during peak hours when electricity is more expensive." (On January 8, 2009, President-elect Obama reiterated the need for this initiative and urged Congress to "act without delay" in implementing it.)

The campaign statement announced Obama's support for construction of a natural gas pipeline from Alaska—a rare point of agreement between him and his Republican opponents—noting that it will create thousands of new jobs.

Once Obama's number-one priority became reversing the economic downturn, he made sure his transition team viewed these energy-related initiatives as ways to create or preserve jobs. The goal stated in their January 2009 paper on the stimulus plan was 459,000 energy-related jobs by the fourth quarter of 2010, with particular emphasis on "green" technologies. The House stimulus bill, as of this writing, includes $54 billion for research and development to increase energy production from renewable sources, of which $11 billion would be directed toward modernizing the electricity grid. The funds are also intended to promote weatherization of public buildings.

But where will the energy-related jobs be? Note the predictions of the transition-team economists regarding the effect of the stimulus package on specific *industries:* Mining and utilities—the two industries where most energy production is concentrated—are expected to have the *smallest* increases in job creation out of the 14 industries identified in the report. The mining industry—which includes oil, gas, and coal extraction—is projected to have 26,000 additional jobs by the fourth quarter of 2010. Only 11,000 jobs are projected for the utilities industry, which includes electric power generation and transmission as well as gas distribution. That's a total of only 37,000 jobs out of the 459,000 energy-related jobs that the transition team predicts.

The remaining 422,000 energy-related jobs will be created in other industries, and this points out a key purpose of the Obama stimulus package: To create jobs in innovative technologies that give America a competitive advantage.

Many past technologies that were developed in the United States and once provided thousands of jobs in manufacturing, research, development, and management have been taken over by foreign competitors—and this includes clean-energy technologies. In his Portsmouth speech, Obama noted, "We see technologies that are invented here in America—like wind turbines, solar panels, and compact fluorescent bulbs—developed overseas and then sold back to American consumers." The problem, he said, is that American companies are unwilling to take the risk of bringing new discoveries to the consumer marketplace. His proposed solution was the Clean Technologies Venture Capital Fund, which he mentioned in the speech and which is part of his stimulus package. It is intended to encourage the jobs that create innovative solutions to energy problems, that manufacture the products that result, and that sell these products to consumers and businesses both here and abroad.

Another reason why many clean-energy jobs being encouraged by Obama will remain in the United States is that they will involve on-site activities, such as putting up solar panels and wind turbines and constructing fuel-efficient buildings.

Therefore, some of the remaining 422,000 energy-related jobs will be in research, development, and management (and will account for some of the 345,000 new jobs projected for the professional and business services industry); some in construction (among the 678,000 new jobs projected); some in manufacturing (among 480,000 jobs); some in wholesale trade (among 158,000 jobs); and some in retail trade (among 604,000 jobs). Doubtless a small number of energy-related jobs will also be created in other industries; for example, any increase in business activity creates demand for information technology.

You may have noticed that at least a few energy-conservation measures advocated by Obama, such as increasing public transportation, may simultaneously be considered infrastructure initiatives. It is not easy to tell from the transition team's paper on the stimulus package where some of these programs are assigned. The smart electric grid and the retrofitting of government buildings with better insulation have been counted as energy programs in the House bill, but probably some energy-conservation programs are considered parts of the infrastructure initiative, which is expected to create or save 377,000 jobs by the fourth quarter of 2010.

Chapter 2 discusses job opportunities in the energy field. If energy conservation interests you, you should also turn to chapter 3, which covers infrastructure—after reading the very next section of this chapter.

Infrastructure

Our economy is built on an infrastructure of roads, bridges, railways, pipelines, power grids, dams, and telecommunications networks. The initial investment in any wisely constructed component of the infrastructure is rewarded by many years of economic payback: improved transportation, communication, or delivery of a resource as vital as water, electric power, or emergency services. Without the infrastructure, we could not do our jobs, live comfortably in our homes, or be secure from threats to our safety as individuals and as a nation. Most components of the infrastructure are subject to decay and obsolescence, and new technologies sometimes demand the creation of new components—for example, the countless cell-phone towers that have gone up over the past two decades. We are required to invest continuously in the infrastructure if we want a thriving economy.

Current State of the Field

Some components of the infrastructure, such as telephone networks and electric power grids, are privately owned. The owners are able to measure the usage of subscribers and charge them a fee that covers the costs of creating and maintaining the facility and returns a profit to the investors. This is also true for some government-owned infrastructure components, such as toll roads, toll bridges, water works, and sewer systems. These user-supported facilities tend to be well maintained and are upgraded to meet new demands.

For many government-owned facilities, however—especially roads and bridges—it is hard to measure usage or inconvenient to charge a toll, so the government raises the necessary revenue through taxes. Taxation has been unpopular over the past quarter century, and even gasoline taxes, which have a clear relationship to highway and bridge usage, are regarded by many people as burdensome. The federal gasoline tax has not been raised in 15 years. You may recall that when gasoline prices spiked last summer, Senators McCain and Clinton both advocated a temporary suspension of this tax. (Obama disagreed.) Although gasoline taxes have not been eliminated, they have not been able to fund all the work that is needed to maintain our highway grid.

The tattered state of the highway grid became a scandal when a well-traveled bridge in the Minneapolis–Saint Paul area collapsed in 2007, killing 13 people, injuring 145, disrupting traffic patterns for over a year, and causing nearby businesses to lose millions of dollars in sales. The state legislature eventually voted to increase the gasoline tax by 5.5 cents per gallon, but they had to override the veto of the governor.

The 2007 bridge collapse called attention to a nationwide neglect of our bridges. According to the Federal Highway Administration, 12.1 percent of highway bridges were structurally deficient in that same year.

Of course, bridge construction and repair have not been totally forgotten by our legislators. One project that was championed by Senator Ted Stevens of Alaska was to build a bridge connecting the mainland of Alaska to an island with only 50 residents—the famous "Bridge to Nowhere." Fortunately, opposition to the bridge outside of Alaska succeeded in blocking the project in 2005, but the incident dramatized how decisions about infrastructure spending were being made on the basis of political influence rather than on the basis of economic benefit.

Another infrastructure failure that shocked the nation was the collapse of the New Orleans levees and flood walls when Hurricane Katrina struck in August 2005. Subsequent investigations demonstrated that the U.S. Army Corps of Engineers had used an inadequate design in their construction of the walls, and maintenance funds had been diverted for decades. Since Katrina, the Corps has spent more than $1 billion patching up the flood-protection system, but many parts of New Orleans are still considered at risk.

Roads, bridges, and floodwalls are not the only parts of our infrastructure in dire need of repair. Here are some relevant facts taken from the text of a 2007 Senate bill jointly sponsored by Senators Christopher J. Dodd (a Democrat) and Senator Chuck Hagel (a Republican):

"According to the American Society of Civil Engineers, the current condition of our nation's major infrastructure systems earns a grade point average of D and jeopardizes the prosperity and quality of life of all Americans.

"According to the Federal Transit Administration, $21.8 billion is needed annually over the next 20 years to maintain and improve the operational capacity of transit systems.

"According to the Department of Housing and Urban Development, there are 1.2 million units of public housing with critical capital needs totaling $18 billion.

"According to the Texas Transportation Institute, the average traveler is delayed 51.5 hours annually due to traffic and infrastructure-related congestion in the nation's 20 largest metropolitan areas. The delays range from 93 hours in Los Angeles to 14 hours in Pittsburgh. Combined, these delays waste 1.78 billion gallons of fuel each year and waste almost $50.3 billion in congestion costs. Furthermore, the average [annual] delay in these metropolitan areas has increased by almost 35.3 hours since 1982.

"According to the Federal Highway Administration, $131.7 billion and $9.4 billion are needed respectively every year over the next 20 years to repair deficient roads and bridges. The average age of bridges is 40 years.

"According to the Environmental Protection Agency, $151 billion and $390 billion are needed respectively every year over the next 20 years to repair obsolete drinking water and wastewater systems. Drinking water and waste-water systems range...from 50 to 100 years in age.

"Current federal financing methods do not adequately distribute funding based on an infrastructure project's size, location, cost, usage, or economic benefit to a region or the entire nation."

Plans for Infrastructure-Related Jobs in the Obama Campaign and Stimulus Package

The Senate bill containing these dire warnings would have established a National Infrastructure Bank charged with evaluating and financing publicly owned mass transit systems, housing properties, roads, bridges, drinking water systems, and wastewater systems. The Bank would have been able to issue government-backed bonds to provide direct subsidies or loan guarantees for infrastructure projects deemed economically necessary.

The bill creating the National Infrastructure Bank has not come to a vote in Congress as of this writing, but Obama has expressed support for it as part of his infrastructure initiative. He intends to fund it with $60 billion over 10 years and views its investments as an addition to, not a replacement for, funds from the federal gasoline tax. In a February 2008 speech to anxious workers at a General Motors plant in Janesville, Wisconsin, the candidate Obama predicted that the investment in the National Infrastructure Bank would "multiply into almost half a trillion dollars of additional infrastructure spending and generate nearly two million new jobs—many of them in the construction industry that's been hard hit by this housing crisis."

In his radio address of December 6, 2008, Obama said his administration "will create millions of jobs by making the single largest new investment in our national infrastructure since the creation of the federal highway system in the 1950s. We'll invest your precious tax dollars in new and smarter ways, and we'll set a simple rule—use it or lose it. If a state doesn't act quickly to invest in roads and bridges in their communities, they'll lose the money." Probably part of his thinking was that the stimulus funding will need to be spent soon to reverse the severe downturn in our economy.

During his campaign and following his election, Obama has identified other specific infrastructure components that he intends to target. One is broadband Internet access. In his December 6, 2008, radio address, he said, "It is unacceptable that the United States ranks 15th in the world in broadband adoption. Here, in the country that invented the Internet, every child should have the chance to get online." According to *BusinessWeek* (January 7, 2009), Obama intends to implement this initiative by offering tax breaks to companies that extend the availability of broadband (as much as 60 percent refund on their investment) or make it run at higher speeds (as much as 40 percent refund). Additional funding may be provided through grants to states. The Obama transition team's site, Change.gov, also mentioned setting new policies about use of the wireless spectrum as a way of extending broadband availability.

Another target for infrastructure funding is improving the energy efficiency of buildings. The Obama campaign's October 2007 policy statement promised that Obama "will create a competitive grant program to award those states and localities that take the first steps in implementing new building codes that prioritize energy efficiency, and provide a federal match for those states with leading-edge public benefits funds that support energy efficiency retrofits of existing buildings." Obama returned to this theme in his December 6, 2008, radio address, when he said, "Our government now pays the highest energy bill in the world. We need to change that. We need to upgrade our federal buildings by replacing old heating systems and installing efficient light bulbs. That won't just save you, the American taxpayer, billions of dollars each year. It will put people back to work." In a speech about the economy one month later, Obama remarked, "We will modernize more than 75 percent of federal buildings and improve the energy efficiency of two million American homes, saving consumers and taxpayers billions on our energy bills."

When Obama appointed Steven Chu, director of the Lawrence Berkeley National Laboratory, as energy secretary, he gave an additional indication of the importance of this initiative. Chu has long advocated improving the energy efficiency of buildings.

Chu's appointment also is consistent with another infrastructure-related (and energy-related) interest of Obama's: research into alternative sources of energy. In a November 2007 position paper and again on the transition Web site in late 2008, the Obama campaign said he planned to "double federal science and research funding for clean energy projects, relying on the resources and ability of our national laboratories, universities, and land grant colleges." The campaign statement also noted, "As a share of the gross domestic product, American federal investment in the physical sciences and engineering research has dropped by half since 1970. Yet, it often has been federally supported basic research that has generated the innovation to create markets and drive economic growth."

Public transportation has been important to Obama since early in his campaign, and now it is a significant piece of his plan for creating infrastructure-related jobs. An August 2007 campaign broadside, "Strengthening America's Transportation Infrastructure," noted Obama's sponsorship of a bill to fund Amtrak's passenger rail service. The bill, which became law in October 2008 after some modifications, funds Amtrak with $2.6 billion per year through 2013. The campaign document added, "As president, Barack Obama will continue to fight for Amtrak funding and reform so that individuals, families, and businesses throughout the country have safe and reliable transportation options." It also mentioned Obama's support for funds to modernize the Mississippi and Illinois Rivers' system of locks and dams and for doubling the federal Jobs Access and Reverse Commute (JARC) program, which provides public transportation to enable low-income urban workers to reach work sites in suburban locations.

In May 2008, the candidate Obama had lunch with an Indiana machinist who was anxious about being laid off by Amtrak. Obama commented, "We are the only advanced country in the world that doesn't have high speed rail.... And it works on the Northeast corridor. They would rather go from New York to Washington by train than they would by plane. It is a lot more reliable and it is a good way for us to start reducing how much gas we are using."

Joe Biden's presence on the ticket probably reinforced Obama's commitment to public transportation. Biden has never established a residence in Washington and instead has commuted from his Delaware home to his Senate job by Amtrak. Amtrak service has long been of vital importance to Delaware, and Biden has been a staunch defender of passenger rail funding.

The specifics of the public-transportation component of the stimulus package began to come together in December of 2008, when Representative Jim Oberstar, chairman of the House Transportation and Infrastructure Committee, held hearings. One important issue was whether there were enough "shovel-ready" projects to enable recovery money to be spent soon. Oberstar noted that the economic slowdown had created a large backlog of projects that could be started up in three or four months, if funded. *The New York Times* reported, "State transportation officials said they could start work on more than 3,000 highway projects totaling $18 billion within 30 to 90 days. Mass transit officials said they could have $8 billion of projects ready to go in 90 days."

According to the *Times,* "The senior Republican on the committee, Representative John L. Mica of Florida, heartily endorsed the effort. 'Every billion dollars of spending on highways and transportation projects results in 35,000 new jobs,' Mr. Mica said, using a figure in the midrange of estimates by economists."

A simultaneous indication of broad-based support for the initiative was a letter appealing to Congress for help that was sent jointly by the National Governors Association, the National Conference of State Legislatures, the National Association of Counties, and the National League of Cities.

One additional infrastructure component that Obama has mentioned as important is the nation's schools. In his radio address of December 6, 2008, he said his recovery plan "will launch the most sweeping effort to modernize and upgrade school buildings that this country has ever seen. We will repair broken schools, make them energy-efficient, and put new computers in our classrooms. Because to help our children compete in a 21st-century economy, we need to send them to 21st-century schools."

The House stimulus bill includes, as of this writing, $90 billion in infrastructure spending. Of this, $10 billion is dedicated to science facilities and research, and $6 billion is for broadband service in rural areas. In the January 2009 report on the job impact of the stimulus package, the transition team's economic advisors estimated that the infrastructure initiatives will create or preserve 377,000 jobs by the fourth quarter of 2010. These will probably account for a large share of the 678,000 jobs the report predicts for the construction industry. Because much of the infrastructure is owned and managed by governments, this initiative also will contribute to the 244,000 jobs expected in government. It will also create jobs in the professional and business services industry (among the 345,000 projected jobs) for engineers, technicians, and others. In the longer term, of course, improved infrastructure contributes to economic growth in all industries.

Chapter 3 discusses specific jobs in the construction industry that are likely to get a boost from the infrastructure stimulus. Education, which will be helped by the planned upgrading of schools, is covered in chapter 5. Chapter 7 describes some other industries and the related jobs that will benefit.

Health Care

During the presidential campaign, most of the discussion about health care was not specifically about jobs. Instead, it was about how to make health care more affordable. Of course, the two issues are related. People cut back on their health-care spending when they can't afford it, and that means fewer health-care jobs or shorter hours for health-care workers.

Current State of the Field

Health care is America's largest and fastest-growing industry. Much of the world's pioneering medical and pharmaceutical research is done in the United States. We lead the world in per-capita spending on health care: $7,026, which is 16 percent of our gross domestic product. However, several measures indicate that Americans are not getting as much health care as they need.

The Commonwealth Fund's *National Scorecard on U.S. Health System Performance, 2008,* gave the U.S. health-care system a grade of 65 out of a possible 100 on 37 measures of performance and noted that performance had not improved since the previous scorecard in 2006. Of greatest concern was the decline in access to health care. "As of 2007, more than 75 million adults—42 percent of all adults ages 19 to 64—were either uninsured during the year or underinsured, up from 35 percent in 2003." This lack of coverage costs us in lives: "The U.S. now ranks last out of 19 countries on a measure of mortality amenable to medical care, falling from 15th as other countries raised the bar on performance. Up to 101,000 fewer people [annually] would die prematurely if the U.S. could achieve leading, benchmark country rates." The health care that people do access is often inefficient. The report notes, "Performance on measures of health system efficiency remains especially low, with the U.S. scoring 53 out of 100 on measures gauging inappropriate, wasteful, or fragmented care; avoidable hospitalizations; variation in quality and costs; administrative costs; and use of information technology."

One inefficiency in our health-care system is its overreliance on paper-and-pencil records. Compared to most other industries, health care lags far behind in the use of information technology. In 2004, it was estimated that fewer than 15 percent of hospitals and between 10 and 30 percent of physician practices had implemented electronic health information systems.

America's costly health-care system also reduces our economic productivity, and not just when workers call in sick. According to a study by economists for the New America Foundation, U.S. manufacturers who provide health-care insurance pay an average of $2.38 per worker per hour for coverage. Health-care insurance premiums continue to rise and are expected to increase by 20 percent in less than four years if nothing is done to reform the system. Employers can pay for these costs by raising the cost of products, but then the products fail to compete with the products of foreign manufacturers, who pay less than half what ours do in health-care costs.

More often, U.S. employers cut workers' wages or trim the workforce, according to the economists Katherine Baicker and Amitabh Chandra. In their 2006 report called "The Labor Market Effects of Rising Health Insurance Premiums," they estimate that "a 20 percent increase in health insurance premiums (smaller than the increase seen in many areas in the last 3 years) would reduce the probability of being employed by 2.4 percentage points—the equivalent of approximately 3.5 million workers. A similar number of workers would move from full-time jobs to part time, reducing the average number of hours worked per week by a little over an hour. Annual (wage) income would be reduced by $1,700 for those who are employed and have [employer-based health insurance]."

Of course, not everyone can get health-care insurance through an employer. Medicare, a federal program, was created in 1965 to provide insurance for people age 65 or older. Although there are concerns about Medicare's funding over the long term, right now the real cause for worry is funding for programs that get some or all of their revenue from the states. Medicaid is jointly funded by the states and the federal government, and the State Children's Health Insurance Program (SCHIP), although funded by the federal government, is administered by the states. In the present economic crisis, many states are running out of funds for these programs and are raising eligibility requirements, cutting benefits, raising premiums (such as copayments), or lowering reimbursements to health-care providers. A report released by Families USA in December 2008 warned that 19 states are in serious trouble and that one million people could lose all their health-care coverage, with many more seeing reductions in benefits.

Plans for Health-Care-Related Jobs in the Obama Campaign and Stimulus Package

Based on the previous discussion, you can understand that any reform of the health-care system that lowers costs will have a positive effect on jobs throughout the economy. And reform of this kind has been one of Obama's highest priorities throughout the 2008 campaign, remaining so as he took office. For the position of Secretary of Health and Human Services, Obama has appointed former Senator Tom Daschle, a longtime advocate of reform and the leader of the Senate Democrats from 1994 to 2004.

This book, however, is not the appropriate place to discuss Obama's plans for changing the way Americans get health-care insurance. The focus of this book is the economic stimulus package and its likely effects on jobs—in this case, health-care jobs.

One relevant initiative that Obama has backed for a long time is increasing use of information technology in the health-care system. (This may also be regarded as an infrastructure initiative.) In his December 6, 2008, radio address, Obama said, "In addition to connecting our libraries and schools to the Internet, we must also ensure that our hospitals are connected to each other through the Internet. That is why the economic recovery plan I'm proposing will help modernize our health-care system—and that won't just save jobs, it will save lives. We will make sure that every doctor's office and hospital in this country is using cutting-edge technology and electronic medical records so that we can cut red tape, prevent medical mistakes, and help save billions of dollars each year."

A similar initiative was proposed in the 2007 Wired for Health Care Quality Act, which Senator Obama co-sponsored (along with 3 Democrats and 12 Republicans) but which never reached a Senate vote. This legislation may be rolled into Obama's stimulus package. One implementation issue that remains hotly contested is the level of confidentiality that will be built into electronic health-care records. Consumers and software publishers want strict protections, but the powerful insurance lobby wants looser controls. Obama has said that he wants strong privacy protections but does not want to slow passage of the bill, so the issue may be resolved after the bill is passed by a ruling from the Department of Health and Human Services.

Another stimulus-package initiative relevant to health care is aid to the states, many of which are running out of funds to disburse through Medicaid and SCHIP. As of this writing, the House stimulus bill contains $87 billion for helping with Medicaid costs, plus $20 billion for health information technology. On January 14, 2009, the House also passed a bill to pump an additional $33 billion into the SCHIP program. Obama urged the Senate to pass the bill (as it did in 2007, when President Bush vetoed it) so it can be among the first measures he signs into law as president.

It's not clear how many dollars of the stimulus package will eventually be targeted at these health-care and aid-to-states initiatives, but the transition team has projected that 244,000 jobs will be saved or created by the fourth quarter of 2010 through the health-care component. The team also projects 821,000 jobs—some of them surely in health care—resulting from aid to the states.

It's also difficult to quantify the expected impact of the stimulus package on jobs in the health-care industry because the economic advisors' report projects a benefit of 240,000 jobs for the education and health-care industries *combined*.

If you add the figures for the two initiatives—244,000 and 821,000 jobs—and compare them to the expected results in the combined education and health-care industries, you can see that these components of the stimulus package are intended to benefit several industries in addition to health care itself. For example, when stimulus money goes to connect health-care offices to the Internet and computerize their records, the information industry will be an obvious beneficiary, and it is targeted for 50,000 jobs by the fourth quarter of 2010.

One health-care chief information officer, blogging on this subject in December 2008, tallied the jobs created when his hospital, Beth Israel

Deaconess, computerized its records. He counted 22 jobs created for rollout and support of the system and calculated that the Obama plan would create tens of thousands of new jobs nationwide.

Turn to chapter 4 to read facts about health-care jobs that will be created and sustained by the stimulus package.

Education

As technology and global trade become more important in our economy, education is becoming more important for our citizens—both young people and adult workers.

Current State of the Field

Every president has pledged to improve American education, but we seem to constantly be slipping further behind as a nation. Although we spend more per pupil than most other industrialized nations, we do not produce outstanding educational results, according to most objective measures.

For example, in the 2007 "Education at a Glance" report of the Organization for Economic Cooperation and Development (OECD), the United States placed 21st out of 27 countries when ranked by percentage of those who graduated from high school. When 26 countries were ranked by percentage of those who graduated from college with an academic degree, the U.S. was in 16th place. The report noted, "Graduation rates have doubled or more during the past 10 years in Austria, Finland, Portugal, the Slovak Republic, and Switzerland, but have been stable in the United States, which—along with New Zealand—had the highest rate in 1995." The U.S. did only a little better when ranked according to percentage of those who graduated with a postsecondary vocational degree: 10th out of 21 countries.

Another OECD report, this one on math and science achievement in 2006, found U.S. teens ranked at 17th of 30 countries in science and 23rd in math.

The U.S. was not scored on the reading section of the OECD assessment (because of a typo), but in a separate report the same year released by Boston College, the Progress in International Reading Literacy Study, American fourth graders ranked 11th of 40 countries on reading. Compare that to 2001, when Americans ranked in fourth place.

For the past two decades, school choice has been offered as a remedy to educational underachievement, but charter schools have not proved they can fulfill their promise. The 2006 National Assessment of Educational Progress found students in public schools scoring higher on reading and math than their charter-school peers. Some studies have produced results more favorable to charter schools, but the NAEP study is thought to have the best methodology. In some assessments, charter schools affiliated with public school districts (rather than for-profit operations) have shown more achievement.

The bipartisan support that the Bush Administration enjoyed for its No Child Left Behind legislation in 2001 has ebbed as the program has become established. Early positive results were reported in 2005, comparing student achievement to that measured in 2001, but these results were actually based on a program that had been in effect only since 2003, and achievement from 2001 to 2003 was as great as that from 2003 to 2005. Although the program was designed to establish accountability by testing students to measure achievement, critics have called the tests too narrow, and because states are free to set their own standards, some states have lowered their passing scores. Most damaging of all, the federal government has not adequately funded the program, and states often have not been able to make up the difference—especially now that a recession has set in.

Plans for Education-Related Jobs in the Obama Campaign and Stimulus Package

One of Obama's first major speeches about education as a candidate was in November 2007 in Manchester, New Hampshire. He announced specific plans for early childhood education: "As president, I will launch a Children's First Agenda that provides care, learning, and support to families with children ages zero to five. We'll create Early Learning Grants to help states create a system of high-quality early care and education for all young children and their families. We'll increase Head Start funding and quadruple Early [Head] Start to include a quarter of a million at-risk children."

In a speech in Flint, Michigan, in June 2008, Obama made these remarks about primary and secondary education: "We can fix the failures of No Child Left Behind while focusing on accountability. That means providing the funding that was promised. More importantly, it means reaching high standards, but not by relying on a single high-stakes standardized test that distorts how teachers teach. Instead, we need to work with governors, educators, and especially teachers to develop better assessment tools that effectively measure student achievement and encourage the kinds of research, scientific investigation, and problem-solving that our children will need to compete.

"And we need to recruit an army of new teachers. I'll make this pledge as president: If you commit your life to teaching, America will pay for your college education. We'll recruit teachers in math and science and deploy them to understaffed school districts in our inner cities and rural America. We'll expand mentoring programs that pair experienced teachers with new recruits. And when our teachers succeed, I won't just talk about how great they are— I'll reward their greatness with better pay and more support."

He also announced his plans to encourage higher education: "I want to give tax breaks to young people in the form of an annual $4,000 tax credit that will cover two-thirds of the tuition at an average public college and make community college completely free. In return, I will ask students to serve, whether it's by teaching, joining the Peace Corps, or working in your community. [He has referred to this as his Service Scholarship program, and it requires recipients to provide 100 hours of community service.] And for those who serve in our military, we'll cover all of your tuition with an even more generous 21st-Century GI Bill."

In September, shortly after a Republican convention at which Senator McCain had advocated school choice, Obama spoke about education in Dayton, Ohio. He noted that in Illinois, he had voted to double the number of charter schools in Chicago and planned to double funding for charter schools as president. He pledged to "work with all our nation's governors to hold all our charter schools accountable. Charter schools that are successful will get the support they need to grow. And charters that aren't will get shut down."

In the Dayton speech he also said he would "help ensure that more of our kids have access to quality after-school and summer school and extended school days for students who need it."

All of these proposals were carried over to the Change.gov site of the transition team, and the House stimulus package introduced on January 15, 2009, included $79 billion to help local school districts and public colleges avoid job cutbacks. In addition, *The New York Times* reported that the bill offered "$41 billion in additional aid, including $13 billion for schools serving mostly impoverished students, $13 billion for disabled students, $14 billion for school construction and modernization, and $1 billion for technology. Another $15.6 billion would be used to increase the size of Pell grants by $500." A few days later the *Times* reported that the education funding in the House bill included $2 billion to be directed to expanding child-care services for the children of low-wage workers, $2.1 billion for Head Start, and $600 million for care of infants and toddlers with disabilities. The House bill also would create a tax credit of as much as $2,500 to offset the college costs of taxpayers earning less than $80,000 (or $160,000 for couples).

The transition team's January 2009 report about the stimulus package projected 250,000 jobs preserved or created by the fourth quarter of 2010 as a result of the educational component of the package. Many of these jobs will not be in the education industry, because the total number of jobs projected for the education and health-care industries *combined* is 240,000. Some of the jobs will probably be among the 244,000 projected for government. Others will be among the 678,000 in construction and among the 50,000 in information, among other industries.

To read about specific jobs in education that are likely to be aided by the recovery funding, see chapter 5.

Manufacturing

The manufacturing sector of the economy produced everything inside your house, with the exceptions of your family members, pets, houseplants, and any raw foodstuffs in your kitchen. Unlike the preceding topics of this chapter, manufacturing is not an initiative within the Obama stimulus package. Rather, it is an industry that is expected to benefit from the various initiatives. However, it is so important as an industry in the United States—and so threatened by recent trends—that it deserves separate discussion here.

Current State of the Field

The mass-production method that the industrialized world uses for manufacturing was invented in the United States, and for many years we led the world in the output of our manufacturers. While the factories hummed, jobs with good pay were plentiful.

But as trade has become more global, more and more manufacturing jobs have been lost to foreign plants. The industries that produce shoes, textiles, furniture, toys, radios, TVs, and computer components have largely shifted their factories to places such as China and other countries with even lower wages. Many manufacturing businesses that used to be major employers are now drastically reduced in size and are threatened with bankruptcy. One very recent symptom of this trend was the attempt by the Big Three automobile manufacturers to persuade Congress to lend them several billion dollars.

Another major trend affecting manufacturing is automation. Many of the factories that survive in the United States have greatly reduced their payroll expenses by laying off workers and installing robots.

Manufacturing in the U.S. is not dead, but it is shrinking rapidly. Since 2000, America has lost 3.7 million manufacturing jobs, a 21 percent decline. Manufacturing still accounts for about 12 percent of our gross domestic product and employs about 14 million workers. But by 2016, long after this recession is over, the industry is projected to employ only about 12.5 million workers—it will be 11 percent smaller.

Plans for Manufacturing-Related Jobs in the Obama Campaign and Stimulus Package

In May 2008, the Obama campaign released a position paper about strengthening domestic manufacturing. The paper said Obama intended to "invest $150 billion over 10 years to advance the next generation of biofuels and fuel infrastructure, accelerate the commercialization of plug-in hybrids, promote development of commercial-scale renewable energy, invest in low-emissions coal plants, and begin transition to a new digital electricity grid." Although this may sound like an energy-related program, it is designed to give a great boost to manufacturing. The policy statement announced plans to double funding for the Manufacturing Extension Partnership (MEP). MEP centers are nonprofit university or state-based organizations that receive a mix of public and private funding and help manufacturers deploy new technologies. The paper called for the creation of an Advanced Manufacturing Fund "to identify and invest in the most compelling advanced manufacturing strategies." It advocated "doubling federal funding for basic research" and "making the research and development tax credit permanent so that firms can effectively plan when making decisions to invest in domestic R&D over multiyear timeframes."

Obama reiterated these plans when he spoke in Flint, Michigan, the next month. Flint has been a hub of manufacturing for General Motors and is a symbol of America's troubled manufacturing industries.

After the election, the Change.gov transition Web site echoed the proposals that Obama had made the previous May. But following the appearance of the auto manufacturers in Washington, the site also noted that Obama "pushed for $50 billion in loan guarantees to help the auto industry retool, develop new battery technologies, and produce the next generation of fuel-efficient cars here in America. Congress passed only half of this amount—it is critical that the administration speed up the implementation of the first half and that Congress move quickly to enact the second half. In addition, Obama and Biden believe that with the tremendous uncertainty facing the auto industry and the small and medium business suppliers who depend on them, it is critical that we keep all options on the table for helping them weather the financial crisis."

As noted earlier in this section, manufacturing is not one of the initiatives in the stimulus plan, but in the January 2009 report of the transition team's economists, this industry is expected to gain or maintain 408,000 jobs by the fourth quarter of 2010 because of the recovery package. The report does not specify which initiatives will contribute to these jobs, but it seems reasonable to suppose that the proposals for energy (projected to support 459,000 jobs total), infrastructure (377,000 jobs), and business tax incentives (470,000 jobs) in particular are targeted to stimulate the manufacturing industries.

Chapter 6 discusses manufacturing jobs that can be expected to benefit from the recovery package. Research and development jobs, which will also gain from a recovery of manufacturing, are described in chapter 7.

Other Priorities of the Obama Plan

In addition to its provisions for preserving and creating jobs, the Obama plan intends to protect the most vulnerable from the recession by increasing expenditures on food stamps ($20 billion in the House bill introduced on January 15, 2009) and by extending the length of time people can collect unemployment insurance when they lose a job ($43 billion). The House bill also sets aside $39 billion to help unemployed people maintain healthcare insurance under the Consolidated Omnibus Budget Reconciliation Act (COBRA) program or get short-term coverage under Medicaid.

Money that gets spent in our economy often has ripple effects that spread far beyond the initial expenditure. For example, if the government gives me a certain sum of money to hire and pay you, you turn around and pay some of that money to the grocer, the hair stylist, and the car mechanic. Those people, in turn, spend these dollars for their own needs, and so on. Economists refer to this as the multiplier effect.

Different types of economic stimulus have different multiplier rates, and the Obama plan is aimed at using methods that have the highest multipliers. Mark Zandi, the chief economist at Moody's Economy.com, estimates that every dollar people gain through a one-time, across-the-board tax cut is felt as $1.03 in its impact on the economy as a whole. By comparison, a dollar spent to increase availability of food stamps has the impact of $1.73 and a dollar for extended unemployment benefits is equivalent to $1.64. For general aid to state governments, the equivalent is $1.36, and for infrastructure spending, it is $1.59.

The economists who prepared the transition team's plan for the recovery package took these differing multipliers into account when computing how many jobs would be created by each kind of stimulus.

CHAPTER 2

JOBS IN ENERGY

Energy-related jobs—which account for 459,000 of the jobs that the transition team predicts by the fourth quarter of 2010—are found in several industries. In this chapter, you'll find descriptions of the **mining** and **utility** industries and some key jobs that will probably have opportunities because of the recovery package. The **machinery manufacturing** industry, which will probably pick up some jobs as clean energy sources are developed, is covered by chapter 6. The **management, scientific, and technical consulting services; scientific research and development services; computer systems design and related services;** and **wholesale trade** industries, all of which will be involved in energy development or will benefit from its economic activity, are described in chapter 7, along with some related jobs.

Mining

Nature of the Industry

The United States has been endowed with a wealth of natural resources that have fostered its growth and development. Extraction of these resources, and finding new deposits, is the work of the mining industry, which provides the foundation for local economies in several regions.

Many resources produced by the mining industry, particularly metals, oil, and gas, are relatively rare and are part of a global market that is highly sensitive to changes in prices. During the 1990s, commodity prices were relatively stable at low levels, causing production to stagnate and limiting the creation of new drilling and mining operations. In recent years, prices have increased dramatically, and exploration and production have likewise risen. Coal is less susceptible to world market conditions, but it also has seen price increases in recent years that have led to expanded production. Demand for nonmetallic minerals is primarily affected by the level of activity in the construction industry, particularly the building of new roads and highways.

Employment in the mining industry has been affected significantly by new technology and more sophisticated mining techniques that increase productivity. Most mining machines and control rooms are now automatic or computer-controlled, requiring fewer, if any, human operators. Many mines also operate with other sophisticated technology such as lasers and robotics, which further increases the efficiency of resource extraction. As a result, mine employment has been falling over time, particularly of workers who are involved in the extraction process itself. These new technologies and techniques have also increased specialization in the industry and led to expanded use of contract mining services companies for specific tasks. These companies also allow mining firms to more easily adjust production levels in response to changes in commodity prices.

Working Conditions

Hours. Work schedules in the mining industry can vary widely. Some sites operate 24 hours a day, 7 days a week, particularly in oil and gas extraction and underground mines. This creates the opportunity for some mining workers to work long shifts several days in a row and then have several days off. The remote location of some sites, such as offshore oil rigs, requires some workers to actually live onsite for weeks at a time, often working 12-hour shifts, followed by an extended leave period onshore. As a result of these conditions, part-time opportunities are rare in this industry, but overtime is common; less than 3 percent of workers were part-time employees in 2006, while nearly 4 in 9 worked more than 40 hours per week, and 1 in 3 worked more than 50 hours per week. The average work week for a production worker in mining was 46.3 hours.

Work environment. Work environments vary by occupation. Scientists and technicians work in office buildings and laboratories, as do executives and administrative and clerical workers. Engineers and managers usually split their time between offices and the mine or well site, where construction and extraction workers spend most of their time. Geologists who specialize in the exploration of natural resources to locate resource deposits may have to travel for extended periods to remote locations in all types of climates.

Working conditions in mines, quarries, and well sites can be unusual and sometimes dangerous. Physical strength and stamina are necessary, as the work involves standing for long periods, lifting moderately heavy objects, and climbing and stooping to work with tools that often are oily and dirty. Workers in surface mines, quarries, and wells are subject to rugged outdoor work in all kinds of weather and climates, though some surface mines and quarries shut down in the winter because snow and ice covering the mine site make work too dangerous. Oil and gas sites, because they are largely automated once deposits have been located, generally operate year round regardless of weather conditions, although offshore oil platforms are evacuated before the onset of dangerous weather such as hurricanes. Surface mining, however, usually is less hazardous than underground mining.

Underground mines are damp and dark, and some can be very hot and noisy. At times, several inches of water may cover tunnel floors. Although underground mines have electric lights along main pathways, many tunnels are illuminated only by the lights on miners' hats. Workers in mines with very low roofs may have to work on their hands and knees, backs, or stomachs in confined spaces. In underground mining operations, unique dangers include the possibility of a cave-in, mine fire, explosion, or exposure to harmful gases. In addition, dust generated by drilling in mines still places miners at risk of developing either of two serious lung diseases: pneumoconiosis, also called "black lung disease," from coal dust or silicosis from rock dust. These days, dust levels in mines are closely monitored and occurrences of lung diseases are rare if proper procedures are followed. Underground miners have the option to have their lungs x-rayed on a periodic basis to monitor for the development of the diseases. Workers who develop black lung disease or silicosis may be eligible for federal aid.

Mine safety is regulated by the Federal Mine Safety and Health Act of 1977 and successive additional legislation, which has resulted in steadily declining rates of mining injuries and illnesses. Increased automation of mining and oil well operations has also reduced the number of workers needed in some of the more dangerous activities. As a result, in 2006, the rate of work-related injury and illness per 100 full-time workers was only 3.5 for the mining industry as a whole, lower than the rate of 4.4 in the entire private sector. Rates for the specific industry sectors were 2.0 in oil and gas extraction, 4.8 in coal mining, 3.1 in metal ore mining, 3.2 in nonmetallic mineral mining and quarrying, and 3.9 in support activities for mining.

Employment

There were approximately 619,000 wage and salary jobs in the mining industry in 2006; around 136,000 in oil and gas extraction; 79,000 in coal mining; 33,000 in metal mining; and 110,000 in nonmetallic mineral mining. Not included in these figures are the thousands of Americans who work abroad for U.S. companies conducting mining or drilling operations around the world. In addition to those employed directly by mining companies, there are also 262,000 jobs in the support activities for mining industry segment.

Mining jobs are heavily concentrated in the parts of the country where large resource deposits exist. Almost 3 out of 4 jobs in the oil and gas extraction industry are located in Texas, California, Oklahoma, and Louisiana. Although there were around 1,400 coal mining operations in 26 states in 2005, over two-thirds of all coal mines, and about half of all mine employees, were located in just three states—Kentucky, Pennsylvania, and West Virginia, according to the Energy Information Administration. Other states employing large numbers of coal miners are Alabama, Illinois, Indiana, Virginia, and Wyoming. Metal mining is more prevalent in the West and Southwest, particularly in Arizona, Nevada, and Montana, and iron ore mining in Minnesota and Michigan. Nonmetallic mineral mining is the most widespread, as quarrying of nonmetallic minerals, such as stone, clay, sand, and gravel, is done in nearly every state. In many rural areas, mining operations are the main employer. About 80 percent of mining establishments employ fewer than 20 workers.

Outlook

Employment in mining will decrease. The growing U.S. and world economies will continue to demand larger quantities of the raw materials produced by mining, but the increased output will be able to be met by new technologies and new extraction techniques that increase productivity and require fewer workers.

Employment change. Wage and salary employment in mining is expected to decline by 2 percent through the year 2016, compared with 11 percent growth projected for the entire economy. Mining production is tied closely with prices and demand for the raw materials produced, and as prices for oil, gas, and metals have risen rapidly in recent years, production and employment in the industry have also grown. Further short-term increases in employment may be likely if prices remain high, but over the course of the projections period, technological advances will increase productivity and cause employment declines in the mining industry as a whole.

Petroleum and natural gas exploration and development in the United States depend upon prices for these resources and the size of accessible reserves. Stable and favorable prices are needed to allow companies enough revenue to expand exploration and production projects. Rising worldwide demand for oil and gas—particularly from developing countries such as India and China—is likely to cause prices to remain high and generate the needed incentive for oil and gas producers to continue exploring and developing oil and gas reserves, at least in the short run. U.S. reserves of oil and gas should remain adequate to support increased production over the projection period. Many U.S. oil services companies operate in overseas oil and gas fields as well and are therefore not limited by domestic reserves.

Environmental concerns, accompanied by strict regulation and limited access to protected federal lands, also continue to have a major impact on this industry. Restrictions on drilling in environmentally sensitive areas and other environmental constraints should continue to limit exploration and development, both onshore and offshore. These factors will cause employment in oil and gas extraction to decline by 2 percent through 2016. However, changes in policy could expand exploration and drilling for oil and natural gas in currently protected areas and add jobs, especially in Alaska and the federally controlled Outer Continental Shelf.

Demand for coal will increase as coal remains the primary fuel source for electricity generation. Although environmental concerns exist regarding coal power—burning coal releases pollutants and carbon dioxide—few alternatives exist on a scale large enough to meet the fuel demand of utilities. Natural gas burns cleaner than coal, but coal power plants equipped with scrubbers reduce this disadvantage, and both fuels emit greenhouse gases. Recent increases in the price of natural gas have also caused some electricity producers to delay their conversion to natural gas, which is helping to maintain demand for coal. Future increased use of nuclear power or renewable energy sources, such as solar or wind power, could reduce demand for coal, and use of all of these may be expanded under Obama's leadership.

Advances in mining technology will adversely affect employment in coal mining as new machinery and processes increase worker productivity. Fewer workers are required for operation and maintenance of new mining machines that are operated remotely by computer and that self-diagnose mechanical problems. Productivity in coal mining has increased with advances in long-wall and surface mining and improvements in transportation and processing that require fewer workers.

Environmental concerns will continue to affect mining operations. Increasingly, government regulations are restricting access to land and restricting the type of mining that is performed in order to protect native plants and animals and decrease the amount of water and air pollution. As population growth expands further into the countryside, new developments and mine operators are competing for land and residents are increasing their opposition to nearby mining activities. These concerns, together with depletion of the most accessible coal deposits in the East, will result in a shift in coal production. Coal mining will increase in the Central, and particularly the Western, United States and decrease in the East. Overall, coal mining employment will experience little employment change as rising demand for coal is met with productivity gains from more efficient and automated production operations.

Job prospects. Despite an overall decline in mining industry employment, job opportunities in most occupations should be very good. Because workers in the mining industry are older than average, some companies may have trouble coping with the loss of many experienced workers to retirement at a time when the industry is expanding production. At the same time, past declines in employment in the industry have dissuaded potential workers from considering employment in the industry, and many colleges and universities have shut down programs designed to train professionals for work in mining. Employment opportunities will be best for those with previous experience and with technical skills, especially qualified professionals and extraction workers who have experience in oil field operations and who can work with new technology.

Utilities

Nature of the Industry

The simple act of walking into a restroom, turning on the light, and washing your hands uses the products of perhaps four different utilities. Electricity powers the light, water supply systems provide water for washing, wastewater treatment plants treat the sewage, and natural gas or electricity heats the water. Some government establishments also provide electric, gas, water, and wastewater treatment services and employ a significant number of workers in similar jobs, but they are part of government and are not included in this industry.

Utilities and the services they provide are so vital to everyday life that they are considered public goods and are typically heavily regulated. Most utility companies that distribute to consumers operate as regulated monopolies because utility distribution tends to require a large investment in plants and equipment and it is generally not desirable to have several competing systems of pipes or power lines in most areas. Since these companies do not face competition, they are regulated by public utility commissions that ensure that companies act in the public interest and set the rates that are charged. However, legislative changes in recent years have established and promoted competition in some parts of the utilities industry. Wholesale providers of electricity now face competition from a number of nonutility generators.

Many utility companies are municipally owned. In the natural gas industry, for example, a majority of the distribution companies in the United States are municipally owned. However, they serve just a fraction of the nationwide customers. Historically, utilities serving large cities had sufficient numbers of customers to justify the large investment in infrastructure needed to run a utility, and so private, investor-owned companies established utility service. In rural areas, where the small number of customers in need of services did not provide an adequate return for private investors, the state or local government, or rural cooperative associations, established utility service.

The various segments of the utilities industry vary in the degree to which their workers are involved in production activities, administration and management, or research and development. Industries such as water supply, that employ relatively few workers, employ more production workers and plant operators. On the other hand, electric utilities generally operate larger plants using very expensive high-technology equipment and thus employ more professional and technical personnel.

The utilities industry is unique in that urban areas with many inhabitants generally have relatively few utility companies. For example, there were about 52,349 community water systems in the United States in 2006 serving more than 281 million people. The 48,275 smallest water systems served only 52 million people while the 4,074 largest systems served more than 229 million. This shows that economies of scale in the utilities industry allow a few large companies to serve large numbers of customers in metropolitan areas more efficiently than many smaller companies. In fact, some utility companies, predominately serving large metropolitan areas, offer more than one type of utility service to their customers.

Unlike most industries, the utilities industry imports and exports only a small portion of its product. To some degree, this is because of the great difficulty in transporting electricity, fresh water, and natural gas. It is also the result of a national policy that utilities should be self-sufficient, without dependence on imports for the basic services our country requires. However, easing trade restrictions, increased pipeline capacity, and shipping natural gas in liquefied form have made international trade in utilities more feasible, especially with Canada and Mexico.

In 2005, Congress passed a new Energy Policy Act, which is the first major legislation on energy since 1992. This will be a major force in the industry through 2016. It was designed to promote conservation and use of cleaner technologies in energy production through higher efficiency standards and tax credits. It is expected that several new power plants will be built as a result of this legislation, including new clean-burning coal and nuclear facilities.

Working Conditions

Hours. Electricity, gas, and water are used continuously throughout each day. As a result, split, weekend, and night shifts are common for utility workers. The average workweek for production workers in utilities was 41.4 hours in 2006, compared with 33.4 hours for all trade, transportation, and utilities industries and 33.9 hours for all private industries. Employees often must work overtime to accommodate peaks in demand and to repair damage caused by storms, cold weather, accidents, and other occurrences. The industry employs relatively few part-time workers.

Work environment. The hazards of working with electricity, natural gas, treatment chemicals, and wastes can be substantial, but generally are avoided by following rigorous safety procedures. Protective gear such as rubber gloves and rubber sleeves, nonsparking maintenance equipment, and body suits with breathing devices designed to filter out any harmful fumes are mandatory for work in dangerous environs. Employees also undergo extensive training on working with hazardous materials and utility company safety measures.

In 2006, the utilities industry reported 4.1 cases of work-related injury or illness per 100 full-time workers, compared with an average of 4.4 cases for all private industries.

Outlook

Employment in utilities is expected to decline, but many job openings will arise because many workers in the industry are approaching retirement age and will need to be replaced.

Employment change. Wage and salary employment in utilities is expected to decline 6 percent between 2006 and 2016, compared with an increase of about 11 percent for all industries combined. Projected employment change varies by industry segment. Although electric power, natural gas, and water continue to be essential to everyday life, employment declines will result from the retirement of much of the industry's workforce. While utilities are doing what they can to replace these workers, the wide variety of careers open to people with technical skills will make it difficult for companies to find enough applicants to fill these openings. Utilities will be forced to further automate their systems, negotiate part-time status with retirees, and contract with employment services to make up for the difference between the desired number of employees and the number of workers actually available.

Reorganization of electric utilities has increased competition and provided incentives for improved efficiency. This has resulted in extensive cost-cutting and a number of mergers, which have led to a decline in employment over the past several years. This has been accomplished by a combination of layoffs and hiring freezes, which have resulted in an older workforce than in most other industries. Because electric utilities tend to be particularly labor intensive and require technically minded people who are in high demand in other industries, they will have the most difficulty recruiting enough replacements. Worker attrition will be managed by further automation of systems and more responsibility for workers.

In the gas transmission and distribution industry, regulatory changes have made it possible for wholesale and even some retail buyers to choose their own natural gas providers. While distributors still maintain local monopolies, they are highly regulated and are not allowed to mark up the wholesale price of natural gas. Their revenues are based on distribution fees, which vary based on infrastructure needs rather than actual use of natural gas. These regulatory changes have resulted in several mergers and an emphasis on cost-cutting. As in the area of electric power, this has led to hiring freezes that have resulted in an older workforce. As these people retire, there will not be enough applicants to replace them, forcing the industry to find new ways to fill its needs.

In the water and sewage systems industries, regulatory changes have had the opposite impact. While most water systems remain locally operated and fairly small in scale, water quality standards for drinking water and disposal of wastewater have been increased for public health and environmental reasons. While hiring freezes have been less common in water than in other parts of the industry, much of the water workforce is nearing retirement age. Water and sewage systems services are projected to grow slightly, as water systems are expanding rapidly despite the difficulty in securing workers. Employment is projected to increase 18.7 percent from 2006 to 2016.

Job prospects. Job prospects for qualified applicants entering the utilities industry are expected to be excellent during the next 10 years. As of 2006, about 55 percent of the utilities industry workforce is over the age of 45. Many of these workers will either retire or prepare to retire within the next 10 years. Because on-the-job training is very intensive in many utilities industry occupations, preparing a new workforce will be one of the industry's highest priorities during the next decade.

In general, persons with college training in advanced technology will have the best opportunities in the utilities industry. Computer systems analysts and network systems and data communications analysts are expected to be among the fastest-growing occupations in the professional and related occupations group as plants emphasize automation and productivity. Some office and administrative support workers, such as utilities meter readers and book-keeping, accounting, and auditing clerks, are among those adversely affected by increasing automation and outsourcing. Technologies including radio-transmitted meter reading and computerized billing procedures are expected to decrease employment.

New and continuing energy policies also provide investment tax credits for research and development of renewable sources of energy and ways to improve the efficiency of equipment used in electric utilities. As a result, electric utilities will continue to increase the productivity of their plants and workers, resulting in a slowdown in new employment. This slowdown will lead to keen competition for some jobs in the industry. However, at the same time, these new technologies will create jobs for highly skilled technical personnel with the education and experience to take advantage of these developments in electric utilities.

Some Energy Jobs That Are Likely to Benefit from the Stimulus Package

Derrick Operators, Oil and Gas

- ❀ Level of Education/Training: Moderate-term on-the-job training
- ❀ Annual Earnings: $37,790
- ❀ Growth: –5.8%
- ❀ Annual Job Openings: 2,018
- ❀ Personality Type: Realistic

Fewer than one-fifth of these workers have education beyond high school.

Rig derrick equipment and operate pumps to circulate mud through drill hole. Inspect derricks or order their inspection prior to being raised or lowered. Inspect derricks for flaws and clean and oil derricks to maintain proper working conditions. Control the viscosity and weight of the drilling fluid. Repair pumps, mud tanks, and related equipment. Set and bolt crown blocks to posts at tops of derricks. Listen to mud pumps and check regularly for vibration and other problems to ensure that rig pumps and drilling mud systems are working properly. Start pumps that circulate mud through drill pipes and boreholes to cool drill bits and flush out drill cuttings. Position and align derrick elements, using harnesses and platform climbing devices. Supervise crew members and provide assistance in training them. Guide lengths of pipe into and out of elevators. Prepare mud reports and instruct crews about the handling of any chemical additives. Clamp holding fixtures on ends of hoisting cables. Weigh clay and mix with water and chemicals to make drilling mud, using portable mixers. String cables through pulleys and blocks. Steady pipes during connection to or disconnection from drill or casing strings.

Work Conditions—Outdoors; noisy; very hot or cold; contaminants; hazardous equipment; minor burns, cuts, bites, or stings.

Electrical and Electronics Repairers, Powerhouse, Substation, and Relay

❀ Level of Education/Training: Postsecondary vocational training
❀ Annual Earnings: $58,970
❀ Growth: –4.7%
❀ Annual Job Openings: 1,591
❀ Personality Type: Realistic

> Consolidation and privatization in utilities industries should improve productivity, reducing employment. Newer equipment will be more reliable and easier to repair, further limiting employment. Job opportunities should be best for applicants with an associate degree in electronics, certification, and related experience.

Inspect, test, repair, or maintain electrical equipment in generating stations, substations, and in-service relays. Construct, test, maintain, and repair substation relay and control systems. Inspect and test equipment and circuits to identify malfunctions or defects, using wiring diagrams and testing devices such as ohmmeters, voltmeters, or ammeters. Consult manuals, schematics, wiring diagrams, and engineering personnel to troubleshoot and solve equipment problems and to determine optimum equipment functioning. Notify facility personnel of equipment shutdowns. Open and close switches to isolate defective relays; then perform adjustments or repairs. Prepare and maintain records detailing tests, repairs, and maintenance. Analyze test data to diagnose malfunctions, to determine performance characteristics of systems, and to evaluate effects of system modifications. Test insulators and bushings of equipment by inducing voltage across insulation, testing current, and calculating insulation loss. Repair, replace, and clean equipment and components such as circuit breakers, brushes, and commutators. Disconnect voltage regulators, bolts, and screws and connect replacement regulators to high-voltage lines. Schedule and supervise the construction and testing of special devices and the implementation of unique monitoring or control systems. Run signal quality and connectivity tests for individual cables and record results. Schedule and supervise splicing or termination of cables in color-code order. Test oil in circuit breakers and transformers for dielectric strength, refilling oil periodically. Maintain inventories of spare parts for all equipment, requisitioning parts as necessary. Set forms and pour concrete footings for installation of heavy equipment.

Work Conditions—Outdoors; noisy; very bright or dim lighting; hazardous conditions; standing; using hands on objects, tools, or controls.

Electrical Power-Line Installers and Repairers

❀ Level of Education/Training: Long-term on-the-job training
❀ Annual Earnings: $52,570
❀ Growth: 7.2%
❀ Annual Job Openings: 6,401
❀ Personality Type: Realistic

> Most new jobs for electrical power-line installers and repairers are
> expected to arise among contracting firms in the construction industry.

Install or repair cables or wires used in electrical power or distribution systems. May erect poles and light- or heavy-duty transmission towers. Adhere to safety practices and procedures, such as checking equipment regularly and erecting barriers around work areas. Open switches or attach grounding devices to remove electrical hazards from disturbed or fallen lines or to facilitate repairs. Climb poles or use truck-mounted buckets to access equipment. Place insulating or fireproofing materials over conductors and joints. Install, maintain, and repair electrical distribution and transmission systems, including conduits; cables; wires; and related equipment such as transformers, circuit breakers, and switches. Identify defective sectionalizing devices, circuit breakers, fuses, voltage regulators, transformers, switches, relays, or wiring, using wiring diagrams and electrical-testing instruments. Drive vehicles equipped with tools and materials to job sites. Coordinate work assignment preparation and completion with other workers. String wire conductors and cables between poles, towers, trenches, pylons, and buildings, setting lines in place and using winches to adjust tension. Inspect and test power lines and auxiliary equipment to locate and identify problems, using reading and testing instruments. Test conductors according to electrical diagrams and specifications to identify corresponding conductors and to prevent incorrect connections. Replace damaged poles with new poles and straighten the poles. Install watt-hour meters and connect service drops between power lines and consumers' facilities. Attach crossarms, insulators, and auxiliary equipment to poles prior to installing them. Travel in trucks, helicopters, and airplanes to inspect lines for freedom from obstruction and adequacy of insulation. Dig holes, using augers, and set poles, using cranes and power equipment. Trim trees that could be hazardous to the functioning of cables or wires. Splice or solder cables together or to overhead transmission lines, customer service lines, or street light lines, using hand tools, epoxies, or specialized equipment. Cut and peel lead sheathing and insulation from defective or newly installed cables and conduits prior to splicing.

Work Conditions—Outdoors; very hot or cold; high places; hazardous conditions; hazardous equipment; using hands on objects, tools, or controls.

Excavating and Loading Machine and Dragline Operators

- ❋ Level of Education/Training: Moderate-term on-the-job training
- ❋ Annual Earnings: $34,050
- ❋ Growth: 8.3%
- ❋ Annual Job Openings: 6,562
- ❋ Personality Type: Realistic

Job openings should be plentiful due to the fact that these occupations are very large. There will be a relatively high number of openings created by the need to replace workers who transfer to other occupations or who retire or leave the labor force for other reasons.

Operate or tend machinery equipped with scoops, shovels, or buckets to excavate and load loose materials. Move levers, depress foot pedals, and turn dials to operate power machinery such as power shovels, stripping shovels, scraper loaders, and backhoes. Set up and inspect equipment prior to operation. Observe hand signals, grade stakes, and other markings when operating machines so that work can be performed to specifications. Become familiar with digging plans, with machine capabilities and limitations, and with efficient and safe digging procedures in a given application. Operate machinery to perform activities such as backfilling excavations, vibrating or breaking rock or concrete, and making winter roads. Lubricate, adjust, and repair machinery and replace parts such as gears, bearings, and bucket teeth. Create and maintain inclines and ramps. Handle slides, mud, and pit cleanings and maintenance. Move materials over short distances, such as around a construction site, factory, or warehouse. Measure and verify levels of rock, gravel, bases, and other excavated material. Receive written or oral instructions regarding material movement or excavation. Adjust dig face angles for varying overburden depths and set lengths. Drive machines to work sites. Perform manual labor, such as shoveling materials by hand, to prepare or finish sites. Direct ground workers engaged in activities such as moving stakes or markers or changing positions of towers. Direct workers engaged in placing blocks and outriggers to prevent capsizing of machines used to lift heavy loads.

Work Conditions—Outdoors; noisy; contaminants; whole-body vibration; sitting; using hands on objects, tools, or controls.

Geological Sample Test Technicians

❀ Level of Education/Training: Associate degree
❀ Annual Earnings: $50,950
❀ Growth: 8.6%
❀ Annual Job Openings: 1,895
❀ Personality Type: Realistic

The job openings listed here are shared with Geophysical Data Technicians.

> Trained job applicants should experience little competition for positions because of the relatively small number of new entrants.

Test and analyze geological samples, crude oil, or petroleum products to detect presence of petroleum, gas, or mineral deposits indicating potential for exploration and production or to determine physical and chemical properties to ensure that products meet quality standards. Test and analyze samples in order to determine their content and characteristics, using laboratory apparatus and testing equipment. Collect and prepare solid and fluid samples for analysis. Assemble, operate, and maintain field and laboratory testing, measuring, and mechanical equipment, working as part of a crew when required. Compile and record testing and operational data for review and further analysis. Adjust and repair testing, electrical, and mechanical equipment and devices. Supervise well exploration and drilling activities and well completions. Inspect engines for wear and defective parts, using equipment and measuring devices. Prepare notes, sketches, geological maps, and cross sections. Participate in geological, geophysical, geochemical, hydrographic, or oceanographic surveys; prospecting field trips; exploratory drilling; well logging; or underground mine survey programs. Plot information from aerial photographs, well logs, section descriptions, and other databases. Assess the environmental impacts of development projects on subsurface materials. Collaborate with hydrogeologists to evaluate groundwater and well circulation. Prepare, transcribe, and/or analyze seismic, gravimetric, well log, or other geophysical and survey data. Participate in the evaluation of possible mining locations.

Work Conditions—Indoors; noisy; contaminants; more often standing than sitting; using hands on objects, tools, or controls.

Geophysical Data Technicians

❀ Level of Education/Training: Associate degree
❀ Annual Earnings: $50,950
❀ Growth: 8.6%
❀ Annual Job Openings: 1,895
❀ Personality Type: Realistic

The job openings listed here are shared with Geological Sample Test Technicians.

> Trained job applicants should experience little competition for positions
> because of the relatively small number of new entrants.

Measure, record, and evaluate geological data by using sonic, electronic, electrical, seismic, or gravity-measuring instruments to prospect for oil or gas. May collect and evaluate core samples and cuttings. Prepare notes, sketches, geological maps, and cross-sections. Read and study reports in order to compile information and data for geological and geophysical prospecting. Interview individuals and research public databases in order to obtain information. Assemble, maintain, and distribute information for library or record systems. Operate and adjust equipment and apparatus used to obtain geological data. Plan and direct activities of workers who operate equipment to collect data. Set up or direct setup of instruments used to collect geological data. Record readings in order to compile data used in prospecting for oil or gas. Supervise oil, water, and gas well drilling activities. Collect samples and cuttings, using equipment and hand tools. Develop and print photographic recordings of information, using equipment. Measure geological characteristics used in prospecting for oil or gas, using measuring instruments. Evaluate and interpret core samples and cuttings and other geological data used in prospecting for oil or gas. Diagnose and repair malfunctioning instruments and equipment, using manufacturers' manuals and hand tools. Prepare and attach packing instructions to shipping containers. Develop and design packing materials and handling procedures for shipping of objects.

Work Conditions—Indoors; sitting.

Geoscientists, Except Hydrologists and Geographers

❀ Level of Education/Training: Master's degree
❀ Annual Earnings: $75,800
❀ Growth: 21.9%
❀ Annual Job Openings: 2,471
❀ Personality Type: Investigative

Graduates with a master's degree should have excellent opportunities, especially in the management, scientific, and technical consulting industry and in the engineering services industries.

Study the composition, structure, and other physical aspects of the Earth. May use knowledge of geology, physics, and mathematics in exploration for oil, gas, minerals, or underground water or in waste disposal, land reclamation, or other environmental problems. May study the Earth's internal composition, atmospheres, and oceans and its magnetic, electrical, and gravitational forces. Includes mineralogists, crystallographers, paleontologists, stratigraphers, geodesists, and seismologists. Analyze and interpret geological, geochemical, and geophysical information from sources such as survey data, well logs, bore holes, and aerial photos. Locate and estimate probable natural gas, oil, and mineral ore deposits and underground water resources, using aerial photographs, charts, or research and survey results. Plan and conduct geological, geochemical, and geophysical field studies and surveys, sample collection, or drilling and testing programs used to collect data for research or application. Analyze and interpret geological data, using computer software. Search for and review research articles or environmental, historical, and technical reports. Assess ground and surface water movement to provide advice regarding issues such as waste management, route and site selection, and the restoration of contaminated sites. Prepare geological maps, cross-sectional diagrams, charts, and reports concerning mineral extraction, land use, and resource management, using results of field work and laboratory research. Investigate the composition, structure, and history of the Earth's crust through the collection, examination, measurement, and classification of soils, minerals, rocks, or fossil remains. Conduct geological and geophysical studies to provide information for use in regional development, site selection, and development of public works projects. Measure characteristics of the Earth, such as gravity and magnetic fields, using equipment such as seismographs, gravimeters, torsion balances, and magnetometers. Inspect construction projects to analyze engineering problems, applying geological knowledge and using test equipment and drilling machinery. Design geological mine maps, monitor mine structural integrity, or advise and monitor mining crews. Identify risks for natural disasters such as mudslides, earthquakes, and volcanic eruptions, providing advice on mitigation of potential damage. Advise construction firms and government agencies on dam and road construction, foundation design, or land use and resource management. Test industrial diamonds and abrasives, soil, or rocks to determine their geological characteristics, using optical, X-ray, heat, acid, and precision instruments.

Work Conditions—Indoors; sitting.

Mining and Geological Engineers, Including Mining Safety Engineers

❀ Level of Education/Training: Bachelor's degree
❀ Annual Earnings: $74,330
❀ Growth: 10.0%
❀ Annual Job Openings: 456
❀ Personality Type: Investigative

> Many mining engineers currently employed are approaching retirement age. Furthermore, relatively few schools offer mining engineering programs, resulting in good job opportunities for graduates. The best opportunities may require frequent travel or even living overseas for extended periods of time as mining operations around the world recruit graduates of U.S. mining engineering programs.

Determine the location and plan the extraction of coal, metallic ores, nonmetallic minerals, and building materials such as stone and gravel. Work involves conducting preliminary surveys of deposits or undeveloped mines and planning their development; examining deposits or mines to determine whether they can be worked at a profit; making geological and topographical surveys; evolving methods of mining best suited to character, type, and size of deposits; and supervising mining operations. Inspect mining areas for unsafe structures, equipment, and working conditions. Select locations and plan underground or surface mining operations, specifying processes, labor usage, and equipment that will result in safe, economical, and environmentally sound extraction of minerals and ores. Examine maps, deposits, drilling locations, or mines to determine the location, size, accessibility, contents, value, and potential profitability of mineral, oil, and gas deposits. Supervise and coordinate the work of technicians, technologists, survey personnel, engineers, scientists, and other mine personnel. Prepare schedules, reports, and estimates of the costs involved in developing and operating mines. Monitor mine production rates to assess operational effectiveness. Design, implement, and monitor the development of mines, facilities, systems, or equipment. Select or develop mineral location, extraction, and production methods based on factors such as safety, cost, and deposit characteristics. Prepare technical reports for use by mining, engineering, and management personnel. Implement and coordinate mine safety programs, including the design and maintenance of protective and rescue equipment and safety devices. Test air to detect toxic gases and recommend measures to remove them, such as installation of ventilation shafts. Design, develop, and implement computer applications for use in mining operations such as mine design, modeling, or mapping or for monitoring mine conditions. Select or devise materials-handling methods and equipment to transport ore, waste materials, and mineral products efficiently and economically. Devise solutions to problems of land reclamation and water and air pollution, such as methods of storing excavated soil and returning exhausted mine sites to natural states. Lay out, direct, and supervise mine construction operations, such as the construction of shafts and tunnels. Evaluate data to develop new mining products, equipment, or processes. Conduct or direct mining experiments to test or prove research findings. Design mining and mineral treatment equipment and machinery in collaboration with other engineering specialists.

Work Conditions—More often indoors than outdoors; very hot or cold; contaminants; hazardous equipment; sitting.

Mobile Heavy Equipment Mechanics, Except Engines
* Level of Education/Training: Postsecondary vocational training
* Annual Earnings: $41,450
* Growth: 12.3%
* Annual Job Openings: 11,037
* Personality Type: Realistic

> Opportunities for heavy vehicle and mobile equipment service technicians and mechanics should be excellent for those who have completed formal training programs in diesel or heavy equipment mechanics. People without formal training are expected to encounter growing difficulty entering these jobs.

Diagnose, adjust, repair, or overhaul mobile mechanical, hydraulic, and pneumatic equipment, such as cranes, bulldozers, graders, and conveyors, used in construction, logging, and surface mining. Test mechanical products and equipment after repair or assembly to ensure proper performance and compliance with manufacturers' specifications. Repair and replace damaged or worn parts. Diagnose faults or malfunctions to determine required repairs, using engine diagnostic equipment such as computerized test equipment and calibration devices. Operate and inspect machines or heavy equipment to diagnose defects. Dismantle and reassemble heavy equipment, using hoists and hand tools. Clean, lubricate, and perform other routine maintenance work on equipment and vehicles. Examine parts for damage or excessive wear, using micrometers and gauges. Read and understand operating manuals, blueprints, and technical drawings. Schedule maintenance for industrial machines and equipment and keep equipment service records.

Overhaul and test machines or equipment to ensure operating efficiency.
Assemble gear systems and align frames and gears. Fit bearings to adjust,
repair, or overhaul mobile mechanical, hydraulic, and pneumatic equipment.
Weld or solder broken parts and structural members, using electric or gas
welders and soldering tools. Clean parts by spraying them with grease solvent
or immersing them in tanks of solvent. Adjust, maintain, and repair or replace
subassemblies, such as transmissions and crawler heads, using hand tools,
jacks, and cranes. Adjust and maintain industrial machinery, using control and
regulating devices. Fabricate needed parts or items from sheet metal. Direct
workers who are assembling or disassembling equipment or cleaning parts.

Work Conditions—Noisy; contaminants; hazardous equipment; minor
burns, cuts, bites, or stings; standing; using hands on objects, tools, or controls.

Nuclear Equipment Operation Technicians

✳ Level of Education/Training: Associate degree

✳ Annual Earnings: $66,140

✳ Growth: 6.7%

✳ Annual Job Openings: 1,021

✳ Personality Type: Realistic

The job openings listed here are shared with Nuclear Monitoring Technicians.

> Although no new nuclear power plants have been built for decades in the
> United States, energy demand has recently renewed interest in this form
> of electricity generation and may lead to future construction.

**Operate equipment used for the release, control, and utilization
of nuclear energy to assist scientists in laboratory and production
activities.** Follow policies and procedures for radiation workers to ensure
personnel safety. Modify, devise, and maintain equipment used in operations.
Set control panel switches, according to standard procedures, to route electric
power from sources and direct particle beams through injector units. Submit
computations to supervisors for review. Calculate equipment operating factors, such as radiation times, dosages, temperatures, gamma intensities, and
pressures, using standard formulas and conversion tables. Perform testing,
maintenance, repair, and upgrading of accelerator systems. Warn maintenance workers of radiation hazards and direct workers to vacate hazardous
areas. Monitor instruments, gauges, and recording devices in control rooms
during operation of equipment under direction of nuclear experiment-
ers. Write summaries of activities and record experimental data, such as

accelerator performance, systems status, particle beam specification, and beam conditions obtained.

Work Conditions—Indoors; noisy; very hot or cold; radiation; hazardous conditions; hazardous equipment.

Nuclear Monitoring Technicians

* Level of Education/Training: Associate degree
* Annual Earnings: $66,140
* Growth: 6.7%
* Annual Job Openings: 1,021
* Personality Type: Realistic

The job openings listed here are shared with Nuclear Equipment Operation Technicians.

> Besides power generation, technicians will be needed to work in defense-related areas, to develop nuclear medical technology, and to improve and enforce waste management and safety standards.

Collect and test samples to monitor results of nuclear experiments and contamination of humans, facilities, and environment. Calculate safe radiation exposure times for personnel, using plant contamination readings and prescribed safe levels of radiation. Provide initial response to abnormal events and to alarms from radiation monitoring equipment. Monitor personnel in order to determine the amounts and intensities of radiation exposure. Inform supervisors when individual exposures or area radiation levels approach maximum permissible limits. Instruct personnel in radiation safety procedures and demonstrate use of protective clothing and equipment. Determine intensities and types of radiation in work areas, equipment, and materials, using radiation detectors and other instruments. Collect samples of air, water, gases, and solids to determine radioactivity levels of contamination. Set up equipment that automatically detects area radiation deviations and test detection equipment to ensure its accuracy. Determine or recommend radioactive decontamination procedures according to the size and nature of equipment and the degree of contamination. Decontaminate objects by cleaning with soap or solvents or by abrading with wire brushes, buffing wheels, or sandblasting machines. Place radioactive waste, such as sweepings and broken sample bottles, into containers for disposal. Calibrate and maintain chemical instrumentation sensing elements and sampling system equipment, using calibration instruments and hand tools. Place irradiated nuclear fuel materials in environmental chambers for testing and observe reactions through cell windows. Enter data into computers in order to record characteristics of nuclear events and locating coordinates of particles. Operate manipulators from outside cells to move specimens into and out of shielded containers, to remove specimens from cells, or to place specimens on benches or equipment workstations. Prepare reports describing contamination tests, material and equipment decontaminated, and methods used in decontamination processes. Confer with scientists directing projects to determine significant events to monitor during tests. Immerse samples in chemical compounds to prepare them for testing.

Work Conditions—Indoors; noisy; very hot or cold; contaminants; radiation; hazardous conditions.

Operating Engineers and Other Construction Equipment Operators

- ❀ Level of Education/Training: Moderate-term on-the-job training
- ❀ Annual Earnings: $38,130
- ❀ Growth: 8.4%
- ❀ Annual Job Openings: 55,468
- ❀ Personality Type: Realistic

> Construction equipment operators who can use a large variety of equipment will have the best prospects. Operators with pipeline experience will have especially good opportunities.

Operate one or several types of power construction equipment, such as motor graders, bulldozers, scrapers, compressors, pumps, derricks, shovels, tractors, or front-end loaders, to excavate, move, and grade earth; erect structures; or pour concrete or other hard-surface pavement. May repair and maintain equipment in addition to other duties. Learn and follow safety regulations. Take actions to avoid potential hazards and obstructions such as utility lines, other equipment, other workers, and falling objects. Adjust handwheels and depress pedals to control attachments such as blades, buckets, scrapers, and swing booms. Start engines; move throttles, switches, and levers; and depress pedals to operate machines such as bulldozers, trench excavators, road graders, and backhoes. Locate underground services, such as pipes and wires, prior to beginning work. Monitor operations to ensure that health and safety standards are met. Align machines, cutterheads, or depth gauge makers with reference stakes and guidelines or ground or position equipment by following hand signals of other workers. Load and move dirt, rocks, equipment, and materials, using trucks, crawler tractors, power cranes, shovels, graders, and related equipment. Drive and maneuver equipment equipped with blades in successive passes over working areas to remove topsoil, vegetation, and rocks and to distribute and level earth or terrain. Coordinate machine actions with other activities, positioning or moving loads in response to hand or audio signals from crew members. Operate tractors and bulldozers to perform such tasks as clearing land, mixing sludge, trimming backfills, and building roadways and parking lots. Repair and maintain equipment, making emergency adjustments or assisting with major repairs as necessary. Check fuel supplies at sites to ensure adequate availability. Connect hydraulic hoses, belts, mechanical linkages, or power takeoff shafts to tractors. Operate loaders to pull out stumps, rip asphalt or concrete, rough-grade properties, bury refuse, or perform general cleanup. Select and fasten bulldozer blades or other attachments to tractors, using hitches. Test atmosphere for adequate oxygen and explosive conditions when working in confined spaces. Operate compactors, scrapers, and rollers to level, compact, and cover refuse at disposal grounds. Talk to clients and study instructions, plans, and diagrams to establish work requirements.

Work Conditions—Outdoors; noisy; very hot or cold; contaminants; whole-body vibration; using hands on objects, tools, or controls.

Petroleum Engineers

❋ Level of Education/Training: Bachelor's degree
❋ Annual Earnings: $103,960
❋ Growth: 5.2%
❋ Annual Job Openings: 1,016
❋ Personality Type: Realistic

> Favorable opportunities are expected for petroleum engineers because the number of job openings is likely to exceed the relatively small number of graduates. Petroleum engineers work around the world; in fact, the best employment opportunities may include some work in other countries.

Devise methods to improve oil and gas well production and determine the need for new or modified tool designs. Oversee drilling and offer technical advice to achieve economical and satisfactory progress. Assess costs and estimate the production capabilities and economic value of oil and gas wells to evaluate the economic viability of potential drilling sites. Monitor production rates and plan rework processes to improve production. Analyze data to recommend placement of wells and supplementary processes to enhance production. Specify and supervise well modification and stimulation programs to maximize oil and gas recovery. Direct and monitor the completion and evaluation of wells, well testing, or well surveys. Assist engineering and other personnel to solve operating problems. Develop plans for oil and gas field drilling and for product recovery and treatment. Maintain records of drilling and production operations. Confer with scientific, engineering, and technical personnel to resolve design, research, and testing problems. Write technical reports for engineering and management personnel. Evaluate findings to develop, design, or test equipment or processes. Assign work to staff to obtain maximum utilization of personnel. Interpret drilling and testing information for personnel. Design and implement environmental controls on oil and gas operations. Coordinate the installation, maintenance, and operation of mining and oilfield equipment. Supervise the removal of drilling equipment, the removal of any waste, and the safe return of land to structural stability when wells or pockets are exhausted. Inspect oil and gas wells to determine that installations are completed. Simulate reservoir performance for different recovery techniques, using computer models. Take samples to assess the amount and quality of oil, the depth at which resources lie, and the equipment needed to properly extract them. Coordinate activities of workers engaged in research, planning, and development. Design or modify mining and oilfield machinery and tools, applying engineering principles. Test machinery and equipment to ensure that it is safe and conforms to performance specifications. Conduct engineering research experiments to improve or modify mining and oil machinery and operations.

Work Conditions—Indoors; sitting.

Pipelayers

* Level of Education/Training: Moderate-term on-the-job training
* Annual Earnings: $31,280
* Growth: 8.7%
* Annual Job Openings: 8,902
* Personality Type: Realistic

> The jobs of pipelayers are generally less sensitive to changes in economic conditions than jobs in other construction trades. Even when construction activity declines, maintenance, rehabilitation, and replacement of existing piping systems provide many jobs.

Lay pipe for storm or sanitation sewers, drains, and water mains. Perform any combination of these tasks: grade trenches or culverts, position pipe, or seal joints. Check slopes for conformance to requirements, using levels or lasers. Cover pipes with earth or other materials. Cut pipes to required lengths. Connect pipe pieces and seal joints, using welding equipment, cement, or glue. Install and repair sanitary and stormwater sewer structures and pipe systems. Install and use instruments such as lasers, grade rods, and transit levels. Grade and level trench bases, using tamping machines and hand tools. Lay out pipe routes, following written instructions or blueprints and coordinating layouts with supervisors. Align and position pipes to prepare them for welding or sealing. Dig trenches to desired or required depths by hand or using trenching tools. Operate mechanized equipment such as pickup trucks, rollers, tandem dump trucks, front-end loaders, and backhoes. Train others in pipe-laying and provide supervision. Tap and drill holes into pipes to introduce auxiliary lines or devices. Locate existing pipes needing repair or replacement, using magnetic or radio indicators.

Work Conditions—Outdoors; noisy; hazardous equipment; standing; using hands on objects, tools, or controls; repetitive motions.

Power Plant Operators

* ❀ Level of Education/Training: Long-term on-the-job training
* ❀ Annual Earnings: $56,640
* ❀ Growth: 2.7%
* ❀ Annual Job Openings: 1,796
* ❀ Personality Type: Realistic

> Prospects should be especially good for people with computer skills and a basic understanding of science and mathematics.

Control, operate, or maintain machinery to generate electric power. Includes auxiliary equipment operators. Operate or control power-generating equipment, including boilers, turbines, generators, and reactors, using control boards or semi-automatic equipment. Monitor and inspect power plant equipment and indicators to detect evidence of operating problems. Adjust controls to generate specified electrical power or to regulate the flow of power between generating stations and substations. Regulate equipment operations and conditions such as water levels based on data from recording and indicating instruments or from computers. Take readings from charts, meters, and gauges at established intervals and take corrective steps as necessary. Inspect records and logbook entries and communicate with other plant personnel to assess equipment operating status. Start or stop generators, auxiliary pumping equipment, turbines, and other power plant equipment and connect or disconnect equipment from circuits. Control and maintain auxiliary equipment, such as pumps, fans, compressors, condensers, feedwater heaters, filters, and chlorinators, to supply water, fuel, lubricants, air, and auxiliary power. Clean, lubricate, and maintain equipment such as generators, turbines, pumps, and compressors in order to prevent equipment failure or deterioration. Communicate with systems operators to regulate and coordinate transmission loads and frequencies and line voltages. Record and compile operational data, completing and maintaining forms, logs, and reports. Open and close valves and switches in sequence upon signals from other workers in order to start or shut down auxiliary units. Collect oil, water, and electrolyte samples for laboratory analysis. Make adjustments or minor repairs, such as tightening leaking gland and pipe joints; report any needs for major repairs. Control generator output to match the phase, frequency, and voltage of electricity supplied to panels. Place standby emergency electrical generators on line in emergencies and monitor the temperature, output, and lubrication of the system. Receive outage calls and call in necessary personnel during power outages and emergencies.

Work Conditions—Indoors; noisy; very hot or cold; contaminants; high places; hazardous conditions.

Rotary Drill Operators, Oil and Gas

❀ Level of Education/Training: Moderate-term on-the-job training
❀ Annual Earnings: $43,480
❀ Growth: –5.4%
❀ Annual Job Openings: 2,145
❀ Personality Type: Realistic

> Fewer than one-fifth of these workers have education beyond high school.

Set up or operate a variety of drills to remove petroleum products from the earth and to find and remove core samples for testing during oil and gas exploration. Train crews and introduce procedures to make drill work more safe and effective. Observe pressure gauge and move throttles and levers to control the speed of rotary tables and to regulate pressure of tools at bottoms of boreholes. Count sections of drill rod to determine depths of boreholes. Push levers and brake pedals to control gasoline, diesel, electric, or steam draw works that lower and raise drill pipes and casings in and out of wells. Connect sections of drill pipe, using hand tools and powered wrenches and tongs. Maintain records of footage drilled, location and nature of strata penetrated, materials and tools used, services rendered, and time required. Maintain and adjust machinery to ensure proper performance. Start and examine operation of slush pumps to ensure circulation and consistency of drilling fluid or mud in well. Locate and recover lost or broken bits, casings, and drill pipes from wells, using special tools. Weigh clay and mix with water and chemicals to make drilling mud. Direct rig crews in drilling and other activities, such as setting up rigs and completing or servicing wells. Monitor progress of drilling operations and select and change drill bits according to the nature of strata, using hand tools. Repair or replace defective parts of machinery, such as rotary drill rigs, water trucks, air compressors, and pumps, using hand tools. Clean and oil pulleys, blocks, and cables. Bolt together pump and engine parts and connect tanks and flow lines. Remove core samples during drilling to determine the nature of the strata being drilled. Cap wells with packers or turn valves to regulate outflow of oil from wells. Line drilled holes with pipes and install all necessary hardware to prepare new wells. Position and prepare truck-mounted derricks at drilling areas that are specified on field maps. Plug observation wells and restore sites. Lower and explode charges in boreholes to start flow of oil from wells. Dig holes, set forms, and mix and pour concrete for foundations of steel or wooden derricks.

Work Conditions—Outdoors; noisy; very hot or cold; contaminants; hazardous equipment; using hands on objects, tools, or controls.

Other Energy Jobs

These jobs play supporting roles in the energy industry, are not expected to have a good outlook (even with help from the recovery plan), or were omitted from the descriptions in this chapter for lack of room.

Accountants (see Management, Scientific, and Technical Consulting Services, chapter 7)

Chief Executives

Computer and Information Systems Managers

Computer Programmers

Computer Software Engineers, Applications (see Computer Systems Design and Related Services, chapter 7)

Computer Support Specialists (see Computer Systems Design and Related Services, chapter 7)

Computer Systems Analysts (see Computer Systems Design and Related Services, chapter 7)

Continuous Mining Machine Operators

Crushing, Grinding, and Polishing Machine Setters, Operators, and Tenders

Dispatchers, Except Police, Fire, and Ambulance

Electro-Mechanical Technicians (see Scientific Research and Development Services, chapter 7)

Engineering Managers (see Manufacturing, chapter 6)

Financial Analysts

Financial Managers

Gas Compressor and Gas Pumping Station Operators

General and Operations Managers

Geological and Petroleum Technicians

Human Resources Managers

Industrial Engineering Technicians (see Manufacturing, chapter 6)

Industrial Engineers (see Manufacturing, chapter 6)

Industrial Production Managers (see Manufacturing, chapter 6)

Industrial Truck and Tractor Operators (see Manufacturing, chapter 6)

Inspectors, Testers, Sorters, Samplers, and Weighers

Loading Machine Operators, Underground Mining

Logisticians

Management Analysts (see Management, Scientific, and Technical Consulting Services, chapter 7)

Marketing Managers (see Management, Scientific, and Technical Consulting Services, chapter 7)

Mechanical Engineering Technicians (see Manufacturing, chapter 6)

Mechanical Engineers (see Manufacturing, chapter 6)

Meter Readers, Utilities

Mine Cutting and Channeling Machine Operators

Network and Computer Systems Administrators (see Computer Systems Design and Related Services, chapter 7)

Nuclear Engineers

Nuclear Power Reactor Operators

Operations Research Analysts

Petroleum Pump System Operators, Refinery Operators, and Gaugers

Power Distributors and Dispatchers

Production, Planning, and Expediting Clerks (see Manufacturing, chapter 6)

Pump Operators, Except Wellhead Pumpers

Roustabouts, Oil and Gas

Sales Managers (see Wholesale Trade, chapter 7)

Security Guards

Separating, Filtering, Clarifying, Precipitating, and Still Machine Setters, Operators, and Tenders

Service Unit Operators, Oil, Gas, and Mining

Shuttle Car Operators

Surveying Technicians

Water and Liquid Waste Treatment Plant and System Operators

Wellhead Pumpers

CHAPTER 3

JOBS IN INFRASTRUCTURE

Obama's plan to repair and expand the American infrastructure is projected to provide 377,000 jobs by the fourth quarter of 2010. Many of these jobs will be in the **construction** industry; in fact, this industry is the one that is expected to benefit most from the recovery package. With 678,000 new or sustained jobs projected for construction, construction obviously is expected to get jobs from several initiatives besides infrastructure.

The infrastructure initiative will also create jobs in the **energy** industry, which is described in chapter 2, and in some of the industries described in chapter 7: **management, scientific, and technical consulting services; computer systems design and related services;** and **wholesale trade.** In each of these chapters you'll find information about key jobs in these industries.

Construction

Nature of the Industry

Houses, apartments, factories, offices, schools, roads, and bridges are only some of the products of the construction industry. This industry's activities include the building of new structures, including site preparation, as well as additions and modifications to existing ones. The industry also includes maintenance, repair, and improvements on these structures.

Construction is heavily dependent upon business cycles. Changes in interest rates and tax laws affect individual and business decisions related to construction activity. State and local budgets affect road construction and maintenance. Changes in regulations can result in new construction or stop planned projects. The effects of these various influences can be short term or long term.

Working Conditions

Hours. Most employees in this industry work full time, and many work more than 40 hours a week. In 2006, about 20 percent of construction workers worked 45 hours or more a week. Construction workers may sometimes work evenings, weekends, and holidays to finish a job or take care of an emergency. Construction workers must often contend with the weather when working outdoors. Rain, snow, or wind may halt construction work. Workers in this industry usually do not get paid if they can't work due to the weather.

Work environment. Workers in this industry need physical stamina because the work frequently requires prolonged standing, bending, stooping, and working in cramped quarters. They also may be required to lift and carry heavy objects. Exposure to weather is common because much of the work is done outside or in partially enclosed structures. Construction workers often work with potentially dangerous tools and equipment amidst a clutter of building materials; some work on temporary scaffolding or at great heights and in bad weather. Consequently, they are more prone to injuries than are workers in other jobs. In 2006, cases of work-related injury and illness were 5.9 per 100 full-time construction workers, which is significantly higher than the 4.4 rate for the entire private sector. Workers who are employed by foundation, structure, and building exterior contractors experienced the highest injury rates. In response, employers increasingly emphasize safe working conditions and habits that reduce the risk of injuries. To avoid injury, employees wear safety clothing, such as gloves and hard hats, and devices to protect their eyes, mouth, or hearing as needed.

Employment

Construction, with 7.7 million wage and salary jobs and 1.9 million self-employed and unpaid family workers in 2006, is one of the nation's largest industries. Construction also maintains the most consistent job growth. About 64 percent of wage and salary jobs in construction are in the specialty trades, primarily plumbing, heating, and air conditioning; electrical; and masonry. Around 24 percent of jobs are mostly in residential and nonresidential construction. The rest are in heavy and civil engineering construction.

Employment in this industry is distributed geographically in much the same way as the nation's population. There were about 883,000 construction establishments in the United States in 2006: 268,000 were building construction contractors, 64,000 were heavy and civil engineering construction or highway contractors, and 550,000 were specialty trade contractors. Most of these establishments tend to be small; 65 percent employ fewer than 5 workers. About 11 percent of workers are employed by small contractors.

Construction offers more opportunities than most other industries for individuals who want to own and run their own business. The 1.9 million self-employed and unpaid family workers in 2006 performed work directly for property owners or acted as contractors on small jobs, such as additions, remodeling, and maintenance projects. The rate of self-employment varies greatly by individual occupation in the construction trades and is partially dependent on the cost of equipment or structure of the work. (Note that the average earnings figures in the job descriptions in this chapter *do not* include self-employed workers.)

Outlook

Long-term job opportunities are expected to be excellent for experienced workers, particularly for certain occupations.

Employment change. The number of wage and salary jobs in the construction industry is expected to grow 10 percent through the year 2016, compared with the 11 percent projected for all industries combined. Employment in this industry depends primarily on the level of construction and remodeling activity that is expected to increase over the coming decade. Construction activity is a key part of the Obama plans for the infrastructure and energy industries.

Although household growth is expected to slow slightly over the coming decade, the increase will create demand for residential construction, especially in the fastest-growing areas in the South and West. Rising numbers of immigrants, as well as the children of the baby boomers, will generate demand for homes and rental apartments. In addition, a desire for larger homes with more amenities will fuel demand for move-up homes, as well as the renovation and expansion of older homes. Townhouses and condominiums in conveniently located suburban and urban settings also are desired types of properties.

Employment is expected to grow faster in nonresidential construction over the decade. Replacement of many industrial plants has been delayed for years, and a large number of structures will have to be replaced or remodeled. Construction of nursing homes and other residential homes for the elderly, as well as all types of health-care facilities, will be necessary to meet the need for more medical treatment facilities, especially by the growing elderly population. Construction of schools will continue to be needed, especially in the South and West where the population is growing the fastest. In other areas, however, replacing and renovating older schools will create jobs.

Employment in heavy and civil engineering construction is projected to increase due to growth in new highway, bridge, and street construction, as well as in maintenance and repairs to prevent further deterioration of the nation's existing highways and bridges. Voters and legislators in most states and localities continue to approve spending on road construction, which will create jobs over the next decade. Another area of expected growth is in power line and related construction. Even with increased conservation and more efficient appliances, there is an increasing demand for power. New power plant construction and connecting these new facilities to the current power grids will increase demand for workers.

The largest number of new jobs is expected to be created in specialty trades contracting because it is the largest segment of the industry and because it is expected to grow about as fast as the rest of the construction industry. The number of jobs will grow as demand increases for subcontractors in new building and heavy construction and as more workers are needed to repair and remodel existing homes, which specialty trade contractors are more likely to perform. Home improvement and repair construction is expected to continue even as new home construction slows. Remodeling should provide many new jobs because of a growing stock of old residential and nonresidential buildings. Many older, smaller homes will be remodeled to appeal to more affluent buyers interested in more space and amenities or in retrofitting for greater energy efficiency. Remodeling tends to be more labor-intensive than new construction. In addition, the construction industry, as well as all types of businesses and institutions, is increasingly contracting out the services of specialty trades workers instead of keeping these workers on their own payrolls.

The number of job openings in construction may fluctuate from year to year. New construction is usually cut back during periods when the economy is not expanding or interest rates are high. However, it is rare that all segments of the construction industry are down at the same time, allowing workers to switch from building houses to working on office building construction, depending on demand.

Although employment in construction trades as a whole is expected to grow about as fast as the industry average, the rate of growth will vary by trade. Employment of boilermakers; roofers; tile and marble setters; and construction and building inspectors is projected to grow faster than the industry average because their specialized services will be in greater demand. On the other hand, employment of carpet installers and floor sanders and finishers is expected to experience little or no growth as the demand for their specialties declines due to lower-cost options and changes in consumer preferences. Employment of rail-track laying and maintenance equipment operators and structural iron and steel workers is expected to grow more slowly than the construction industry as a whole as workers become more productive. Employment of paperhangers and floor layers, except carpet, wood, and hard tile, is expected to decline rapidly due to changes in consumer preferences, lower-cost options, and movement towards tile and prefinished hardwood floors.

Employment of construction managers is expected to grow as a result of the increasing complexity of construction work that needs to be managed, including the need to deal with the proliferation of laws dealing with building construction, worker safety, and environmental issues. Also, the growth of self-employment in this industry is leading to a larger number of managers who own small construction businesses.

Job prospects. Job opportunities are expected to be excellent in the construction industry, especially for construction trades workers, because of the need to replace the large number of workers anticipated to leave these occupations over the next decade, coupled with continued job growth. Furthermore, fewer people are expected to enter the construction trades, reflecting "blue collar bias," the perception that nonprofessional occupations are associated with relatively low status.

Experienced construction workers, and new entrants with a good work history or prior military service, should enjoy the best job prospects. A variety of factors can affect job prospects and competition for positions. Entering specialties requiring specific education, certification, or licensure is likely to improve job prospects for those willing to get the needed certifications, licenses, training, and education. Jobs that cause a worker to be at great heights, are physically demanding, or expose workers to extreme conditions are also more likely to have less competition for positions and often have conditions related to high replacement needs. Occupations that have few training needs are likely to have increased competition and less favorable job prospects.

Certain occupations should have particularly good job opportunities. Because of the difficulty in obtaining certification as a crane operator, some employers have been unable to fill all their construction equipment operator job openings. Electricians, plumbers, pipefitters, and steamfitters are also licensed occupations that should have a favorable outlook due to projected job growth. Roofers should have favorable opportunities due to job growth and difficult working conditions, which lead to high replacement needs. Boilermakers; brickmasons, blockmasons, and stonemasons; and structural and reinforcing iron and rebar workers should have excellent opportunities because of the skills required to perform their duties and the difficult working conditions. Installation and maintenance occupations—including line installers and heating and air-conditioning mechanics and installers—also should have especially favorable prospects because of a growing stock of homes that will require service to maintain interior systems. Construction managers who have a bachelor's degree in construction science with an emphasis on construction management and related work experience in construction management services firms should have especially good prospects as well. Employment growth among administrative support occupations will continue to be limited by office automation. Construction laborers needing less training should face competition for work, as there are few barriers to entrance to this occupation. The outlook for carpenters will be heavily dependent upon residential construction activity, which is unlikely to grow as fast as in recent years. Painters should have good opportunities because of demand for their work, while paperhangers should have less favorable opportunities because of the reduced demand for their work.

Some Infrastructure Jobs That Are Likely to Benefit from the Stimulus Package

Civil Drafters

❋ Level of Education/Training: Postsecondary vocational training
❋ Annual Earnings: $43,310
❋ Growth: 6.1%
❋ Annual Job Openings: 16,238
❋ Personality Type: Realistic

The job openings listed here are shared with Architectural Drafters.

> Opportunities should be best for individuals with at least two years of postsecondary training in drafting and considerable skill and experience using computer-aided design and drafting systems.

Prepare drawings and topographical and relief maps used in civil engineering projects such as highways, bridges, pipelines, flood control projects, and water and sewerage control systems. Produce drawings by using computer-assisted drafting systems (CAD) or drafting machines or by hand, using compasses, dividers, protractors, triangles, and other drafting devices. Draw maps, diagrams, and profiles, using cross-sections and surveys, to represent elevations, topographical contours, subsurface formations, and structures. Draft plans and detailed drawings for structures, installations, and construction projects such as highways, sewage disposal systems, and dikes, working from sketches or notes. Determine the order of work and method of presentation such as orthographic or isometric drawing. Finish and duplicate drawings and documentation packages according to required mediums and specifications for reproduction, using blueprinting, photography, or other duplication methods. Review rough sketches, drawings, specifications, and other engineering data received from civil engineers to ensure that they conform to design concepts. Calculate excavation tonnage and prepare graphs and fill-hauling diagrams for use in earth-moving operations. Supervise and train other technologists, technicians, and drafters. Correlate, interpret, and modify data obtained from topographical surveys, well logs, and geophysical prospecting reports. Determine quality, cost, strength, and quantity of required materials and enter figures on materials lists. Locate and identify symbols located on topographical surveys to denote geological and geophysical formations or oil field installations. Calculate weights, volumes, and stress factors and their implications for technical aspects of designs. Supervise or conduct field surveys, inspections, or technical investigations to obtain data required to revise construction drawings. Explain drawings to production or construction teams and provide adjustments as necessary. Plot characteristics of boreholes for oil and gas wells from photographic subsurface survey recordings and other data, representing depth, degree, and direction of inclination.

Work Conditions—Indoors; sitting; using hands on objects, tools, or controls; repetitive motions.

Construction and Building Inspectors

- ❀ Level of Education/Training: Work experience in a related occupation
- ❀ Annual Earnings: $48,330
- ❀ Growth: 18.2%
- ❀ Annual Job Openings: 12,606
- ❀ Personality Type: Conventional

> Opportunities should be best for experienced construction supervisors and craftworkers who have some college education, engineering or architectural training, or certification as construction inspectors or plan examiners.

Inspect structures using engineering skills to determine structural soundness and compliance with specifications, building codes, and other regulations. Inspections may be general in nature or may be limited to a specific area, such as electrical systems or plumbing. Issue violation notices and stop-work orders, conferring with owners, violators, and authorities to explain regulations and recommend rectifications. Inspect bridges, dams, highways, buildings, wiring, plumbing, electrical circuits, sewers, heating systems, and foundations during and after construction for structural quality, general safety, and conformance to specifications and codes. Approve and sign plans that meet required specifications. Review and interpret plans, blueprints, site layouts, specifications, and construction methods to ensure compliance to legal requirements and safety regulations.

Monitor installation of plumbing, wiring, equipment, and appliances to ensure that installation is performed properly and is in compliance with applicable regulations. Inspect and monitor construction sites to ensure adherence to safety standards, building codes, and specifications. Measure dimensions and verify level, alignment, and elevation of structures and fixtures to ensure compliance to building plans and codes. Maintain daily logs and supplement inspection records with photographs. Use survey instruments, metering devices, tape measures, and test equipment such as concrete strength measurers to perform inspections. Train, direct, and supervise other construction inspectors. Issue permits for construction, relocation, demolition, and occupancy. Examine lifting and conveying devices such as elevators, escalators, moving sidewalks, lifts and hoists, inclined railways, ski lifts, and amusement rides to ensure safety and proper functioning. Compute estimates of work completed or of needed renovations or upgrades and approve payment for contractors. Evaluate premises for cleanliness, including proper garbage disposal and lack of vermin infestation.

Work Conditions—More often outdoors than indoors; very hot or cold; very bright or dim lighting; contaminants; cramped work space, awkward positions.

Construction Carpenters

❈ Level of Education/Training: Long-term on-the-job training
❈ Annual Earnings: $37,660
❈ Growth: 10.3%
❈ Annual Job Openings: 223,225
❈ Personality Type: Realistic

The job openings listed here are shared with Rough Carpenters.

> About one-third of all carpenters—the largest construction trade—are self-employed.

Construct, erect, install, and repair structures and fixtures of wood, plywood, and wallboard, using carpenter's hand tools and power tools. Measure and mark cutting lines on materials, using ruler, pencil, chalk, and marking gauge. Follow established safety rules and regulations and maintain a safe and clean environment. Verify trueness of structure, using plumb bob and level. Shape or cut materials to specified measurements, using hand tools, machines, or power saw. Study specifications in blueprints, sketches, or building plans to prepare project layout and determine dimensions and materials required. Assemble and fasten materials to make framework or props, using hand tools and wood screws, nails, dowel pins, or glue. Build or repair cabinets, doors, frameworks, floors, and other wooden fixtures used in buildings, using woodworking machines, carpenter's hand tools, and power tools. Erect scaffolding and ladders for assembling structures above ground level. Remove damaged or defective parts or sections of structures and repair or replace, using hand tools. Install structures and fixtures, such as windows, frames, floorings, and trim, or hardware, using carpenter's hand and power tools. Select and order lumber and other required materials. Maintain records, document actions, and present written progress reports. Finish surfaces of woodwork or wallboard in houses and buildings, using paint, hand tools, and paneling. Prepare cost estimates for clients or employers. Arrange for subcontractors to deal with special areas such as heating and electrical wiring work. Inspect ceiling or floor tile, wall coverings, siding, glass, or woodwork to detect broken or damaged structures. Work with or remove hazardous material. Construct forms and chutes for pouring concrete. Cover subfloors with building paper to keep out moisture and lay hardwood, parquet, and wood-strip-block floors by nailing floors to subfloor or cementing them to mastic or asphalt base. Fill cracks and other defects in plaster or plasterboard and sand patch, using patching plaster, trowel, and sanding tool. Perform minor plumbing, welding, or concrete mixing work. Apply shock-absorbing, sound-deadening, and decorative paneling to ceilings and walls.

Work Conditions—Outdoors; noisy; hazardous equipment; standing; walking and running; using hands on objects, tools, or controls.

Construction Managers

- Level of Education/Training: Bachelor's degree
- Annual Earnings: $76,230
- Growth: 15.7%
- Annual Job Openings: 44,158
- Personality Type: Enterprising

> Although certification is not required, there is a growing movement toward certification of construction managers.

Plan, direct, coordinate, or budget, usually through subordinate supervisory personnel, activities concerned with the construction and maintenance of structures, facilities, and systems. Participate in the conceptual development of a construction project and oversee its organization, scheduling, and implementation. Schedule the project in logical steps and budget time required to meet deadlines. Confer with supervisory personnel, owners, contractors, and design professionals to discuss and resolve matters such as work procedures, complaints, and construction problems. Prepare contracts and negotiate revisions, changes, and additions to contractual agreements with architects, consultants, clients, suppliers, and subcontractors. Prepare and submit budget estimates and progress and cost tracking reports. Interpret and explain plans and contract terms to administrative staff, workers, and clients, representing the owner or developer. Plan, organize, and direct activities concerned with the construction and maintenance of structures, facilities, and systems. Take actions to deal with the results of delays, bad weather, or emergencies at construction sites. Inspect and review projects to monitor compliance with building and safety codes and other regulations. Study job specifications to determine appropriate construction methods. Select, contract, and oversee workers who complete specific pieces of the project, such as painting or plumbing. Obtain all necessary permits and licenses. Direct and supervise workers. Develop and implement quality control programs. Investigate damage, accidents, or delays at construction sites to ensure that proper procedures are being carried out. Determine labor requirements and dispatch workers to construction sites. Evaluate construction methods and determine cost-effectiveness of plans, using computers. Requisition supplies and materials to complete construction projects. Direct acquisition of land for construction projects.

Work Conditions—More often outdoors than indoors; noisy; contaminants; hazardous equipment; sitting.

Cost Estimators

- ❋ Level of Education/Training: Work experience in a related occupation
- ❋ Annual Earnings: $54,920
- ❋ Growth: 18.5%
- ❋ Annual Job Openings: 38,379
- ❋ Personality Type: Conventional

> Voluntary certification can be valuable to cost estimators; some individual employers may require professional certification for employment.

Prepare cost estimates for product manufacturing, construction projects, or services to aid management in bidding on or determining prices of products or services. May specialize according to particular service performed or type of product manufactured. Consult with clients, vendors, personnel in other departments, or construction foremen to discuss and formulate estimates and resolve issues. Analyze blueprints and other documentation to prepare time, cost, materials, and labor estimates. Prepare estimates for use in selecting vendors or subcontractors. Confer with engineers, architects, owners, contractors, and subcontractors on changes and adjustments to cost estimates. Prepare estimates used by management for purposes such as planning, organizing, and scheduling work. Prepare cost and expenditure statements and other necessary documentation at regular intervals for the duration of the project. Assess cost-effectiveness of products, projects, or services, tracking actual costs relative to bids as projects develop. Set up cost-monitoring and cost-reporting systems and procedures. Conduct special studies to develop and establish standard hour and related cost data or to effect cost reductions. Review material and labor requirements to decide whether it is more cost-effective to produce or purchase components. Prepare and maintain a directory of suppliers, contractors, and subcontractors. Establish and maintain tendering processes and conduct negotiations. Visit sites and record information about access, drainage and topography, and availability of services such as water and electricity.

Work Conditions—Indoors; sitting.

Electricians

* Level of Education/Training: Long-term on-the-job training
* Annual Earnings: $44,780
* Growth: 7.4%
* Annual Job Openings: 79,083
* Personality Type: Realistic

> Most electricians acquire their skills by completing an apprenticeship program lasting four to five years.

Install, maintain, and repair electrical wiring, equipment, and fixtures. Ensure that work is in accordance with relevant codes. May install or service street lights, intercom systems, or electrical control systems. Maintain current electrician's license or identification card to meet governmental regulations. Connect wires to circuit breakers, transformers, or other components. Repair or replace wiring, equipment, and fixtures, using hand tools and power tools. Assemble, install, test, and maintain electrical or electronic wiring, equipment, appliances, apparatus, and fixtures, using hand tools and power tools. Test electrical systems and continuity of circuits in electrical wiring, equipment, and fixtures, using testing devices such as ohmmeters, voltmeters, and oscilloscopes, to ensure compatibility and safety of system. Use a variety of tools and equipment such as power construction equipment, measuring devices, power tools, and testing equipment, including oscillo-scopes, ammeters, and test lamps. Plan layout and installation of electrical wiring, equipment, and fixtures based on job specifications and local codes. Inspect electrical systems, equipment, and components to identify hazards, defects, and the need for adjustment or repair and to ensure compliance with codes. Direct and train workers to install, maintain, or repair electrical wiring, equipment, and fixtures. Diagnose malfunctioning systems, apparatus, and components, using test equipment and hand tools, to locate the cause of a breakdown and correct the problem. Prepare sketches or follow blueprints to determine the location of wiring and equipment and to ensure conformance to building and safety codes. Install ground leads and connect power cables to equipment such as motors. Work from ladders, scaffolds, and roofs to install, maintain, or repair electrical wiring, equipment, and fixtures. Perform business management duties such as maintaining records and files, preparing reports, and ordering supplies and equipment. Fasten small metal or plastic boxes to walls to house electrical switches or outlets. Place conduit, pipes, or tubing inside designated partitions, walls, or other concealed areas and pull insulated wires or cables through the conduit to complete circuits between boxes. Advise management on whether continued operation of equipment could be hazardous.

Work Conditions—Noisy; cramped work space, awkward positions; hazardous conditions; hazardous equipment; standing; using hands on objects, tools, or controls.

Environmental Engineering Technicians

- ❀ Level of Education/Training: Associate degree
- ❀ Annual Earnings: $40,690
- ❀ Growth: 24.8%
- ❀ Annual Job Openings: 2,162
- ❀ Personality Type: No data available

> Because the type and quality of training programs vary considerably, pro-spective students should carefully investigate training programs before enrolling.

Apply theory and principles of environmental engineering to modify, test, and operate equipment and devices used in the prevention, control, and remediation of environmental pollution, including waste treatment and site remediation. May assist in the development of envi-ronmental pollution remediation devices under direction of engineer.

Receive, set up, test, and decontaminate equipment. Maintain project logbook records and computer program files. Perform environmental quality work in field and office settings. Conduct pollution surveys, collecting and analyzing samples such as air and groundwater. Review technical documents to ensure completeness and conformance to requirements. Perform laboratory work such as logging numerical and visual observations, preparing and packaging samples, recording test results, and performing photo documentation. Review work plans to schedule activities. Obtain product information, identify vendors and suppliers, and order materials and equipment to maintain inventory. Arrange for the disposal of lead, asbestos, and other hazardous materials. Inspect facilities to monitor compliance with regulations governing substances such as asbestos, lead, and wastewater. Provide technical engineering support in the planning of projects such as wastewater treatment plants to ensure compliance with environmental regulations and policies. Improve chemical processes to reduce toxic emissions. Oversee support staff. Assist in the cleanup of hazardous material spills. Produce environmental assessment reports, tabulating data and preparing charts, graphs, and sketches. Maintain process parameters and evaluate process anomalies. Work with customers to assess the environmental impact of proposed construction and to develop pollution prevention programs. Perform statistical analysis and correction of air or water pollution data submitted by industry and other agencies. Develop work plans, including writing specifications and establishing material, manpower, and facilities needs.

Work Conditions—More often indoors than outdoors; contaminants; hazardous conditions; hazardous equipment; standing.

Helpers—Electricians

- ❋ Level of Education/Training: Short-term on-the-job training
- ❋ Annual Earnings: $24,880
- ❋ Growth: 6.8%
- ❋ Annual Job Openings: 35,109
- ❋ Personality Type: Realistic

Although most workers are employed in the construction industry, there also will be opportunities in other industries.

Help electricians by performing duties of lesser skill. Duties include using, supplying, or holding materials or tools and cleaning work area and equipment. Trace out short circuits in wiring, using test meter. Measure, cut, and bend wire and conduit, using measuring instruments and hand tools. Maintain tools, vehicles, and equipment and keep parts and supplies in order. Drill holes and pull or push wiring through openings, using hand and power tools. Perform semi-skilled and unskilled laboring duties related to the installation, maintenance, and repair of a wide variety of electrical systems and equipment. Disassemble defective electrical equipment, replace defective or worn parts, and reassemble equipment, using hand tools. Transport tools, materials, equipment, and supplies to worksite by hand; handtruck; or heavy, motorized truck. Examine electrical units for loose connections and broken insulation and tighten connections, using hand tools. Strip insulation from wire ends, using wire-stripping pliers, and attach wires to terminals for subsequent soldering. Construct controllers and panels, using power drills, drill presses, taps, saws, and punches. Thread conduit ends, connect couplings, and fabricate and secure conduit support brackets, using hand tools. String transmission lines or cables through ducts or conduits, under the ground, through equipment, or to towers. Clean work area and wash parts. Erect electrical system components and barricades and rig scaffolds, hoists, and shoring. Install copper-clad ground rods, using a manual post driver. Raise, lower, or position equipment, tools, and materials, using hoist, hand line, or block and tackle. Dig trenches or holes for installation of conduit or supports. Requisition materials, using warehouse requisition or release forms. Bolt component parts together to form tower assemblies, using hand tools. Paint a variety of objects related to electrical functions. Operate cutting torches and welding equipment while working with conduit and metal components to construct devices associated with electrical functions. Break up concrete, using air hammer, to facilitate installation, construction, or repair of equipment. Solder electrical connections, using soldering iron. Trim trees and clear undergrowth along right-of-way.

Work Conditions—Outdoors; very hot or cold; contaminants; high places; standing; using hands on objects, tools, or controls.

Rail-Track Laying and Maintenance Equipment Operators

❀ Level of Education/Training: Moderate-term on-the-job training
❀ Annual Earnings: $42,120
❀ Growth: 4.8%
❀ Annual Job Openings: 1,817
❀ Personality Type: Realistic

Almost one-third of workers have some education beyond high school.

Lay, repair, and maintain track for standard or narrow-gauge railroad equipment used in regular railroad service or in plant yards, quarries, sand and gravel pits, and mines. Includes ballast-cleaning-machine operators and roadbed-tamping-machine operators. Drive vehicles that automatically move and lay tracks or rails over sections of track to be constructed, repaired, or maintained. Operate track-wrench machines to tighten or loosen bolts at joints that hold ends of rails together. Clean, grade, and level ballast on railroad tracks. Dress and reshape worn or damaged railroad switch points and frogs, using portable power grinders. Push controls to close grasping devices on track or rail sections so that they can be raised or moved. Drive graders, tamping machines, brooms, and ballast cleaning/spreading machines to redistribute gravel and ballast between rails. Adjust controls of machines that spread, shape, raise, level, and align track according to specifications. Engage mechanisms that lay tracks or rails to specified gauges. Grind ends of new or worn rails to attain smooth joints, using portable grinders. Observe leveling indicator arms to verify levelness and alignment of tracks. Operate single- or multiple-head spike-driving machines to drive spikes into ties and secure rails. Operate single- or multiple-head spike pullers to pull old spikes from ties. Operate tie-adzing machines to cut ties and permit insertion of fishplates that hold rails. Drill holes through rails, tie plates, and fishplates for insertion of bolts and spikes, using power drills. Repair and adjust track switches, using wrenches and replacement parts. Spray ties, fishplates, and joints with oil to protect them from weathering. String and attach wire-guidelines machine to rails so that tracks or rails can be aligned or leveled. Cut rails to specified lengths, using rail saws. Patrol assigned track sections so that damaged or broken track can be located and reported. Paint railroad signs, such as speed limits and gate-crossing warnings. Lubricate machines, change oil, and fill hydraulic reservoirs to specified levels. Clean tracks and clear ice and snow from tracks and switch boxes. Clean and make minor repairs to machines and equipment. Turn wheels of machines, using lever controls, to adjust guidelines for track alignments and grades, following specifications.

Work Conditions—Outdoors; noisy; very hot or cold; hazardous equipment; standing; using hands on objects, tools, or controls.

Reinforcing Iron and Rebar Workers

❋ Level of Education/Training: Long-term on-the-job training
❋ Annual Earnings: $37,890
❋ Growth: 11.5%
❋ Annual Job Openings: 4,502
❋ Personality Type: Realistic

> Most employers recommend completion of a formal three- or four-year apprenticeship, but some workers learn on the job.

Position and secure steel bars or mesh in concrete forms to reinforce concrete. Use a variety of fasteners, rod-bending machines, blowtorches, and hand tools. Cut rods to required lengths, using metal shears, hacksaws, bar cutters, or acetylene torches. Determine quantities, sizes, shapes, and locations of reinforcing rods from blueprints, sketches, or oral instructions. Space and fasten together rods in forms according to blueprints, using wire and pliers. Place blocks under rebar to hold the bars off the deck when reinforcing floors. Bend steel rods with hand tools and rod-bending machines and weld them with arc-welding equipment. Cut and fit wire mesh or fabric, using hooked rods, and position fabric or mesh in concrete to reinforce concrete. Position and secure steel bars, rods, cables, or mesh in concrete forms, using fasteners, rod-bending machines, blowtorches, and hand tools.

Work Conditions—Outdoors; contaminants; standing; walking and running; using hands on objects, tools, or controls; repetitive motions.

Telecommunications Line Installers and Repairers

❀ Level of Education/Training: Long-term on-the-job training
❀ Annual Earnings: $47,220
❀ Growth: 4.6%
❀ Annual Job Openings: 14,719
❀ Personality Type: Realistic

> A growing number of retirements should create very good job opportunities, especially for electrical power-line installers and repairers.

String and repair telephone and television cable, including fiber optics and other equipment for transmitting messages or television programming. Travel to customers' premises to install, maintain, and repair audio and visual electronic reception equipment and accessories. Inspect and test lines and cables, recording and analyzing test results, to assess transmission characteristics and locate faults and malfunctions. Splice cables, using hand tools, epoxy, or mechanical equipment. Measure signal strength at utility poles, using electronic test equipment. Set up service for customers, installing, connecting, testing, and adjusting equipment. Place insulation over conductors and seal splices with moisture-proof covering. Access specific areas to string lines and install terminal boxes, auxiliary equipment, and appliances, using bucket trucks, or by climbing poles and ladders or entering tunnels, trenches, or crawl spaces. String cables between structures and lines from poles, towers, or trenches and pull lines to proper tension. Install equipment such as amplifiers and repeaters to maintain the strength of communications transmissions. Lay underground cable directly in trenches or string it through conduits running through trenches. Pull up cable by hand from large reels mounted on trucks; then pull lines through ducts by hand or with winches. Clean and maintain tools and test equipment. Explain cable service to subscribers after installation and collect any installation fees that are due. Compute impedance of wires from poles to houses to determine additional resistance needed for reducing signals to desired levels. Use a variety of construction equipment to complete installations, including digger derricks, trenchers, and cable plows. Dig trenches for underground wires and cables. Dig holes for power poles, using power augers or shovels, set poles in place with cranes, and hoist poles upright, using winches. Fill and tamp holes, using cement, earth, and tamping devices. Participate in the construction and removal of telecommunication towers and associated support structures.

Work Conditions—Outdoors; very hot or cold; contaminants; cramped work space, awkward positions; hazardous equipment; using hands on objects, tools, or controls.

Welders, Cutters, and Welder Fitters

* Level of Education/Training: Long-term on-the-job training
* Annual Earnings: $32,270
* Growth: 5.1%
* Annual Job Openings: 61,125
* Personality Type: Realistic

The job openings listed here are shared with Solderers and Brazers.

> Job prospects should be excellent because employers report difficulty finding enough qualified people.

Use hand-welding or flame-cutting equipment to weld or join metal components or to fill holes, indentations, or seams of fabricated metal products. Operate safety equipment and use safe work habits. Weld components in flat, vertical, or overhead positions. Ignite torches or start power supplies and strike arcs by touching electrodes to metals being welded, completing electrical circuits. Clamp, hold, tack-weld, heat-bend, grind, or bolt component parts to obtain required configurations and positions for welding.

Detect faulty operation of equipment or defective materials and notify supervisors. Operate manual or semi-automatic welding equipment to fuse metal segments, using processes such as gas tungsten arc, gas metal arc, flux-cored arc, plasma arc, shielded metal arc, resistance welding, and submerged arc welding. Monitor the fitting, burning, and welding processes to avoid overheating of parts or warping, shrinking, distortion, or expansion of material. Examine workpieces for defects and measure workpieces with straightedges or templates to ensure conformance with specifications. Recognize, set up, and operate hand and power tools common to the welding trade, such as shielded metal arc and gas metal arc welding equipment. Lay out, position, align, and secure parts and assemblies prior to assembly, using straightedges, combination squares, calipers, and rulers. Chip or grind off excess weld, slag, or spatter, using hand scrapers or power chippers, portable grinders, or arc-cutting equipment. Analyze engineering drawings, blueprints, specifications, sketches, work orders, and material safety data sheets to plan layout, assembly, and welding operations. Connect and turn regulator valves to activate and adjust gas flow and pressure so that desired flames are obtained. Weld separately or in combination, using aluminum, stainless steel, cast iron, and other alloys. Determine required equipment and welding methods, applying knowledge of metallurgy, geometry, and welding techniques. Mark or tag material with proper job number, piece marks, and other identifying marks as required. Prepare all material surfaces to be welded, ensuring that there is no loose or thick scale, slag, rust, moisture, grease, or other foreign matter.

Work Conditions—Noisy; contaminants; minor burns, cuts, bites, or stings; standing; using hands on objects, tools, or controls; repetitive motions.

Other Infrastructure Jobs

These jobs play supporting roles in the construction industry, are not expected to have a good outlook (even with help from the recovery plan), or were omitted from the descriptions in this chapter for lack of room.

Accountants (see Management, Scientific, and Technical Consulting Services, chapter 7)

Architectural Drafters

Bookkeeping, Accounting, and Auditing Clerks (see Management, Scientific, and Technical Consulting Services, chapter 7)

Carpet Installers

Cartographers and Photogrammetrists

Cement Masons and Concrete Finishers

City and Regional Planning Aides

Civil Engineering Technicians

Civil Engineers (see Scientific Research and Development Services, chapter 7)

Cleaners of Vehicles and Equipment

Construction Laborers

Conveyor Operators and Tenders

Crane and Tower Operators

Dredge Operators

Driver/Sales Workers

Electrical Engineering Technicians (see Management, Scientific, and Technical Consulting Services, chapter 7)

Electrical Engineers (see Management, Scientific, and Technical Consulting Services, chapter 7)

Electrical Power-Line Installers and Repairers (see Energy, chapter 2)

Elevator Installers and Repairers

Environmental Engineers (see Scientific Research and Development Services, chapter 7)

Excavating and Loading Machine and Dragline Operators (see Energy, chapter 2)

Explosives Workers, Ordnance Handling Experts, and Blasters

Fence Erectors

Fire-Prevention and Protection Engineers

First-Line Supervisors/Managers of Construction Trades and Extraction Workers

First-Line Supervisors/Managers of Mechanics, Installers, and Repairers

Floor Layers, Except Carpet, Wood, and Hard Tiles

Floor Sanders and Finishers

Forest and Conservation Technicians

General and Operations Managers

Glaziers

Hazardous Materials Removal Workers

Heating, Air Conditioning, and Refrigeration Mechanics and Installers

Helpers—Brickmasons, Blockmasons, Stonemasons, and Tile and Marble Setters

Helpers—Carpenters

Helpers—Painters, Paperhangers, Plasterers, and Stucco Masons

Helpers—Pipelayers, Plumbers, Pipefitters, and Steamfitters

Helpers—Roofers

Highway Maintenance Workers

Hoist and Winch Operators

Industrial Engineers (see Manufacturing, chapter 6)

Industrial Machinery Mechanics (see Manufacturing, chapter 6)

Industrial Safety and Health Engineers

Industrial Truck and Tractor Operators (see Manufacturing, chapter 6)

Insulation Workers, Floor, Ceiling, and Wall

Insulation Workers, Mechanical

Janitors and Cleaners, Except Maids and Housekeeping Cleaners

Laborers and Freight, Stock, and Material Movers, Hand

Machine Feeders and Offbearers

Mapping Technicians

Mobile Heavy Equipment Mechanics, Except Engines (see Energy, chapter 2)

Operating Engineers and Other Construction Equipment Operators (see Energy, chapter 2)

Painters, Construction and Maintenance

Paperhangers

Paving, Surfacing, and Tamping Equipment Operators

Pile-Driver Operators

Pipelayers (see Energy, chapter 2)

Plasterers and Stucco Masons

Pump Operators, Except Wellhead Pumpers

Receptionists and Information Clerks

Riggers

Rough Carpenters

Sales Representatives, Wholesale and Manufacturing, Except Technical and Scientific Products (see Wholesale Trade, chapter 7)

Secretaries, Except Legal, Medical, and Executive

Segmental Pavers

Septic Tank Servicers and Sewer Pipe Cleaners

Sheet Metal Workers

Soil and Water Conservationists

Structural Iron and Steel Workers

Surveying Technicians

Surveyors

Tapers

Telecommunications Equipment Installers and Repairers, Except Line Installers

Truck Drivers, Heavy and Tractor-Trailer (see Wholesale Trade, chapter 7)

Truck Drivers, Light or Delivery Services (see Wholesale Trade, chapter 7)

Urban and Regional Planners

CHAPTER 4

JOBS IN HEALTH CARE

H ealth care is already the nation's largest and fastest-growing industry—and is therefore an excellent place to plan a career. The Obama recovery plan is projected to add or sustain 100,000 jobs to the industry, more or less, by the fourth quarter of 2010. (The figure is very imprecise because the transition team does not project a separate figure for health care; it projects 240,000 for health care and education combined.) Two Obama initiatives in particular, targeted at health care and state relief, will boost health-care jobs.

The health-care initiative will also create jobs in other sectors of our economy, especially the **management, scientific, and technical consulting services** industry and the **computer systems design and related services** industry, both of which are described in chapter 7, along with important jobs in those industries.

Health Care

Nature of the Industry

Combining medical technology and the human touch, the health-care industry administers care around the clock, responding to the needs of millions of people—from newborns to the critically ill.

Technological advances have made many new medical procedures and methods of diagnosis and treatment possible. Clinical developments such as infection control, less-invasive surgical techniques, advances in reproductive technology, and gene therapy for cancer treatment continue to increase the longevity and improve the quality of life of many Americans. Advances in medical technology also have improved the survival rates of trauma victims and the severely ill, who need extensive care from therapists and social workers as well as other support personnel.

In addition, advances in information technology continue to improve patient care and worker efficiency with devices such as handheld computers that record notes on each patient. Information on vital signs and orders for tests are transferred electronically to a main database; this process eliminates the need for paper and reduces recordkeeping errors. The Obama administration's budgetary plans are based partly on the assumption that expansion of electronic medical records will help bring down health-care costs.

Cost containment is shaping the health-care industry in many other ways, such as the growing emphasis on providing services on an outpatient, ambulatory basis; limiting unnecessary or low-priority services; and stressing preventive care, which reduces the potential cost of undiagnosed, untreated medical conditions. Enrollment in managed care programs—predominantly preferred provider organizations, health maintenance organizations, and hybrid plans such as point-of-service programs—continues to grow. These prepaid plans provide comprehensive coverage to members and control health insurance costs by emphasizing preventive care. Cost effectiveness also is improved with the increased use of integrated delivery systems, which combine two or more segments of the industry to increase efficiency through the streamlining of functions, primarily financial and managerial. These changes will continue to reshape not only the nature of the health-care workforce, but also the manner in which health care is provided.

Working Conditions

Hours. Average weekly hours of nonsupervisory workers in private health care varied among the different segments of the industry. Workers in offices of dentists averaged only 27.1 hours per week in 2006, while those in psychiatric and substance abuse hospitals averaged 35.7 hours, compared with 33.9 hours for all private industry.

Many workers in the health-care industry are on part-time schedules. Part-time workers made up about 19 percent of the health-care workforce as a whole in 2006, but accounted for 38 percent of workers in offices of dentists and 31 percent of those in offices of other health practitioners. Many health-care establishments operate around the clock and need staff at all hours. Shift work is common in some occupations, such as registered nurses. Numerous health-care workers hold more than one job.

Work environment. In 2006, the incidence of occupational injury and illness in hospitals was 8.1 cases per 100 full-time workers, compared with an average of 4.4 for private industry overall. Nursing care facilities had a higher rate of 9.8. Health-care workers involved in direct patient care must take precautions to prevent back strain from lifting patients and equipment; to minimize exposure to radiation and caustic chemicals; and to guard against infectious diseases such as AIDS, tuberculosis, and hepatitis. Home care personnel who make house calls are exposed to the possibility of being injured in highway accidents, all types of overexertion when assisting patients, and falls inside and outside homes.

Employment

As the largest industry in 2006, health care provided 14 million jobs—13.6 million jobs for wage and salary workers and about 438,000 jobs for self-employed and unpaid family workers. Of the 13.6 million wage and salary jobs, 40 percent were in hospitals, another 21 percent were in nursing and residential care facilities, and 16 percent were in offices of physicians. The majority of jobs for self-employed and unpaid family workers in health care were in offices of physicians, dentists, and other health practitioners—about 295,000 out of the 438,000 total self-employed.

Health-care jobs are found throughout the country, but they are concentrated in the largest states—in particular, California, New York, Florida, Texas, and Pennsylvania.

Workers in health care tend to be older than workers in other industries. Health-care workers also are more likely to remain employed in the same occupation, in part because of the high level of education and training required for many health occupations.

Outlook

Health care will generate 3 million new wage and salary jobs between 2006 and 2016, more than any other industry. Seven of the twenty fastest-growing occupations are related to health care. Job opportunities should be good in all employment settings.

Employment change. Wage and salary employment in the health-care industry is projected to increase 22 percent through 2016, compared with 11 percent for all industries combined. Employment growth is expected to account for about 3 million new wage and salary jobs—20 percent of all wage and salary jobs added to the economy over the 2006–2016 period. Projected rates of employment growth for the various segments of the industry range from 13 percent in hospitals, the largest and slowest-growing industry segment, to 55 percent in the much smaller home health-care services.

Employment in health care will continue to grow for several reasons. The number of people in older age groups, with much-greater-than-average health-care needs, will grow faster than the total population between 2006 and 2016; as a result, the demand for health care will increase. Employment in home health care and nursing and residential care should increase rapidly as life expectancies rise and as aging children are less able to care for their parents and rely more on long-term-care facilities. Advances in medical technology will continue to improve the survival rate of severely ill and injured patients, who will then need extensive therapy and care. New technologies will make it possible to identify and treat conditions that were previously not treatable. Medical group practices and integrated health systems will become larger and more complex, increasing the need for office and administrative support workers. Industry growth also will occur as a result of the shift from inpatient to less expensive outpatient and home health care because of improvements in diagnostic tests and surgical procedures, along with patients' desires to be treated at home.

Many of the occupations projected to grow the fastest in the economy are concentrated in the health-care industry. For example, over the 2006–2016 period, total employment of home health aides—including the self-employed—is projected to increase by 49 percent, medical assistants by 35 percent, physical therapist assistants by 32 percent, and physician assistants by 27 percent.

Rapid growth is expected for workers in occupations concentrated outside the inpatient hospital sector, such as pharmacy technicians and personal and home care aides. Because of cost pressures, many health-care facilities will adjust their staffing patterns to reduce labor costs. Where patient care demands and regulations allow, health-care facilities will substitute lower-paid providers and will cross-train their workforces. Many facilities have cut the number of middle managers while simultaneously creating new managerial positions as the facilities diversify. Traditional inpatient hospital positions are no longer the only option for many future health-care workers; persons seeking a career in the field must be willing to work in various employment settings. Hospitals will be the slowest-growing segment within the health-care industry because of efforts to control hospital costs and the increasing use of outpatient clinics and other alternative care sites.

Demand for dental care will rise due to population growth, greater retention of natural teeth by middle-aged and older persons, greater awareness of the importance of dental care, and an increased ability to pay for services. Dentists will use support personnel such as dental hygienists and assistants to help meet their increased workloads.

In some management, business, and financial operations occupations, rapid growth will be tempered by restructuring to reduce administrative costs and streamline operations. Office automation and other technological changes will slow employment growth in office and administrative support occupations, but because the employment base is large, replacement needs will continue to create substantial numbers of job openings. Slower-growing service occupations also will provide job openings that are due to replacement needs.

Job prospects. Job opportunities should be good in all employment settings because of high job turnover, particularly from the large number of expected retirements and tougher immigration rules that are slowing the numbers of foreign health-care workers entering the United States.

Occupations with the most replacement openings are usually large, with high turnover stemming from low pay and status, poor benefits, low training requirements, and a high proportion of young and part-time workers. Nursing aides, orderlies, and attendants and home health aides are among the occupations adding the most new jobs between 2006 and 2016, about 647,000 combined. By contrast, occupations with relatively few replacement openings—such as physicians and surgeons—are characterized by high pay and status, lengthy training requirements, and a high proportion of full-time workers.

Another occupation that is expected to have many openings is registered nurses. The median age of registered nurses is increasing, and not enough younger workers are replacing them. As a result, employers in some parts of the country are reporting difficulties in attracting and retaining nurses. Imbalances between the supply of and the demand for qualified workers should spur efforts to attract and retain qualified registered nurses. For example, employers may restructure workloads and job responsibilities, improve compensation and working conditions, and subsidize training or continuing education.

Health-care workers at all levels of education and training will continue to be in demand. In many cases, it may be easier for job seekers with health-specific training to obtain jobs and advance in their careers. Specialized clinical training is a requirement for many jobs in health care and is an asset even for many administrative jobs that do not specifically require it.

Office automation and other technological changes will slow employment growth in office and administrative support occupations, but because the employment base is large, replacement needs will continue to create substantial numbers of job openings. Slower-growing service occupations also will provide job openings created by replacement needs.

Some Health-Care Jobs That Are Likely to Benefit from the Stimulus Package

Dentists, General

❀ Level of Education/Training: First professional degree
❀ Annual Earnings: $137,630
❀ Growth: 9.2%
❀ Annual Job Openings: 7,106
❀ Personality Type: Investigative

> Job prospects should be good. Average employment growth will generate
> some job openings, but most openings will result from the need to replace
> the large number of dentists expected to retire.

Diagnose and treat diseases, injuries, and malformations of teeth and gums and related oral structures. May treat diseases of nerve, pulp, and other dental tissues affecting vitality of teeth. Use masks, gloves, and safety glasses to protect themselves and their patients from infectious diseases. Administer anesthetics to limit the amount of pain experienced by patients during procedures. Examine teeth, gums, and related tissues, using dental instruments, X-rays, and other diagnostic equipment, to evaluate dental health, diagnose diseases or abnormalities, and plan appropriate treatments. Formulate plan of treatment for patient's teeth and mouth tissue. Use air turbine and hand instruments, dental appliances, and surgical implements. Advise and instruct patients regarding preventive dental care, the causes and treatment of dental problems, and oral health-care services. Design, make, and fit prosthodontic appliances such as space maintainers, bridges, and dentures or write fabrication instructions or prescriptions for denturists and dental technicians. Diagnose and treat diseases, injuries, and malformations of teeth, gums, and related oral structures and provide preventive and corrective services. Fill pulp chamber and canal with endodontic materials. Write prescriptions for antibiotics and other medications. Analyze and evaluate dental needs to determine changes and trends in patterns of dental disease. Treat exposure of pulp by pulp capping, removal of pulp from pulp chamber, or root canal, using dental instruments. Eliminate irritating margins of fillings and correct occlusions, using dental instruments. Perform oral and periodontal surgery on the jaw or mouth. Remove diseased tissue, using surgical instruments. Apply fluoride and sealants to teeth. Manage business, employing and supervising staff and handling paperwork and insurance claims. Bleach, clean, or polish teeth to restore natural color. Plan, organize, and maintain dental health programs. Produce and evaluate dental health educational materials.

Work Conditions—Indoors; contaminants; radiation; disease or infections; sitting; using hands on objects, tools, or controls.

Emergency Medical Technicians and Paramedics

* Level of Education/Training: Postsecondary vocational training
* Annual Earnings: $28,400
* Growth: 19.2%
* Annual Job Openings: 19,513
* Personality Type: Social

Competition will be greater for jobs in local fire, police, and rescue squad departments than in private ambulance services; opportunities will be best for those who have advanced certification.

Assess injuries, administer emergency medical care, and extricate trapped individuals. Transport injured or sick persons to medical facilities. Administer first-aid treatment and life-support care to sick or injured persons in prehospital setting. Perform emergency diagnostic and treatment procedures, such as stomach suction, airway management, or heart monitoring, during ambulance ride. Observe, record, and report to physician the patient's condition or injury, the treatment provided, and reactions to drugs and treatment. Immobilize patient for placement on stretcher and ambulance transport, using backboard or other spinal immobilization device. Maintain vehicles and medical and communication equipment and replenish first-aid equipment and supplies. Assess nature and extent of illness or injury to establish and prioritize medical procedures. Communicate with dispatchers and treatment center personnel to provide information about situation, to arrange reception of victims, and to receive instructions for further treatment. Comfort and reassure patients. Decontaminate ambulance interior following treatment of patient with infectious disease and report case to proper authorities. Operate equipment such as electrocardiograms (EKGs), external defibrillators, and bag-valve mask resuscitators in advanced life-support environments. Drive mobile intensive care unit to specified location, following instructions from emergency medical dispatcher. Coordinate with treatment center personnel to obtain patients' vital statistics and medical history, to determine the circumstances of the emergency, and to administer emergency treatment. Coordinate work with other emergency medical team members and police and fire department personnel. Attend training classes to maintain certification licensure, keep abreast of new developments in the field, or maintain existing knowledge. Administer drugs orally or by injection and perform intravenous procedures under a physician's direction.

Work Conditions—More often outdoors than indoors; noisy; very hot or cold; very bright or dim lighting; disease or infections.

Medical Assistants

❈ Level of Education/Training: Moderate-term on-the-job training

❈ Annual Earnings: $27,430

❈ Growth: 35.4%

❈ Annual Job Openings: 92,977

❈ Personality Type: Social

Job prospects should be best for medical assistants with formal training or experience, particularly those with certification.

Perform administrative and certain clinical duties under the direction of physicians. Administrative duties may include scheduling appointments, maintaining medical records, billing, and coding for insurance purposes. Clinical duties may include taking and recording vital signs and medical histories, preparing patients for examination, drawing blood, and administering medications as directed by physician. Record patients' medical history, vital statistics, and information such as test results in medical records. Prepare treatment rooms for patient examinations, keeping the rooms neat and clean. Interview patients to obtain medical information and measure their vital signs, weights, and heights. Authorize drug refills and provide prescription information to pharmacies. Clean and sterilize instruments and dispose of contaminated supplies. Prepare and administer medications as directed by a physician. Show patients to examination rooms and prepare them for the physician. Explain treatment procedures, medications, diets, and physicians' instructions to patients. Help physicians examine and treat patients, handing them instruments and materials or performing such tasks as giving injections or removing sutures. Collect blood, tissue, or other laboratory specimens, log the specimens, and prepare them for testing. Perform routine laboratory tests and sample analyses. Contact medical facilities or departments to schedule patients for tests or admission. Operate X-ray, electrocardiogram (EKG), and other equipment to administer routine diagnostic tests. Change dressings on wounds. Set up medical laboratory equipment. Perform general office duties such as answering telephones, taking dictation, or completing insurance forms. Greet and log in patients arriving at office or clinic. Schedule appointments for patients. Inventory and order medical, lab, or office supplies and equipment. Keep financial records and perform other bookkeeping duties, such as handling credit and collections and mailing monthly statements to patients.

Work Conditions—Indoors; disease or infections; standing; walking and running; using hands on objects, tools, or controls; repetitive motions.

Medical Records and Health Information Technicians

- ❀ Level of Education/Training: Associate degree
- ❀ Annual Earnings: $29,290
- ❀ Growth: 17.8%
- ❀ Annual Job Openings: 39,048
- ❀ Personality Type: Conventional

> This is one of the few health occupations in which there is little or no direct contact with patients.

Compile, process, and maintain medical records of hospital and clinic patients in a manner consistent with medical, administrative, ethical, legal, and regulatory requirements of the health-care system. Process, maintain, compile, and report patient information for health requirements and standards. Protect the security of medical records to ensure that confidentiality is maintained. Review records for completeness, accuracy, and compliance with regulations. Retrieve patient medical records for physicians, technicians, or other medical personnel. Release information to persons and agencies according to regulations. Plan, develop, maintain, and operate a variety of health record indexes and storage and retrieval systems to collect, classify, store, and analyze information. Enter data such as demographic characteristics, history and extent of disease, diagnostic procedures, and treatment into computer. Process and prepare business and government forms. Compile and maintain patients' medical records to document condition and treatment and to provide data for research or cost control and care improvement efforts. Process patient admission and discharge documents. Assign the patient to diagnosis-related groups (DRGs), using appropriate computer software. Transcribe medical reports. Identify, compile, abstract, and code patient data, using standard classification systems. Resolve or clarify codes and diagnoses with conflicting, missing, or unclear information by consulting with doctors or others or by participating in the coding team's regular meetings. Compile medical care and census data for statistical reports on diseases treated, surgeries performed, or use of hospital beds.

Post medical insurance billings. Train medical records staff. Prepare statistical reports, narrative reports, and graphic presentations of information such as tumor registry data for use by hospital staff, researchers, or other users. Manage the department and supervise clerical workers, directing and controlling activities of personnel in the medical records department. Develop in-service educational materials. Consult classification manuals to locate information about disease processes.

Work Conditions—Indoors; disease or infections; sitting; using hands on objects, tools, or controls; repetitive motions.

Nursing Aides, Orderlies, and Attendants

❀ Level of Education/Training: Postsecondary vocational training
❀ Annual Earnings: $23,160
❀ Growth: 18.2%
❀ Annual Job Openings: 321,036
❀ Personality Type: Social

> Most jobs are in nursing and residential care facilities, hospitals, and home health-care services.

Provide basic patient care under direction of nursing staffs. Perform duties such as feeding, bathing, dressing, grooming, or moving patients or changing linens. Answer patients' call signals. Turn and reposition bedridden patients, alone or with assistance, to prevent bedsores. Observe patients' conditions, measuring and recording food and liquid intake and output and vital signs, reporting changes to professionals. Feed patients who are unable to feed themselves. Provide patients with help walking, exercising, and moving in and out of bed. Provide patient care by supplying and emptying bed pans, applying dressings, and supervising exercise routines. Bathe, groom, shave, dress, or drape patients to prepare them for surgery, treatment, or examination. Transport patients to treatment units, using a wheelchair or stretcher. Clean rooms and change linens. Collect specimens such as urine, feces, or sputum. Prepare, serve, and collect food trays. Deliver messages, documents, and specimens. Answer phones and direct visitors. Restrain patients if necessary. Set up equipment such as oxygen tents, portable X-ray machines, and overhead irrigation bottles. Explain medical instructions to patients and family members. Work as part of a medical team that examines and treats clinic outpatients. Maintain inventories by storing, preparing, sterilizing, and issuing supplies such as dressing packs and treatment trays. Administer medications and treatments such as catheterizations, suppositories, irrigations, enemas, massages, and douches as directed by a physician or nurse. Perform clerical duties such as processing documents and scheduling appointments.

Work Conditions—Disease or infections; standing; walking and running; using hands on objects, tools, or controls; bending or twisting the body; repetitive motions.

Pharmacists

❀ Level of Education/Training: First professional degree
❀ Annual Earnings: $100,480
❀ Growth: 21.7%
❀ Annual Job Openings: 16,358
❀ Personality Type: Investigative

> As a result of rapid growth and the need to replace workers who leave the occupation, job prospects should be excellent.

Compound and dispense medications, following prescriptions issued by physicians, dentists, or other authorized medical practitioners. Review prescriptions to assure accuracy, to ascertain the needed ingredients, and to evaluate their suitability. Provide information and advice regarding drug interactions, side effects, dosage, and proper medication storage. Analyze prescribing trends to monitor patient compliance and to prevent excessive usage or harmful interactions. Order and purchase pharmaceutical supplies, medical supplies, and drugs, maintaining stock and storing and handling it properly. Maintain records, such as pharmacy files; patient profiles; charge system files; inventories; control records for radioactive nuclei; and registries of poisons, narcotics, and controlled drugs. Provide specialized services to help patients manage conditions such as diabetes, asthma, smoking cessation, or high blood pressure. Advise customers on the selection of medication brands, medical equipment, and health-care supplies. Collaborate with other health-care professionals to plan, monitor, review, and evaluate the quality and effectiveness of drugs and drug regimens, providing advice on drug applications and characteristics. Compound and dispense medications as prescribed by doctors and dentists by calculating, weighing, measuring, and mixing ingredients or oversee these activities. Offer health promotion and prevention activities—for example, training people to use devices such as blood-pressure or diabetes monitors. Refer patients to other health professionals and agencies when appropriate. Prepare sterile solutions and infusions for use in surgical procedures, emergency rooms, or patients' homes. Plan, implement, and maintain procedures for mixing, packaging, and labeling pharmaceuticals according to policy and legal requirements to ensure quality, security, and proper disposal. Assay radiopharmaceuticals, verify rates of disintegration, and calculate the volume required to produce the desired results to ensure proper dosages. Manage pharmacy operations, hiring and supervising staff, performing administrative duties, and buying and selling nonpharmaceutical merchandise. Work in hospitals, clinics, or for health maintenance organizations (HMOs), dispensing prescriptions, serving as a medical team consultant, or specializing in specific drug therapy areas such as oncology or nuclear pharmacotherapy.

Work Conditions—Indoors; disease or infections; standing; repetitive motions.

Pharmacy Aides

- ❊ Level of Education/Training: Short-term on-the-job training
- ❊ Annual Earnings: $19,530
- ❊ Growth: –11.1%
- ❊ Annual Job Openings: 7,586
- ❊ Personality Type: No data available

Many pharmacy aides work evenings, weekends, and holidays.

Record drugs delivered to the pharmacy, store incoming merchandise, and inform the supervisor of stock needs. May operate cash register and accept prescriptions for filling. Accept prescriptions for filling, gathering and processing necessary information. Answer telephone inquiries, referring callers to pharmacist when necessary. Prepare solid and liquid dosage medications for dispensing into bottles and unit dose packaging. Greet customers and help them locate merchandise. Unpack, sort, count, and label incoming merchandise, including items requiring special handling or refrigeration. Prepare prescription labels by typing or operating a computer and printer. Receive, store, and inventory pharmaceutical supplies, notifying pharmacist when levels are low. Operate cash register to process cash and credit sales. Restock storage areas, replenishing items on shelves. Perform clerical tasks such as filing, compiling and maintaining prescription records, and composing letters. Maintain and clean equipment, work areas, and shelves. Provide customers with information about the uses and effects of drugs. Prepare, maintain, and record records of inventories, receipts, purchases, and deliveries, using a variety of computer screen formats. Process medical insurance claims, posting bill amounts and calculating co-payments.

Compound, package, and label pharmaceutical products under direction of pharmacist. Operate capsule- and tablet-counting machine that automatically distributes a certain number of capsules or tablets into smaller containers. Calculate anticipated drug usage for a prescribed period. Deliver medication to treatment areas, living units, residences, and clinics, using various means of transportation.

Work Conditions—Indoors; disease or infections; standing; walking and running; using hands on objects, tools, or controls; repetitive motions.

Physical Therapist Assistants

❋ Level of Education/Training: Associate degree

❋ Annual Earnings: $44,130

❋ Growth: 32.4%

❋ Annual Job Openings: 5,957

❋ Personality Type: Social

About 60 percent of jobs are in hospitals or offices of physical therapists.

Assist physical therapists in providing physical therapy treatments and procedures. May, in accordance with state laws, assist in the development of treatment plans, carry out routine functions, document the progress of treatment, and modify specific treatments in accordance with patient status and within the scope of treatment plans established by physical therapists. Generally requires formal training. Instruct, motivate, safeguard, and assist patients as they practice exercises and functional activities. Observe patients during treatments to compile and evaluate data on their responses and progress; provide results to physical therapists in person or through progress notes. Confer with physical therapy staffs or others to discuss and evaluate patient information for planning, modifying, and coordinating treatment. Transport patients to and from treatment areas, lifting and transferring them according to positioning requirements. Secure patients into or onto therapy equipment. Administer active and passive manual therapeutic exercises; therapeutic massages; aquatic physical therapy; and heat, light, sound, and electrical modality treatments such as ultrasound. Communicate with or instruct caregivers and family members on patient therapeutic activities and treatment plans. Measure patients' ranges-of-joint motion, body parts, and vital signs to determine effects of treatments or for patient evaluations. Monitor operation of equipment and record use of equipment and administration of treatment. Fit patients for orthopedic braces, prostheses, and supportive devices such as crutches. Train patients in the use of orthopedic braces, prostheses, or supportive devices. Clean work areas and check and store equipment after treatments. Assist patients to dress; undress; or put on and remove supportive devices such as braces, splints, and slings. Attend or conduct continuing education courses, seminars, or in-service activities. Perform clerical duties such as taking inventory, ordering supplies, answering telephones, taking messages, and filling out forms. Prepare treatment areas and electrotherapy equipment for use by physiotherapists. Administer traction to relieve neck and back pain, using intermittent and static traction equipment. Perform postural drainage, percussions, and vibrations and teach deep breathing exercises to treat respiratory conditions.

Work Conditions—Indoors; disease or infections; standing; walking and running.

Physical Therapists

* Level of Education/Training: Master's degree
* Annual Earnings: $69,760
* Growth: 27.1%
* Annual Job Openings: 12,072
* Personality Type: Social

> Job opportunities should be good, particularly in acute hospital, rehabilitation, and orthopedic settings.

Assess, plan, organize, and participate in rehabilitative programs that improve mobility, relieve pain, increase strength, and decrease or prevent deformity of patients suffering from disease or injury. Perform and document initial exams, evaluating data to identify problems and determine diagnoses prior to interventions. Plan, prepare, and carry out individually designed programs of physical treatment to maintain, improve, or restore physical functioning; alleviate pain; and prevent physical dysfunction in patients. Record prognoses, treatments, responses, and progresses in patients' charts or enter information into computers. Identify and document goals, anticipated progresses, and plans for reevaluation. Evaluate effects of treatments at various stages and adjust treatments to achieve maximum benefits. Administer manual exercises, massages, or traction to help relieve pain, increase patient strength, or decrease or prevent deformity or crippling. Test and measure patients' strength, motor development and function, sensory perception, functional capacity, and respiratory and circulatory efficiency and record data. Instruct patients and families in treatment procedures to be continued at home. Confer with patients, medical practitioners, and appropriate others to plan, implement, and assess intervention programs. Review physicians' referrals and patients' medical records to help determine diagnoses and physical therapy treatments required. Obtain patients' informed consent to proposed interventions. Discharge patients from physical therapy when goals or projected outcomes have been attained and provide for appropriate follow-up care or referrals. Provide information to patients about proposed interventions, material risks, and expected benefits and any reasonable alternatives. Inform patients when diagnoses reveal findings outside the scope of physical therapy to treat and refer to appropriate practitioners. Direct, supervise, assess, and communicate with supportive personnel. Provide educational information about physical therapy and physical therapists, injury prevention, ergonomics, and ways to promote health. Refer clients to community resources and services. Administer treatment involving application of physical agents, using equipment, moist packs, ultraviolet and infrared lamps, and ultrasound machines.

Work Conditions—Indoors; disease or infections; standing.

Registered Nurses

* Level of Education/Training: Associate degree
* Annual Earnings: $60,010
* Growth: 23.5%
* Annual Job Openings: 233,499
* Personality Type: Social

> Individuals considering nursing should carefully weigh the advantages and disadvantages of enrolling in a bachelor's program because if they do, their advancement opportunities usually are broader. In fact, some career paths for nurses are open only to those with a bachelor's or master's degree.

Assess patient health problems and needs, develop and implement nursing care plans, and maintain medical records. Administer nursing care to ill, injured, convalescent, or disabled patients. May advise patients on health maintenance and disease prevention or provide case management. Licensing or registration required. Includes advance practice nurses such as nurse practitioners, clinical nurse specialists, certified nurse midwives, and certified registered nurse anesthetists. Advanced practice nursing is practiced by RNs who have specialized formal, post-basic education and who function in highly autonomous and specialized roles. Monitor, record, and report symptoms and changes in patients' conditions. Maintain accurate, detailed reports and records.

Record patients' medical information and vital signs. Order, interpret, and evaluate diagnostic tests to identify and assess patients' conditions. Modify patient treatment plans as indicated by patients' responses and conditions. Direct and supervise less skilled nursing or health-care personnel or supervise particular units. Consult and coordinate with health-care team members to assess, plan, implement, and evaluate patient care plans. Monitor all aspects of patient care, including diet and physical activity. Instruct individuals, families, and other groups on topics such as health education, disease prevention, and childbirth and develop health improvement programs. Prepare patients for, and assist with, examinations and treatments. Assess the needs of individuals, families, or communities, including assessment of individuals' home or work environments to identify potential health or safety problems. Provide health care, first aid, immunizations, and assistance in convalescence and rehabilitation in locations such as schools, hospitals, and industry. Prepare rooms, sterile instruments, equipment, and supplies and ensure that stock of supplies is maintained. Inform physicians of patients' conditions during anesthesia. Administer local, inhalation, intravenous, and other anesthetics. Perform physical examinations, make tentative diagnoses, and treat patients en route to hospitals or at disaster site triage centers. Observe nurses and visit patients to ensure proper nursing care. Conduct specified laboratory tests. Direct and coordinate infection control programs, advising and consulting with specified personnel about necessary precautions. Prescribe or recommend drugs; medical devices; or other forms of treatment such as physical therapy, inhalation therapy, or related therapeutic procedures. Perform administrative and managerial functions such as taking responsibility for a unit's staff, budget, planning, and long-range goals. Hand items to surgeons during operations.

Work Conditions—Indoors; disease or infections; standing; walking and running; using hands on objects, tools, or controls.

Respiratory Therapy Technicians

❀ Level of Education/Training: Associate degree
❀ Annual Earnings: $40,590
❀ Growth: 0.9%
❀ Annual Job Openings: 2,655
❀ Personality Type: No data available

> The vast majority of job openings will continue to be in hospitals. However, a growing number of openings are expected to be outside of hospitals, especially in home health-care services, offices of physicians or other health practitioners, consumer-goods rental firms, or as temporary workers.

Provide specific, well-defined respiratory care procedures under the direction of respiratory therapists and physicians. Use ventilators and various oxygen devices and aerosol and breathing treatments in the provision of respiratory therapy. Work with patients in areas such as the emergency room, neonatal or pediatric intensive care, and surgical intensive care, treating conditions including emphysema, chronic bronchitis, asthma, cystic fibrosis, and pneumonia. Read and evaluate physicians' orders and patients' chart information to determine patients' condition and treatment protocols. Keep records of patients' therapy, completing all necessary forms. Set equipment controls to regulate the flow of oxygen, gases, mists, or aerosols. Assess patients' response to treatments and modify treatments according to protocol if necessary. Provide respiratory care involving the application of well-defined therapeutic techniques under the supervision of a respiratory therapist and a physician. Prepare and test devices such as mechanical ventilators, therapeutic gas administration apparatus, environmental control systems, aerosol generators, and electrocardiogram (EKG) machines. Monitor patients during treatment and report any unusual reactions to the respiratory therapist. Explain treatment procedures to patients. Clean, sterilize, check, and maintain respiratory therapy equipment. Perform diagnostic procedures to assess the severity of respiratory dysfunction in patients. Follow and enforce safety rules applying to equipment. Administer breathing and oxygen procedures such as intermittent positive pressure breathing treatments, ultrasonic nebulizer treatments, and incentive spirometer treatments. Recommend and review bedside procedures, X-rays, and laboratory tests. Interview and examine patients to collect clinical data. Teach patients how to use respiratory equipment at home. Teach or oversee other workers who provide respiratory care services.

Work Conditions—Indoors; contaminants; disease or infections; standing; walking and running; using hands on objects, tools, or controls.

Other Health-Care Jobs

These jobs play supporting roles in the health-care industry, are not expected to have a good outlook (even with help from the recovery plan), or were omitted from the descriptions in this chapter for lack of room.

Anesthesiologists

Audiologists

Cardiovascular Technologists and Technicians

Chiropractors

Dental Assistants

Dental Hygienists

Dentists, All Other Specialists

Diagnostic Medical Sonographers

Dietetic Technicians

Dietitians and Nutritionists

Family and General Practitioners

Home Health Aides

Internists, General

Licensed Practical and Licensed
Vocational Nurses

Massage Therapists

Medical and Clinical Laboratory
Technicians

Medical and Clinical Laboratory
Technologists

Medical Equipment Preparers

Medical Transcriptionists

Nuclear Medicine Technologists

Obstetricians and Gynecologists

Occupational Health and Safety
Specialists

Occupational Health and Safety
Technicians

Occupational Therapist Aides

Occupational Therapist Assistants

Occupational Therapists

Opticians, Dispensing

Optometrists

Oral and Maxillofacial Surgeons

Orthodontists

Orthotists and Prosthetists

Pediatricians, General

Pharmacy Technicians

Physical Therapist Aides

Physician Assistants

Physicians and Surgeons, All Other

Podiatrists

Prosthodontists

Psychiatric Aides

Psychiatric Technicians

Psychiatrists

Radiation Therapists

Radiologic Technicians

Radiologic Technologists

Recreational Therapists

Respiratory Therapists

Speech-Language Pathologists

Surgeons

Surgical Technologists

Therapists, All Other

CHAPTER 5

JOBS IN EDUCATION

ducation is vital for maintaining America's competitiveness in a global and increasingly high-tech economy. The Obama recovery plan
specifically targets education and will also benefit schools through
its state-relief initiative. The transition team projects that the recovery package will create or sustain a total of 240,000 jobs that this industry will share
with the **health-care** industry (described in chapter 4). This chapter describes
the **educational services** and **child day-care services** industries and some
important related jobs that are expected to be stimulated by the recovery
package.

The **management, scientific, and technical consulting services; computer systems design and related services;** and **wholesale trade** industries will probably also benefit from the education initiative in the stimulus
package, and you can find descriptions of those three industries and related
key jobs in chapter 7.

Educational Services

Nature of the Industry

Education is an important part of life. The amount and type of education
that individuals receive are major influences on both the types of jobs they
are able to hold and their earnings. Lifelong learning is important in acquiring new knowledge and upgrading one's skills, particularly in this age of
rapid technological and economic changes. The educational services industry
includes a variety of institutions that offer academic education, vocational or
career and technical instruction, and other education and training to millions
of students each year.

In recent decades, the nation has focused attention on the educational system because of the growing importance of producing a trained and educated
workforce. Many institutions, including government, private industry, and
research organizations, are involved in improving the quality of education.
The passage of the No Child Left Behind Act of 2001 established federal
guidelines to ensure that all students in public elementary through secondary

schools receive a high-quality education. Through this act, individual states are given more flexibility on how to spend the educational funds they are allocated. In return, the Act requires standardized testing of all students in core subject areas. In this manner, students, teachers, and all staff involved in education are held accountable for the results of testing, and teachers and teacher assistants must demonstrate that they are sufficiently qualified in the subjects or areas in which they teach. States are responsible for following these guidelines and can lose federal funding if the standards are not met. Despite the increased federal role, state and local governments are still the most important regulators of public education. Many states had already begun to introduce performance standards individually prior to passage of the Act, and the Act still allows states a considerable amount of discretion in how they implement many of its provisions.

In an effort to promote innovation in public education, many local and state governments have authorized the creation of public charter schools in the belief that, by presenting students and their parents with a greater range of instructional options, schools and students will be encouraged to strive for excellence. Charter schools, which usually are run by teachers and parents or, increasingly, by private firms, operate independently of the school system, set their own standards, and practice a variety of innovative teaching methods. Businesses strive to improve education by donating instructional equipment, lending personnel for teaching and mentoring, hosting visits to the workplace, and providing job-shadowing and internship opportunities. Businesses also collaborate with educators to develop curricula that will provide students with the skills they need to cope with new technology in the workplace.

Quality improvements also are being made to career and technical education at secondary and postsecondary schools. Academics are playing a more important role in career and technical curricula, and programs are being made more relevant to the local job market. Often, students must meet rigorous standards, set in consultation with private industry, before receiving a certificate or degree. Career and technical students in secondary school programs must pass the same standardized tests in core subject areas as students who are enrolled in academic programs of study. A growing number of career and technical programs emphasize general workplace skills, such as problem solving, teamwork, and customer service. Many high schools now offer technical preparatory ("tech-prep") programs, which are developed jointly by high schools and community colleges to provide a continuous course of study leading to an associate degree or other postsecondary credential.

Computer technology continues to affect the education industry. Computers simplify administrative tasks and make it easier to track student performance. Teachers use the Internet in classrooms as well as to communicate with colleagues around the country; students use the Internet for research projects. Distance learning continues to expand as more postsecondary institutions use Internet-based technology to conduct lessons and coursework electronically, allowing students in distant locations access to educational opportunities formerly available only on campus. Increasing Internet access for schools is part of the Obama plan for economic recovery.

Despite these improvements in quality, problems remain. High school completion rates remain low, particularly for minority students, and employers contend that numerous high school graduates still lack many of the math and communication skills needed in today's workplace. School budgets often are not sufficient to meet the institution's various goals, particularly in the inner cities, where aging facilities and chronic teacher shortages make educating children more difficult.

Working Conditions

Hours. Elementary and secondary schools generally operate 10 months a year, but summer sessions for special education or remedial students are common. In addition, education administrators, office and administrative support workers, and janitors and cleaners often work the entire year. Postsecondary institutions operate year-round, but may have reduced offerings during summer months. Institutions that cater to adult students, and those that offer educational support services such as tutoring, generally operate year-round as well. Night and weekend work is common for teachers of adult literacy and remedial and self-enrichment education, for postsecondary teachers, and for library workers in postsecondary institutions. Part-time work is common for this same group of teachers, as well as for teacher assistants and school bus drivers. The latter often work a split shift, driving one or two routes in the morning and afternoon; drivers who are assigned to drive students on field trips, to athletic and other extracurricular activities, or to midday kindergarten programs work additional hours during or after school. Many teachers spend significant time outside of school preparing for class, doing administrative tasks, conducting research, writing articles and books, and pursuing advanced degrees.

Work environment. Elementary and secondary school conditions often vary from town to town. Some schools in poorer neighborhoods may be run down, have few supplies and equipment, and lack air conditioning. Other schools may be new and well equipped and maintained. Conditions at postsecondary institutions are generally very good. Regardless of the type of conditions facing elementary and secondary schools, seeing students develop and enjoy learning can be rewarding for teachers and other education workers.

However, dealing with unmotivated students or those with social or behavioral problems can be stressful and require patience and understanding.

Despite occurrences of violence in some schools, the educational services industry is relatively safe. There were 2.3 cases of occupational injury and illness per 100 full-time workers in private educational establishments in 2006, compared with 4.4 in all industries combined.

Employment

The educational services industry was the second-largest industry in the economy in 2006, providing jobs for about 13.3 million workers—about 13.2 million wage and salary workers and 195,000 self-employed and unpaid family workers. Most jobs are found in elementary and secondary schools, either public or private. Public schools employ more workers than private schools because most students attend public educational institutions. According to the latest data from the Department of Education's National Center for Education Statistics, close to 90 percent of students attend public primary and secondary schools, and about 75 percent attend public postsecondary institutions.

Outlook

Greater numbers of children and adults enrolled in all types of schools will generate employment growth in this industry. A large number of retirements will add additional job openings and create good job prospects for many of those seeking work in educational services.

Employment change. Wage and salary employment growth of 11 percent is expected in the educational services industry over the 2006–2016 period, comparable to the 11 percent increase projected for all industries combined. Over the long term, the overall demand for workers in educational services will increase as a result of a growing emphasis on improving education and making it available not only to more children and young adults, but also to those currently employed and in need of improving their skills. Much of the demand for educational services is driven by growth in the population of students at each level. Low enrollment growth projections at the elementary, middle, and secondary school level are likely to limit growth somewhat, resulting in average growth for these teachers. However, reforms, such as universal preschool and all-day kindergarten, will require more preschool and kindergarten teachers.

Among other workers in primary and secondary education, the number of special education teachers is projected to experience faster-than-average growth through 2016 because of continued emphasis on the inclusion of disabled students in general education classrooms and an effort to reach students with problems at younger ages. Employment of teacher assistants will grow about as fast as the average. School reforms calling for more individual attention to students will require additional teacher assistants, particularly to work with special education and English-as-a-second-language students.

Enrollments are expected to grow at a faster rate in postsecondary institutions as more high school graduates attend college and as more working adults return to school to enhance or update their skills. As a result, employment of postsecondary teachers is expected to experience much-faster-than-average growth.

Despite expected increases in education expenditures over the next decade, budget constraints at all levels of government may place restrictions on educational services, particularly in light of the rapidly escalating costs associated with increased college enrollments, special education, construction of new schools, and other services. Funding constraints generally affect student services (such as school busing, library and educational materials, and extracurricular activities) before employment of administrative, instructional, and support staff, though supplementary programs, such as music and foreign language instruction, also often face cuts when budgets become tight. Even if no reductions are required, budget considerations may affect attempts to expand school programs, such as increasing the number of counselors and teacher assistants in elementary schools. The Obama recovery plan includes funding to help relieve some of these budget constraints.

Job prospects. In addition to job openings due to employment growth, retirements will create large numbers of job openings as a greater-than-average number of workers are over the age of 45 in nearly all the major occupations that make up the industry—from janitors to education administrators.

School districts, particularly those in urban and rural areas, continue to report difficulties in recruiting qualified teachers, administrators, and support personnel. Fast-growing areas of the country—including several states and cities in the South and West—also report difficulty recruiting education workers, especially teachers. Retirements are expected to remain high over the 2006–2016 period, so the number of students graduating with education degrees may not be sufficient to meet this industry's growing needs, making job opportunities for graduates in many education fields good to excellent. Currently, alternative licensing programs are helping to attract more people into teaching, especially those from other career paths, but opportunities should continue to be very good for highly qualified teachers, especially those in subject areas with the highest needs, such as math, science, and special education.

At the postsecondary level, increases in student enrollments and projected retirements of current faculty should contribute to a favorable job market for postsecondary teachers. However, candidates applying for tenured positions will continue to face keen competition as many colleges and universities rely on adjunct or part-time faculty and graduate students to make up a larger share of the total instructional staff than in the past.

Child Day-Care Services

Nature of the Industry

Obtaining affordable, quality child day care, especially for children under age 5, is a major concern for many parents, particularly in recent years with the rise in families with two working parents. As the need for child day care has increased in the last decade, the child day-care services industry began to fill the need of non-relative child care.

Child day-care needs are met in different ways. Care in a child's home, care in an organized child care center, and care in a provider's home—known as family child care—are all common arrangements for preschool-aged children. Older children also may receive child day-care services when they are not in school, generally through before- and after-school programs or private summer school programs. With the increasing number of households in which both parents work full time, this industry has been one of the fastest growing in the U.S. economy.

The industry consists of establishments that provide paid care for infants, toddlers, preschool children, or older children in before- and after-school programs.

Two main types of child care make up the child day-care services industry: center-based care and family child care. Formal child day-care centers include preschools, child care centers, and Head Start centers. Family child care providers care for children in their home for a fee and are the majority of self-employed workers in this industry. This does not include persons who provide unpaid care in their homes for the children of relatives or friends or occasional babysitters. Also, child care workers who work in the child's home, such as nannies, are included primarily in the private household industry, not this industry.

The for-profit part of this industry includes centers that operate independently or as part of a local or national company. The number of for-profit establishments has grown rapidly in response to demand for child care services. Nonprofit child day-care organizations may provide services in religious institutions, YMCAs and other social and recreation centers, colleges, public schools, social service agencies, and worksites ranging from factories to office complexes. Within the nonprofit sector, there has been strong growth in Head Start, the federally funded child care program designed to provide disadvantaged children with social, educational, and health services.

Some employers offer child care benefits to their employees, recognizing that the unavailability of child care is a barrier to the employment of many parents, especially qualified women, and that the cost of the benefits is offset by increased employee morale and productivity and reduced absenteeism. Some employers sponsor child care centers in or near the workplace, while others provide direct financial assistance, vouchers, or discounts for child care or after-school or sick-child care services. Still others offer a dependent-care option in a flexible benefits plan.

Working Conditions

Hours. The hours of child day-care workers vary. Many centers are open 12 or more hours a day and cannot close until all of the children are picked up by their parents or guardians. Unscheduled overtime, traffic jams, and other types of emergencies can cause parents or guardians to be late. Nearly 18 percent of full-time employees in the child day-care services industry work more than 40 hours per week. Self-employed workers tend to work longer hours than do their salaried counterparts. The industry also offers many opportunities for part-time work: More than 26 percent of all employees worked part time in 2006.

Work environment. Helping children grow, learn, and gain new skills can be very rewarding. Preschool teachers and child care workers often improve their own communication, learning, and other personal skills by working with children. The work is sometimes routine; however, new activities and challenges mark each day. Child care can be physically and emotionally taxing, as workers constantly stand, walk, bend, stoop, and lift to attend to each child's needs, interests, and problems. Child care workers must be constantly alert, anticipate and prevent trouble, deal effectively with disruptive children, and provide fair but firm discipline.

Many child day-care workers become dissatisfied with their jobs' stressful conditions, low pay, and lack of benefits and eventually leave.

Employment

Child day-care services provided about 807,000 wage and salary jobs in 2006. There were an additional 467,000 self-employed and unpaid family workers in the industry, most of whom were family child care providers, although some were self-employed managers of child care centers.

Jobs in child day care are found across the country, mirroring the distribution of the population. However, day-care centers are less common in rural areas, where there are fewer children to support a separate facility. Child day-care operations vary in size, from the self-employed person caring for a few children in a private home to the large corporate-sponsored center employing a sizable staff. Almost half of all wage and salary jobs in 2006 were located in establishments with fewer than 20 employees. Nearly all establishments have fewer than 50 workers.

Opportunities for self-employment in this industry are among the best in the economy. About 37 percent of all workers in the industry are self-employed or unpaid family workers, compared with only 8 percent in all industries. This disparity reflects the ease of entering the child day-care business. (Note that the average earnings figures for jobs in this chapter *do not* include self-employed workers.)

The median age of child day-care providers is 38, compared with 44 for all workers. About 21 percent of all care providers are 24 years or younger as opposed to about 14 percent for all industries. About 6 percent of these workers are below the age of 20, reflecting the minimal training requirements for many child day-care positions.

Outlook

Employment in child day-care services is projected to increase rapidly, and an unusually large number of job openings will result each year from that growth and the need to replace the large numbers of experienced workers who leave the industry for other jobs.

Employment change. Wage and salary jobs in the child day-care services industry are projected to grow about 34 percent over the 2006–2016 period, compared with the 11 percent employment growth projected for all industries combined. The rising demand for child day-care services driving industry growth reflects in part demographic trends. Over the same period, the number of children under age 5 is expected to increase at a faster rate than in previous years, and many of them will continue to be raised in households with two working parents or a single working parent. Furthermore, growing numbers of parents will hold jobs that require work during weekends, evenings, and late nights. As a result, demand will grow significantly for child care programs that can provide care during not only traditional weekday hours, but nontraditional hours as well. In addition, school-aged children, who generally require child care only before and after school, increasingly are being cared for in centers.

Center-based day care should continue to expand its share of the industry because an increasing number of parents prefer its more formal setting and believe that it provides a better foundation for children before they begin traditional schooling. However, family child care providers will continue to remain an important source of care for many young children because some parents prefer the more personal attention that such a setting can provide. Demand for child care centers and preschool teachers to staff them could increase even further if more states implement preschool programs for 3- and 4-year-old children, which some states have begun and others are planning to start. In addition, subsidies for children from low-income families attending child day-care programs also could result in more children being served in centers, as could the increasing involvement of employers in funding and operating day-care centers. Legislation requiring more welfare recipients to work also could contribute to growing demand for child day-care services. Finally, expanded access to day care is among the goals of the Obama recovery plan.

Job prospects. Opportunities within this industry are expected to be excellent because of the need to replace workers who choose to leave the industry to return to school or enter a new occupation or industry. Replacement needs are substantial, reflecting the low wages and relatively meager benefits provided to most workers. The substantial replacement needs, coupled with faster-than-average employment growth, should create numerous employment opportunities.

Some Education Jobs That Are Likely to Benefit from the Stimulus Package

Adult Literacy, Remedial Education, and GED Teachers and Instructors

- ❀ Level of Education/Training: Bachelor's degree
- ❀ Annual Earnings: $44,710
- ❀ Growth: 14.2%
- ❀ Annual Job Openings: 17,340
- ❀ Personality Type: Social

> Job opportunities are expected to be favorable, particularly for teachers of English to speakers of other languages.

Teach or instruct out-of-school youths and adults in remedial education classes, preparatory classes for the General Educational Development test, literacy, or English as a Second Language. Teaching may or may not take place in a traditional educational institution. Adapt teaching methods and instructional materials to meet students' varying needs, abilities, and interests. Observe and evaluate students' work to determine progress and make suggestions for improvement. Instruct students individually and in groups, using various teaching methods such as lectures, discussions, and demonstrations. Plan and conduct activities for a balanced program of instruction, demonstration, and work time that provides students with opportunities to observe, question, and investigate. Maintain accurate and complete student records as required by laws or administrative policies. Prepare materials and classrooms for class activities. Establish clear objectives for all lessons, units, and projects and communicate those objectives to students. Conduct classes, workshops, and demonstrations to teach principles, techniques, or methods in subjects such as basic English language skills, life skills, and workforce entry skills. Prepare students for further education by encouraging them to explore learning opportunities and to persevere with challenging tasks. Establish and enforce rules for behavior and procedures for maintaining order among the students for whom they are responsible. Provide information, guidance, and preparation for the General Equivalency Diploma (GED) examination. Assign and grade classwork and homework. Observe students to determine qualifications, limitations, abilities, interests, and other individual characteristics. Register, orient, and assess new students according to standards and procedures. Prepare and implement remedial programs for students requiring extra help. Prepare and administer written, oral, and performance tests and issue grades in accordance with performance. Use computers, audiovisual aids, and other equipment and materials to supplement presentations. Prepare objectives and outlines for courses of study, following curriculum guidelines or requirements of states and schools. Guide and counsel students with adjustment or academic problems or special academic interests. Enforce administration policies and rules governing students.

Work Conditions—Indoors; more often standing than sitting.

Child Care Workers

- ❋ Level of Education/Training: Short-term on-the-job training
- ❋ Annual Earnings: $18,350
- ❋ Growth: 17.8%
- ❋ Annual Job Openings: 471,956
- ❋ Personality Type: Social

The job openings listed here are shared with Nannies.

Many workers leave these jobs every year, creating good job opportunities. About 35 percent of child-care workers are self-employed, most of whom provided child care in their homes.

Attend to children at schools, businesses, private households, and child care institutions. Perform a variety of tasks, such as dressing, feeding, bathing, and overseeing play. Support children's emotional and social development, encouraging understanding of others and positive self-concepts. Care for children in institutional setting, such as group homes, nursery schools, private businesses, or schools for the handicapped. Sanitize toys and play equipment. Discipline children and recommend or initiate other measures to control behavior, such as caring for own clothing and picking up toys and books. Identify signs of emotional or developmental problems in children and bring them to parents' or guardians' attention. Observe and monitor children's play activities. Keep records on individual children, including daily observations and information about activities, meals served, and medications administered. Instruct children in health and personal habits such as eating, resting, and toilet habits. Read to children and teach them simple painting, drawing, handicrafts, and songs. Organize and participate in recreational activities, such as games. Assist in preparing food for children, serve meals and refreshments to children, and regulate rest periods. Organize and store toys and materials to ensure order in activity areas. Operate in-house daycare centers within businesses. Sterilize bottles and prepare formulas. Provide counseling or therapy to mentally disturbed, delinquent, or handicapped children. Dress children and change diapers. Help children with homework and school work. Perform housekeeping duties such as laundry, cleaning, dishwashing, and changing of linens. Accompany children to and from school, on outings, and to medical appointments. Place or hoist children into baths or pools.

Work Conditions—Indoors; noisy; disease or infections; standing.

Child, Family, and School Social Workers

* Level of Education/Training: Bachelor's degree
* Annual Earnings: $38,620
* Growth: 19.1%
* Annual Job Openings: 35,402
* Personality Type: Social

Competition for jobs is expected in cities, but opportunities should be good in rural areas.

Provide social services and assistance to improve the social and psychological functioning of children and their families and to maximize the family well-being and the academic functioning of children. May assist single parents, arrange adoptions, and find foster homes for abandoned or abused children. In schools, they address such problems as teenage pregnancy, misbehavior, and truancy. May also advise teachers on how to deal with problem children. Interview clients individually, in families, or in groups, assessing their situations, capabilities, and problems, to determine what services are required to meet their needs. Counsel individuals, groups, families, or communities regarding issues including mental health, poverty, unemployment, substance abuse, physical abuse, rehabilitation, social adjustment, child care, or medical care. Maintain case history records and prepare reports. Counsel students whose behavior, school progress, or mental or physical impairment indicate a need for assistance, diagnosing students' problems and arranging for needed services. Consult with parents, teachers, and other school personnel to determine causes of problems such as truancy and misbehavior and to implement solutions. Counsel parents with child rearing problems, interviewing the child and family to determine whether further action is required. Develop and review service plans in consultation with clients and perform follow-ups assessing the quantity and quality of services provided. Collect supplementary information needed to assist clients, such as employment records, medical records, or school reports. Address legal issues, such as child abuse and discipline, assisting with hearings and providing testimony to inform custody arrangements. Provide, find, or arrange for support services, such as child care, homemaker service, prenatal care, substance abuse treatment, job training, counseling, or parenting classes, to prevent more serious problems from developing. Refer clients to community resources for services such as job placement, debt counseling, legal aid, housing, medical treatment, or financial assistance and provide concrete information, such as where to go and how to apply. Arrange for medical, psychiatric, and other tests that may disclose causes of difficulties and indicate remedial measures. Work in child and adolescent residential institutions. Administer welfare programs. Evaluate personal characteristics and home conditions of foster home or adoption applicants. Serve as liaisons between students, homes, schools, family services, child guidance clinics, courts, protective services, doctors, and other contacts to help children who face problems such as disabilities, abuse, or poverty.

Work Conditions—Indoors; sitting.

Education Administrators, Elementary and Secondary School

❋ Level of Education/Training: Work experience plus degree
❋ Annual Earnings: $80,580
❋ Growth: 7.6%
❋ Annual Job Openings: 27,143
❋ Personality Type: Social

> Excellent opportunities are expected because a large proportion of education administrators is expected to retire over the next 10 years.

Plan, direct, or coordinate the academic, clerical, or auxiliary activities of public or private elementary or secondary-level schools. Review and approve new programs or recommend modifications to existing programs, submitting program proposals for school board approval as necessary. Prepare, maintain, or oversee the preparation and maintenance of attendance, activity, planning, or personnel reports and records. Confer with parents and staff to discuss educational activities, policies, and student behavioral or learning problems. Prepare and submit budget requests and recommendations or grant proposals to solicit program funding. Direct and coordinate school maintenance services and the use of school facilities. Counsel and provide guidance to students regarding personal, academic, vocational, or behavioral issues. Organize and direct committees of specialists, volunteers, and staff to provide technical and advisory assistance for programs. Teach classes or courses to students. Advocate for new schools to be built or for existing facilities to be repaired or remodeled. Plan and develop instructional methods and content for educational, vocational, or student activity programs. Develop partnerships with businesses, communities, and other organizations to help meet identified educational needs and to provide school-to-work programs. Direct and coordinate activities of teachers, administrators, and support staff at schools, public agencies, and institutions. Evaluate curricula, teaching methods, and programs to determine their effectiveness, efficiency, and utilization and to ensure that school activities comply with federal, state, and local regulations. Set educational standards and goals and help establish policies and procedures to carry them out. Recruit, hire, train, and evaluate primary and supplemental staff. Enforce discipline and attendance rules. Observe teaching methods and examine learning materials to evaluate and standardize curricula and teaching techniques and to determine areas where improvement is needed. Establish, coordinate, and oversee particular programs across school districts, such as programs to evaluate student academic achievement. Review and interpret government codes and develop programs to ensure adherence to codes and facility safety, security, and maintenance.

Work Conditions—Indoors; standing.

Education Administrators, Preschool and Child Care Center/Program

- ❀ Level of Education/Training: Work experience plus degree
- ❀ Annual Earnings: $38,580
- ❀ Growth: 23.5%
- ❀ Annual Job Openings: 8,113
- ❀ Personality Type: Social

> Preschool and child care center administrators are expected to experience substantial growth due to increasing enrollments in formal child care programs. Additionally, as more states implement or expand public preschool programs, more preschool directors will be needed.

Plan, direct, or coordinate the academic and nonacademic activities of preschool and child care centers or programs. Confer with parents and staff to discuss educational activities and policies and students' behavioral or learning problems. Prepare and maintain attendance, activity, planning, accounting, or personnel reports and records for officials and agencies or direct preparation and maintenance activities. Set educational standards and goals and help establish policies, procedures, and programs to carry them out. Monitor students' progress and provide students and teachers with assistance in resolving any problems. Determine allocations of funds for staff, supplies, materials, and equipment and authorize purchases. Recruit, hire, train, and evaluate primary and supplemental staff and recommend personnel actions for programs and services. Direct and coordinate activities of teachers or administrators at day-care centers, schools, public agencies, or institutions. Plan, direct, and monitor instructional methods and content of educational, vocational, or student activity programs. Review and interpret government codes and develop procedures to meet codes and to ensure facility safety, security, and maintenance. Determine the scope of educational program offerings and prepare drafts of program schedules and descriptions to estimate staffing and facility requirements. Review and evaluate new and current programs to determine their efficiency; effectiveness; and compliance with state, local, and federal regulations, and recommend any necessary modifications. Teach classes or courses or provide direct care to children. Prepare and submit budget requests or grant proposals to solicit program funding. Write articles, manuals, and other publications and assist in the distribution of pro-motional literature about programs and facilities. Collect and analyze survey data, regulatory information, and demographic and employment trends to forecast enrollment patterns and the need for curriculum changes. Inform businesses, community groups, and governmental agencies about educational needs, available programs, and program policies. Organize and direct com-mittees of specialists, volunteers, and staff to provide technical and advisory assistance for programs.

Work Conditions—Indoors; standing.

Educational, Vocational, and School Counselors

❋ Level of Education/Training: Master's degree
❋ Annual Earnings: $49,450
❋ Growth: 12.6%
❋ Annual Job Openings: 54,025
❋ Personality Type: Social

> Job opportunities for counselors should be very good because job open-ings are expected to exceed the number of graduates from counseling programs.

Counsel individuals and provide group educational and vocational guidance services. Counsel students regarding educational issues such as course and program selection, class scheduling, school adjustment, truancy, study habits, and career planning. Counsel individuals to help them under-stand and overcome personal, social, or behavioral problems affecting their educational or vocational situations. Maintain accurate and complete student records as required by laws, district policies, and administrative regulations. Confer with parents or guardians, teachers, other counselors, and administra-tors to resolve students' behavioral, academic, and other problems. Provide crisis intervention to students when difficult situations occur at schools. Identify cases involving domestic abuse or other family problems affecting students' development. Meet with parents and guardians to discuss their chil-dren's progress and to determine their priorities for their children and their resource needs. Prepare students for later educational experiences by encour-aging them to explore learning opportunities and to persevere with challenging tasks. Encourage students and/or parents to seek additional assistance from mental health professionals when necessary. Observe and evaluate students' performance, behavior, social development, and physical health. Enforce all administration policies and rules governing students. Meet with other professionals to discuss individual students' needs and progress. Provide students with information on such topics as college degree programs and admission requirements, financial aid opportunities, trade and technical schools, and apprenticeship programs. Evaluate individuals' abilities, interests, and personality characteristics, using tests, records, interviews, and professional sources. Collaborate with teachers and administrators in the development, evaluation, and revision of school programs. Establish and enforce behavioral rules and procedures to maintain order among students. Teach classes and present self-help or information sessions on subjects related to education and career planning. Attend professional meetings, educational conferences, and teacher training workshops to maintain and improve professional competence.

Work Conditions—Indoors; sitting.

Elementary School Teachers, Except Special Education

❋ Level of Education/Training: Bachelor's degree
❋ Annual Earnings: $47,330
❋ Growth: 13.6%
❋ Annual Job Openings: 181,612
❋ Personality Type: Social

> Job prospects should be better in inner cities and rural areas than in suburban districts.

Teach pupils in public or private schools at the elementary level basic academic, social, and other formative skills. Establish and enforce rules for behavior and procedures for maintaining order among the students for whom they are responsible. Observe and evaluate students' performance, behavior, social development, and physical health. Prepare materials and classrooms for class activities. Adapt teaching methods and instructional materials to meet students' varying needs and interests. Plan and conduct activities for a balanced program of instruction, demonstration, and work time that provides students with opportunities to observe, question, and investigate. Instruct students individually and in groups, using various teaching methods such as lectures, discussions, and demonstrations. Establish clear objectives for all lessons, units, and projects and communicate those objectives to students. Assign and grade classwork and homework. Read books to entire classes or small groups. Prepare, administer, and grade tests and assignments in order to evaluate students' progress. Confer with parents or guardians, teachers, counselors, and administrators to resolve students' behavioral and academic problems. Meet with parents and guardians to discuss their children's progress and to determine their priorities for their children and their resource needs. Prepare students for later grades by encouraging them to explore learning opportunities and to persevere with challenging tasks. Maintain accurate and complete student records as required by laws, district policies, and administrative regulations. Guide and counsel students with adjustment or academic problems or special academic interests. Prepare and implement remedial programs for students requiring extra help. Prepare objectives and outlines for courses of study, following curriculum guidelines or requirements of states and schools. Provide a variety of materials and resources for children to explore, manipulate, and use, both in learning activities and in imaginative play. Enforce administration policies and rules governing students. Confer with other staff members to plan and schedule lessons promoting learning, following approved curricula.

Work Conditions—Indoors; noisy; disease or infections; standing.

Kindergarten Teachers, Except Special Education

* Level of Education/Training: Bachelor's degree
* Annual Earnings: $45,120
* Growth: 16.3%
* Annual Job Openings: 27,603
* Personality Type: Social

> You may want to attain professional certification in order to demonstrate competency beyond that required for a license.

Teach elemental natural and social science, personal hygiene, music, art, and literature to children from 4 to 6 years old. Promote physical, mental, and social development. May be required to hold state certification. Teach basic skills such as color, shape, number, and letter recognition; personal hygiene; and social skills. Establish and enforce rules for behavior and policies and procedures to maintain order among students. Observe and evaluate children's performance, behavior, social development, and physical health. Instruct students individually and in groups, adapting teaching methods to meet students' varying needs and interests. Read books to entire classes or to small groups. Demonstrate activities to children. Provide a variety of materials and resources for children to explore, manipulate, and use, both in learning activities and in imaginative play. Plan and conduct activities for a balanced program of instruction, demonstration, and work time that provides students with opportunities to observe, question, and investigate. Confer with parents or guardians, other teachers, counselors, and administrators to resolve students' behavioral and academic problems. Prepare children for later grades by encouraging them to explore learning opportunities and to persevere with challenging tasks. Establish clear objectives for all lessons, units, and projects and communicate those objectives to children. Prepare and implement remedial programs for students requiring extra help. Meet with parents and guardians to discuss their children's progress and to determine their priorities for their children and their resource needs. Prepare objectives and outlines for courses of study, following curriculum guidelines or requirements of states and schools. Organize and lead activities designed to promote physical, mental, and social development, such as games, arts and crafts, music, and storytelling. Guide and counsel students with adjustment or academic problems or special academic interests. Identify children showing signs of emotional, developmental, or health-related problems and discuss them with supervisors, parents or guardians, and child development specialists. Instruct and monitor students in the use and care of equipment and materials to prevent injuries and damage. Assimilate arriving children to the school environment by greeting them, helping them remove outerwear, and selecting activities of interest to them.

Work Conditions—Indoors; disease or infections; standing.

Librarians

* Level of Education/Training: Master's degree
* Annual Earnings: $50,970
* Growth: 3.6%
* Annual Job Openings: 18,945
* Personality Type: Artistic

> Despite slower-than-average projected employment growth, job opportunities are still expected to be favorable because a large number of librarians are expected to retire in the coming decade.

Administer libraries and perform related library services. Work in a variety of settings, including public libraries, schools, colleges and universities, museums, corporations, government agencies, law firms, non-profit organizations, and health-care providers. Tasks may include selecting, acquiring, cataloguing, classifying, circulating, and maintaining library materials and furnishing reference, bibliographical, and readers' advisory services. May perform in-depth, strategic

research and synthesize, analyze, edit, and filter information. May set up or work with databases and information systems to catalogue and access information. Search standard reference materials, including online sources and the Internet, to answer patrons' reference questions. Analyze patrons' requests to determine needed information and assist in furnishing or locating that information. Teach library patrons to search for information by using databases. Keep records of circulation and materials. Supervise budgeting, planning, and personnel activities. Check books in and out of the library. Explain use of library facilities, resources, equipment, and services and provide information about library policies. Review and evaluate resource material, such as book reviews and catalogs, to select and order print, audiovisual, and electronic resources. Code, classify, and catalog books, publications, films, audiovisual aids, and other library materials based on subject matter or standard library classification systems. Locate unusual or unique information in response to specific requests. Direct and train library staff in duties such as receiving, shelving, researching, cataloging, and equipment use. Respond to customer complaints, taking action as necessary. Organize collections of books, publications, documents, audiovisual aids, and other reference materials for convenient access. Develop library policies and procedures. Evaluate materials to determine outdated or unused items to be discarded. Develop information access aids such as indexes and annotated bibliographies, Web pages, electronic pathfinders, and online tutorials. Plan and deliver client-centered programs and services such as special services for corporate clients, storytelling for children, newsletters, or programs for special groups. Compile lists of books, periodicals, articles, and audiovisual materials on particular subjects. Arrange for interlibrary loans of materials not available in a particular library. Assemble and arrange display materials. Confer with teachers, parents, and community organizations to develop, plan, and conduct programs in reading, viewing, and communication skills. Compile lists of overdue materials and notify borrowers that their materials are overdue.

Work Conditions—Indoors; sitting; using hands on objects, tools, or controls; repetitive motions.

Library Technicians

- ❈ Level of Education/Training: Postsecondary vocational training
- ❈ Annual Earnings: $27,680
- ❈ Growth: 8.5%
- ❈ Annual Job Openings: 29,075
- ❈ Personality Type: Conventional

Training requirements range from a high school diploma to an associate degree, but computer skills are necessary for all workers. Opportunities will be best for those with specialized postsecondary library training.

Assist librarians by helping readers in the use of library catalogs, databases, and indexes to locate books and other materials and by answering questions that require only brief consultation of standard reference. Compile records; sort and shelve books; remove or repair damaged books; register patrons; check materials in and out of the circulation process. Replace materials in shelving area (stacks) or files. Includes bookmobile drivers who operate bookmobiles or light trucks that pull trailers to specific locations on a predetermined schedule and assist with providing services in mobile libraries. Reserve, circulate, renew, and discharge books and other materials. Enter and update patrons' records on computers. Provide assistance to teachers and students by locating materials and helping to complete special projects. Guide patrons in finding and using library resources, including reference materials, audiovisual equipment, computers, and electronic resources. Answer routine reference inquiries and refer patrons needing further assistance to librarians. Train other staff, volunteers, or student assistants, and schedule and supervise their work. Sort books, publications, and other items according to procedure and return them to shelves, files, or other designated storage areas. Conduct reference searches, using printed materials and in-house and online databases. Deliver and retrieve items throughout the library by hand or using pushcart. Take actions to halt disruption of library activities by problem patrons. Process interlibrary loans for patrons. Process print and non-print library materials to prepare them for inclusion in library collections. Retrieve information from central databases for storage in a library's computer. Organize and maintain periodicals and reference materials. Compile and maintain records relating to circulation, materials, and equipment. Collect fines and respond to complaints about fines. Issue identification cards to borrowers. Verify bibliographical data for materials, including author, title, publisher, publication date, and edition. Review subject matter of materials to be classified and select classification numbers and headings according to classification systems. Send out notices about lost or overdue books. Prepare order slips for materials to be acquired, checking prices and figuring costs. Design, customize, and maintain databases, Web pages, and local area networks. Operate and maintain audiovisual equipment such as projectors, tape recorders, and videocassette recorders. File catalog cards according to system used. Prepare volumes for binding. Conduct children's programs and other specialized programs such as library tours. Compose explanatory summaries of contents of books and other reference materials.

Work Conditions—Indoors; sitting; using hands on objects, tools, or controls; repetitive motions.

Preschool Teachers, Except Special Education

※ Level of Education/Training: Postsecondary vocational training

※ Annual Earnings: $23,130

※ Growth: 26.3%

※ Annual Job Openings: 78,172

※ Personality Type: Social

> Preschool teachers working in day-care settings often work year round. Part-time schedules are common.

Instruct children (normally up to 5 years of age) in activities designed to promote social, physical, and intellectual growth needed for primary school in preschool, day-care center, or other child development facility. May be required to hold state certification. Provide a variety of materials and resources for children to explore, manipulate, and use, both in learning activities and in imaginative play. Attend to children's basic needs by feeding them, dressing them, and changing their diapers. Establish and enforce rules for behavior and procedures for maintaining order. Read books to entire classes or to small groups. Teach basic skills such as color, shape, number, and letter recognition; personal hygiene; and social skills. Organize and lead activities designed to promote physical, mental, and social development, such as games, arts and crafts, music, storytelling, and field trips. Observe and evaluate children's performance, behavior, social development, and physical health. Meet with parents and guardians to discuss their children's progress and needs, determine their priorities for their children, and suggest ways that they can promote learning and development. Identify children showing signs of emotional, developmental, or health-related problems and discuss them with supervisors, parents or guardians, and child development specialists. Enforce all administration policies and rules governing students. Prepare materials and classrooms for class activities. Serve meals and snacks in accordance with nutritional guidelines. Teach proper eating habits and personal hygiene. Assimilate arriving children to the school environment by greeting them, helping them remove outerwear, and selecting activities of interest to them. Adapt teaching methods and instructional materials to meet students' varying needs and interests. Establish clear objectives for all lessons, units, and projects and communicate those objectives to children. Demonstrate activities to children. Arrange indoor and outdoor space to facilitate creative play, motor-skill activities, and safety. Plan and conduct activities for a balanced program of instruction, demonstration, and work time that provides students with opportunities to observe, question, and investigate. Maintain accurate and complete student records as required by laws, district policies, and administrative regulations.

Work Conditions—Indoors; standing; walking and running; bending or twisting the body.

Secondary School Teachers, Except Special and Vocational Education

❋ Level of Education/Training: Bachelor's degree
❋ Annual Earnings: $49,420
❋ Growth: 5.6%
❋ Annual Job Openings: 93,166
❋ Personality Type: Social

> Currently, many school districts have difficulty hiring qualified teachers in some subject areas—most often mathematics, science (especially chemistry and physics), bilingual education, and foreign languages.

Instruct students in secondary public or private schools in one or more subjects at the secondary level, such as English, mathematics, or social studies. May be designated according to subject matter specialty, such as typing instructors, commercial teachers, or English teachers. Establish and enforce rules for behavior and procedures for maintaining order among the students for whom they are responsible. Instruct through lectures, discussions, and demonstrations in one or more subjects such as English, mathematics, or social studies. Establish clear objectives for all lessons, units, and projects and communicate those objectives to students. Prepare, administer, and grade tests and assignments to evaluate students' progress. Prepare materials and classrooms for class activities. Adapt teaching methods and instructional materials to meet students' varying needs and interests. Assign and grade classwork and homework. Maintain accurate and complete student records as required by laws, district policies, and administrative regulations. Enforce all administration policies and rules governing students. Observe and evaluate students' performance, behavior, social development, and physical health. Plan and conduct activities for a balanced program of instruction, demonstration, and work time that provides students with opportunities to observe, question, and investigate. Prepare students for later grades by encouraging them to explore learning opportunities and to persevere with challenging tasks. Guide and counsel students with adjustment and/or academic problems or special academic interests. Instruct and monitor students in the use and care of equipment and materials to prevent injuries and damage. Prepare for assigned classes and show written evidence of preparation upon request of immediate supervisors. Meet with parents and guardians to discuss their children's progress and to determine their priorities for their children and their resource needs. Confer with parents or guardians, other teachers, counselors, and administrators in order to resolve students' behavioral and academic problems. Use computers, audiovisual aids, and other equipment and materials to supplement presentations. Prepare objectives and outlines for courses of study, following curriculum guidelines or requirements of states and schools. Meet with other professionals to discuss individual students' needs and progress.

Work Conditions—Indoors; noisy; standing.

Special Education Teachers, Preschool, Kindergarten, and Elementary School

❋ Level of Education/Training: Bachelor's degree
❋ Annual Earnings: $48,350
❋ Growth: 19.6%
❋ Annual Job Openings: 20,049
❋ Personality Type: Social

> Excellent job prospects are expected because of rising enrollments of special education students and reported shortages of qualified teachers.

Teach elementary and preschool school subjects to educationally and physically handicapped students. Includes teachers who specialize and work with audibly and visually handicapped students and those who teach basic academic and life processes skills to the mentally impaired. Instruct students in academic subjects, using a variety of techniques such as phonetics, multisensory learning, and repetition to reinforce learning and to meet students' varying needs and interests. Employ special educational strategies and techniques during instruction to improve the development of sensory- and perceptual-motor skills, language, cognition, and memory. Teach socially acceptable behavior, employing techniques such as behavior modification and positive reinforcement. Modify the general education curriculum for special-needs students based upon a variety of instructional techniques and technologies. Meet with parents and guardians to discuss their children's progress and to determine their priorities for their children and their resource needs. Plan and conduct activities for a balanced program of instruction, demonstration, and work time that provides students with opportunities to observe, question, and investigate. Establish and enforce rules for behavior and policies and procedures to maintain order among the students for whom they are responsible. Confer with parents, administrators, testing specialists, social workers, and professionals to develop individual educational plans designed to promote students' educational, physical, and social development. Maintain accurate and complete student records and prepare reports on children and activities as required by laws, district policies, and administrative regulations. Establish clear objectives for all lessons, units, and projects and communicate those objectives to students. Develop and implement strategies to meet the needs of students with a variety of handicapping conditions. Prepare classrooms for class activities and provide a variety of materials and resources for children to explore, manipulate, and use, both in learning activities and imaginative play. Confer with parents or guardians, teachers, counselors, and administrators to resolve students' behavioral and academic problems. Observe and evaluate students' performance, behavior, social development, and physical health. Teach students personal development skills such as goal setting, independence, and self-advocacy.

Work Conditions—Indoors; noisy; standing.

Special Education Teachers, Secondary School

✽ Level of Education/Training: Bachelor's degree
✽ Annual Earnings: $49,640
✽ Growth: 8.5%
✽ Annual Job Openings: 10,601
✽ Personality Type: Social

Excellent job prospects are expected because of rising enrollments of special education students and reported shortages of qualified teachers.

Teach secondary school subjects to educationally and physically handicapped students. Includes teachers who specialize and work with audibly and visually handicapped students and those who teach basic academic and life processes skills to the mentally impaired. Maintain accurate and complete student records and prepare reports on children and activities as required by laws, district policies, and administrative regulations. Prepare materials and classrooms for class activities. Teach socially acceptable behavior, employing techniques such as behavior modification and positive reinforcement. Establish and enforce rules for behavior and policies and procedures to maintain order among students. Confer with parents, administrators, testing specialists, social workers, and professionals to develop individual educational plans designed to promote students' educational, physical, and social development. Instruct through lectures, discussions, and demonstrations in one or more subjects such as English, mathematics, or social studies. Employ special educational strategies and techniques during instruction to improve the development of sensory- and perceptual-motor skills, language, cognition, and memory. Plan and conduct activities for a balanced program of instruction, demonstration, and work time that provides students with opportunities to observe, question, and investigate. Prepare students for later grades by encouraging them to explore learning opportunities and to persevere with challenging tasks. Teach personal development skills such as goal setting, independence, and self-advocacy. Establish clear objectives for all lessons, units, and projects and communicate those objectives to students. Develop and implement strategies to meet the needs of students with a variety of handicapping conditions. Modify the general education curriculum for special-needs students based upon a variety of instructional techniques and technologies. Meet with other professionals to discuss individual students' needs and progress. Confer with parents or guardians, other teachers, counselors, and administrators to resolve students' behavioral and academic problems. Meet with parents and guardians to discuss their children's progress and to determine their priorities for their children and their resource needs. Guide and counsel students with adjustment or academic problems or special academic interests.

Work Conditions—Indoors; noisy; standing.

Teacher Assistants

* Level of Education/Training: Short-term on-the-job training
* Annual Earnings: $21,580
* Growth: 10.4%
* Annual Job Openings: 193,986
* Personality Type: Social

About 4 in 10 teacher assistants work part time.

Perform duties that are instructional in nature or deliver direct services to students or parents. Serve in a position for which a teacher or another

professional has ultimate responsibility for the design and implementation of educational programs and services. Provide extra assistance to students with special needs, such as non-English-speaking students or those with physical and mental disabilities. Tutor and assist children individually or in small groups to help them master assignments and to reinforce learning concepts presented by teachers. Supervise students in classrooms, halls, cafeterias, school yards, and gymnasiums or on field trips. Enforce administration policies and rules governing students. Observe students' performance and record relevant data to assess progress. Discuss assigned duties with classroom teachers to coordinate instructional efforts. Instruct and monitor students in the use and care of equipment and materials to prevent injuries and damage. Present subject matter to students under the direction and guidance of teachers, using lectures, discussions, or supervised role-playing methods. Organize and label materials and display students' work in a manner appropriate for their eye levels and perceptual skills. Distribute tests and homework assignments and collect them when they are completed. Type, file, and duplicate materials. Distribute teaching materials such as textbooks, workbooks, papers, and pencils to students. Use computers, audiovisual aids, and other equipment and materials to supplement presentations. Attend staff meetings and serve on committees as required. Prepare lesson materials, bulletin board displays, exhibits, equipment, and demonstrations. Carry out therapeutic regimens such as behavior modification and personal development programs under the supervision of special education instructors, psychologists, or speech-language pathologists. Provide disabled students with assistive devices, supportive technology, and assistance accessing facilities such as restrooms. Assist in bus loading and unloading. Take class attendance and maintain attendance records. Grade homework and tests, and compute and record results, using answer sheets or electronic marking devices. Organize and supervise games and other recreational activities to promote physical, mental, and social development.

Work Conditions—Indoors; noisy; standing.

Vocational Education Teachers, Secondary School

- ❀ Level of Education/Training: Work experience plus degree
- ❀ Annual Earnings: $50,090
- ❀ Growth: –4.6%
- ❀ Annual Job Openings: 7,639
- ❀ Personality Type: Social

Qualified vocational teachers are currently in demand in a variety of fields at both the middle school and secondary school levels.

Teach or instruct vocational or occupational subjects at the secondary school level. Prepare materials and classroom for class activities. Maintain accurate and complete student records as required by law, district policy, and administrative regulations. Instruct students individually and in groups, using various teaching methods such as lectures, discussions, and demonstrations. Observe and evaluate students' performance, behavior, social development, and physical health. Establish and enforce rules for behavior and procedures for maintaining order among the students for whom they are responsible. Instruct and monitor students the in use and care of equipment and materials to prevent injury and damage. Plan and conduct activities for a balanced program of instruction, demonstration, and work time that provides students with opportunities to observe, question, and investigate. Prepare, administer, and grade tests and assignments to evaluate students' progress. Enforce all administration policies and rules governing students. Assign and grade classwork and homework. Instruct students in the knowledge and skills required in a specific occupation or occupational field, using a systematic plan of lectures; discussions; audiovisual presentations; and laboratory, shop, and field studies. Establish clear objectives for all lessons, units, and projects and communicate those objectives to students. Use computers, audiovisual aids, and other equipment and materials to supplement presentations. Plan and supervise work-experience programs in businesses, industrial shops, and school laboratories. Prepare students for later grades by encouraging them to explore learning opportunities and to persevere with challenging tasks. Confer with parents or guardians, other teachers, counselors, and administrators in order to resolve students' behavioral and academic problems. Guide and counsel students with adjustment or academic problems or special academic interests. Prepare objectives and outlines for courses of study, following curriculum guidelines or requirements of states and schools. Keep informed about trends in education and subject matter specialties.

Work Conditions—Indoors; noisy; standing; using hands on objects, tools, or controls.

Other Education Jobs

These jobs play supporting roles in the education industries, are not expected to have a good outlook (even with help from the recovery plan), or were omitted from the descriptions in this chapter for lack of room.

Bus Drivers, School

Chief Executives

Clinical, Counseling, and School
  Psychologists

Coaches and Scouts

Computer Support Specialists (see
  Computer Systems Design and
  Related Services, chapter 7)

Cooks, Fast Food

Cooks, Institution and Cafeteria

Education Administrators, Postsecondary

First-Line Supervisors/Managers of Personal Service Workers

Instructional Coordinators

Janitors and Cleaners, Except Maids and Housekeeping Cleaners

Library Assistants, Clerical

Maintenance and Repair Workers, General

Middle School Teachers, Except Special and Vocational Education

Network and Computer Systems Administrators (see Computer Systems Design and Related Services, chapter 7)

Office Clerks, General

Registered Nurses (see Health Care, chapter 4)

Secretaries, Except Legal, Medical, and Executive

Security Guards

Self-Enrichment Education Teachers

Special Education Teachers, Middle School

Speech-Language Pathologists

Teachers, Postsecondary

CHAPTER 6

JOBS IN MANUFACTURING

Manufacturing in the United States has been in decline for several years, but Obama's recovery plan is designed to add or maintain 408,000 manufacturing jobs by the fourth quarter of 2010. No single initiative in the stimulus package is labeled "manufacturing," but the energy and infrastructure components of the package, plus the business tax incentives, will probably provide the greatest boosts to manufacturing jobs.

This chapter describes the manufacturing industries that are most likely to benefit from the recovery initiatives. Obama has spoken specifically about the need to help Detroit transition to a new generation of vehicles, so the **motor vehicle and parts manufacturing** industry is included here. The **machinery manufacturing** and **computer and electronic product manufacturing** industries are also included here because they are two of the biggest manufacturing employers. At the end of the chapter, you'll find descriptions of important related jobs.

You may note that many of these jobs are projected to shrink rather than grow over the next decade, and it is unlikely that the stimulus package can completely reverse this trend. However, manufacturing employs so many workers that even as it grows smaller, it will still create many jobs as workers retire, die, or move on to other jobs.

The same initiatives that encourage manufacturing will also stimulate jobs in the **management, scientific, and technical consulting services** and **scientific research and development services** industries. You can read about those two industries and related jobs in chapter 7.

Motor Vehicle and Parts Manufacturing

Nature of the Industry

Despite news of plant closures and unemployed auto workers, the motor vehicle and parts manufacturing industry continues to be one of the largest employers in the country and a major contributor to our economy's success. Motor vehicle and parts manufacturing is continually evolving to improve efficiency and provide products that consumers want in a highly competitive market, which at times may mean that outdated plants are forced to close. It also means that companies and workers must adapt more quickly to changes in demand and production practices so that new technologies can be implemented and work can be done on a number of different vehicles at one time. Teamwork and continual retraining are key components to the success of this industry and the ability of the workforce to adapt.

Motor vehicle and parts manufacturers have a major influence on other industries in the economy as well. Building motor vehicles requires vast quantities of materials from, and creates many jobs in, industries that manufacture steel, rubber, plastics, glass, and other basic materials. It also spurs employment for automobile and other motor vehicle dealers; automotive repair and maintenance shops; gasoline stations; highway construction companies; and automotive parts, accessories, and tire stores.

The motor vehicle and parts manufacturing industry in the United States is increasingly a global industry. Even "domestic" vehicles are produced using parts manufactured around the world. This healthy competition among both domestic and foreign manufacturers has dramatically increased productivity and improved efficiency.

Competition has also led the U.S. automotive market to be increasingly fragmented. To compete for consumers' attention, automakers have greatly increased the number of models in the market, which has put a strain on the manufacturing process. To adapt, firms have had to be fast and flexible in implementing new production techniques, such as replacing traditional assembly lines with modern systems using computers, robots, and flexible production techniques. Plants designed for production flexibility put resources in the right place at the right time, allowing manufacturers to quickly and efficiently shift from slow-selling models to popular models. Flexible plants allow manufacturers to produce multiple vehicles on the same assembly line.

Working Conditions

Hours. In 2006, about 30 percent of workers in the motor vehicle and parts manufacturing industry worked, on average, more than 40 hours per week. Overtime is especially common during periods of peak demand. Most employees, however, usually work an 8-hour shift: either from 7 a.m. to 3:30 p.m. or from 4 p.m. to 12:30 a.m. A third shift often is reserved for maintenance and cleanup.

Work environment. Although working conditions have improved in recent years, some production workers still are subject to uncomfortable conditions. Heat, fumes, noise, and repetition are not uncommon in this industry.

In addition, many workers come into contact with oil and grease and may have to lift and fit heavy objects, although hydraulic lifts and other equipment have eliminated much of the heavy lifting. Employees also may operate powerful, high-speed machines that can be dangerous. Accidents and injuries usually are avoided when protective equipment and clothing are worn and safety practices are observed. Additionally, companies use carefully designed work stations and physical conditioning to reduce injuries from repetitive motions.

Newer plants are more automated and have safer, more comfortable conditions. For example, cars on the assembly line can be raised, lowered, and sometimes even rotated to work on the bottom of the car or to adjust to the worker's height. Workers also typically function as part of a team, doing more than one job and thus reducing the repetitiveness of assembly line work.

Workers in this industry experience higher rates of injury and illness than do workers in most other industries. In 2006, motor vehicle manufacturing, on average, sustained 11.4 cases of work-related injury and illness per 100 full-time workers, 13.2 in motor vehicle body and trailer manufacturing, and 7.7 in motor vehicle parts manufacturing—compared with 6.0 in all manufacturing industries and 4.4 in the entire private sector.

As in other industries, professional and managerial workers normally have clean, comfortable offices and are not subject to the hazards of assembly line work. However, many supervisors and plant managers still need to visit the assembly line and face some of the same hazards as assembly line workers.

Employment

Motor vehicle and parts manufacturing was among the largest of the manufacturing industries in 2006, providing 1.1 million jobs. The majority of jobs, about 61 percent, were in firms that make motor vehicle parts. About 23 percent of workers in the industry were employed in firms assembling complete motor vehicles, while about 16 percent worked in firms producing truck trailers; motor homes; travel trailers; campers; and car, truck, and bus bodies placed on separately purchased chassis.

Although motor vehicle and parts manufacturing jobs are scattered throughout the nation, jobs are concentrated in the Midwest and South. Michigan, which houses the headquarters for the three major domestic manufacturers, accounts for 21 percent of all jobs. Michigan, Ohio, Indiana, Tennessee, and Illinois combined have 54 percent of all the jobs in this industry. Other states that account for significant numbers of jobs include Kentucky, New York, California, Pennsylvania, and North Carolina. Automotive employment is shifting away from its traditional base in the Midwest to southeastern states such as Alabama, Mississippi, South Carolina, and Tennessee.

Employment is concentrated in a relatively small number of large establishments. More than half of all motor vehicle and parts manufacturing jobs were in establishments employing 500 or more workers. Motor vehicle manufacturing employment, in particular, is concentrated in these large establishments, whereas many motor vehicle parts manufacturing jobs are found in small and medium-sized establishments.

Motor vehicle manufacturing corporations employ many additional workers in establishments that are parts of other industries. Many of these jobs are located in Michigan. Jobs in corporate headquarters often are in separate establishments and so would be classified as part of a different industry. Likewise, workers in research and development (R&D) establishments that are separate from a manufacturing facility are included in a separate industry—scientific research and development services. (This industry is covered in chapter 7.)

Outlook

Continued productivity improvements and more foreign outsourcing of parts will cause overall employment to decline over the next decade.

Employment change. Overall wage and salary employment in the motor vehicle and parts manufacturing industry is expected to decline by 14 percent over the 2006–2016 period, compared with 11 percent growth for all industries combined. Although projections are for more automobiles and light trucks to be manufactured in the U.S. over this period, productivity improvements will enable manufacturers to produce more vehicles and parts with fewer workers. Also, as the foreign-based manufacturers gain market share, employment in the parts industry will be affected because these companies generally import more of their parts than the domestic manufacturers.

The growing intensity of international and domestic competition has increased cost pressures on manufacturers. In response, they have sought to improve productivity and quality with high-technology production techniques, including computer-assisted design, production, and testing. In addition to automation, both domestic and foreign-based manufacturers will reduce costs by shifting some parts and vehicle production to lower-wage countries.

The automotive industry also is increasingly turning to contract employees in an effort to reduce costs. Contract workers are employed by staffing agencies or employment services firms that provide workers to companies on a temporary or as-needed basis. Although they work in the manufacturing plants alongside auto manufacturing employees, they are considered workers in the employment services industry and thus are not counted in this industry. Contract workers are less costly to hire and lay off than are permanent employees and they enable plants to expand or reduce production quickly without the need to lay off or rehire permanent employees. Contract jobs also serve as a screening tool by employers to search for candidates for permanent jobs that are more complex and require more skills.

Expanding factory automation, robotics, efficiency gains, and the need to cut costs will cause nearly all production occupations to decline, but some occupations will decline more than others. Increasing automation will affect more basic machine operator occupations, but not as much skilled workers who program robots. Assemblers who only perform one or two tasks will be replaced by team assemblers who are interchangeable on a team and can perform multiple functions. Greater automation will boost demand for maintenance workers who service and repair the robots and automated systems essential to a factory. As employers seek more flexible workers in these positions, employment will shift from specialized occupations, such as electricians, to more generalized occupations such as industrial machinery mechanics and maintenance workers.

Employment of management, computer, office, and administrative support occupations will decline as the number of production workers, who these workers manage, supervise, and support, decline. Industrial production engineers are expected to increase as the need to streamline production and reduce costs continues to be important to this industry.

Job prospects. In light of the increasingly automated and sophisticated nature of motor vehicle manufacturing and assembly, employers are seeking a better educated workforce. While applicants for assembly jobs may face competition, opportunities will be best for those with a two-year degree in a technical area. Applicants for maintenance jobs also face competition. As automakers shift to multi-skilled maintenance personnel, opportunities will be best for those with skills across a range of areas, such as hydraulics, electrical, and welding. Employers use screening tests for new applicants and state that both strong math and communications skills are necessary to pass these tests.

Although employment may be declining, there are expected to be a significant number of openings due to the large number of auto workers who are expected to retire in the coming decade. Some of the earlier foreign plants that were built in the 1980s will see much turnover as a large proportion of their workers retire.

Machinery Manufacturing

Nature of the Industry

The development and implementation of machinery was responsible for one of the great advances in human history, the industrial revolution. Machinery encompasses a vast range of products, ranging from huge industrial turbines costing millions of dollars to the common lawn mower, but all machinery has one common defining feature: It either reduces or eliminates the amount of human work required to accomplish a task. Machinery is critical to the production of much of the nation's goods and services because nearly every workplace in every industry uses some form of machinery. From the oil derrick that pumps out oil to the commercial refrigerator in use by your favorite restaurant, machinery is necessary for the way we live today. Thus, while people never use or even see most of the machinery that makes their lifestyles possible, they use the products it makes every day.

Most machinery is made of metal, which gives the end product strength and durability, but which necessitates specialized procedures in production. Each part needs to be designed to exacting specifications to ensure proper function of the finished product. Techniques such as forging, stamping, bending, forming, and machining are used to create each piece of metal, thousands of which then need to be welded or assembled together in the largest machines. At each stage of production and assembly, extensive testing takes place to maintain quality control standards. Because of the great variety of machinery produced by this industry, firms specialize in designing and producing certain types of equipment for specific applications.

The machinery manufacturing industry, like all U.S. manufacturers, continues to evolve. Domestic and foreign competition have required the industry to adopt new technologies and techniques to lower costs and raise the productivity of its workforce. For example, using high-technology production techniques, including robots, computers, and programmable equipment, results in productivity gains and helps to maximize the use of available equipment and workers. Increasing technology and automation also reduces the number of unskilled workers needed in the production process.

Pressures to reduce costs and maximize profits have also caused manufacturers in the industry to adopt new business practices. One example is the practice of contracting out support functions such as janitorial and security jobs and, increasingly, some administrative services and warehouse and shipping jobs. Rather than employ workers directly for these jobs, a manufacturer will often contract with another company that specializes in providing these services. This practice reduces costs by forcing service providers to compete for the work, allows manufacturers to focus on their core design and production activities, and increases manufacturers' flexibility by letting them add and subtract contract workers more easily than they could hire and fire employees.

These changes have had a profound effect on the machinery manufacturing workforce. Automation of many of the production processes and outsourcing of many of the administrative and support functions have reduced the need for many less-skilled workers and increased the skill level required for the remaining workers. These changes are allowing the industry to remain competitive and meet the demand for machinery that other industries rely on.

Working Conditions

Hours. Most workers in machinery manufacturing work 8-hour shifts 5 days a week. Overtime can be common, especially during periods of peak demand. As a result, the average production worker worked 42.4 hours per week in 2006, with about 35 percent of all workers in the industry averaging more than 40 hours a week and 20 percent of workers averaging more than 50 hours per week. Opportunities for part-time work are rare, as less than 4 percent of workers were employed part time in 2006. Some plants are capable of operating 24 hours a day, but some shifts are able to operate with a reduced workforce because of the automated nature of the production process.

Work environment. Production workers in the machinery manufacturing industry generally encounter conditions that are much improved from the past. New facilities in particular tend to be clean, well lighted, and temperature controlled. Noise can still be a factor, however, especially in larger production facilities. Most of the labor-intensive work is now automated, but some heavy lifting may still be required. Some workers may also have to work with oil and grease or chemicals that require special handling. Certain types of machinery also require special care in their use. Nevertheless, injuries are rare when proper safety procedures are observed. In 2006, the rate of work-related injuries and illnesses per 100 workers was 6.2, compared with 6.0 for all manufacturing industries. The rate for the private sector as a whole was 4.4.

Employment

The machinery manufacturing industry provided 1.2 million wage and salary jobs in 2006. Employment was relatively evenly distributed among all segments of the industry. There were about 31,000 establishments in the industry; about half employed fewer than 10 workers. However, 39 percent of workers were employed in establishments of 250 workers or more.

Although machinery manufacturing jobs are located throughout the country, certain states account for the greatest numbers of jobs. About a third of all jobs were located in the Midwestern states of Illinois, Indiana, Michigan, Ohio, and Wisconsin. Populous states such as California, Texas, New York, and Pennsylvania also had large numbers of jobs.

Outlook

Employment in machinery manufacturing is expected to continue its long-term decline as productivity increases allow companies to produce more goods with fewer workers.

Employment change. Wage and salary employment in the machinery manufacturing industry is expected to decrease 12 percent over the 2006–2016 period compared with an 11 percent increase for all industries combined. All segments of the industry are expected to experience some employment declines.

The main factor affecting the level of employment in the machinery manufacturing industry is the high rate of productivity growth. Increases in productivity allow companies to produce more goods with the same number of workers. Even though output in machinery manufacturing is expected to increase significantly, firms will be able to meet the increase through higher productivity of existing workers rather than by creating new jobs.

A second factor expected to cause some employment declines in machinery manufacturing is the growing number of imported parts. This industry is less likely to lose a large part of its output to imports from other countries than some other manufacturing industries. The large size and complexity of many of the types of machinery made by this industry and the relatively skilled workforce it requires is an advantage that many manufacturing industries do not share. However, while most finished machines are made in the United States, it is increasingly common for manufacturers to have some parts of the final product made in other countries and then shipped to U.S. manufacturers for final assembly. While still expected to account for only a small part of the total process, this increased offshore outsourcing of production will have a negative effect on machinery manufacturing employment.

Demand for machinery is expected to remain strong. Machinery is important for all industries because it boosts their productivity, and advances in technology will make machinery even more efficient and thus more desirable. Demand for machinery is highly sensitive to cyclical swings in the economy, however, causing employment in machinery manufacturing to fluctuate. During periods of economic prosperity, companies invest in new equipment, such as machinery, in order to boost production. When economic growth slows, however, many companies are reluctant to purchase new machinery. These changes in demand cause machinery manufacturers to replace fewer workers who leave or even lay off some workers.

Although overall employment in the machinery manufacturing industry is expected to decline, the outlook for occupations will vary; some will experience larger declines than others, while some will even experience growth instead. Increased automation and more efficient production processes will cause employment declines in assembler and fabricator occupations. Office and administrative support workers will also experience declines as a result of increased automation and contracting out. Employment in professional and management occupations will experience smaller declines relative to other occupations in the industry; engineers in particular will experience very good employment opportunities, as they are responsible for increasing innovation and competitiveness in the industry.

Job prospects. Despite the decline in employment projected for this sizeable industry, a significant number of job openings will become available because of the need to replace workers who retire or move to jobs outside of the industry. However, not all jobs that are vacated will be filled because attrition is one of the main ways that establishments reduce the number of employees. It is also a way the establishments upgrade the skill mix of their workforce. Machinery manufacturing establishments will continually be seeking to hire more highly skilled workers, especially persons with good basic educational skills who make good candidates to be trained for the high-skilled jobs of 21st-century manufacturing. Workers with these skills are expected to experience excellent job prospects.

Computer and Electronic Product Manufacturing

Nature of the Industry

The computer and electronic product manufacturing industry produces computers; computer-related products, including printers; communications equipment; and home electronic equipment, as well as a wide range of goods used for both commercial and military purposes. In addition, many electronic products or components are incorporated into other industries' products, such as cars, toys, and appliances.

The rapid pace of innovation in electronic technology makes for a constant demand for newer and faster products and applications. This demand puts a greater emphasis on research and development (R&D) than is typical in most manufacturing operations. Being the first firm to market a new or better product can mean success for both the product and the firm. Even for many relatively commonplace items, R&D continues to result in better, cheaper products with more desirable features. For example, a company that develops a new kind of computer chip to be used in many brands of computers can earn millions of dollars in sales until a competitor is able to improve on that design. Many employees, therefore, are research scientists, engineers, and technicians whose job it is to continually develop and improve products.

The product design process includes not only the initial design, but also development work, which ensures that the product functions properly and can be manufactured as inexpensively as possible. When a product is manufactured, the components are assembled, usually by soldering them to a printed circuit board by means of automated equipment. Hand assembly of small parts requires both good eyesight and coordination, but because of the cost and precision involved, assembly and packaging are becoming highly automated.

Working Conditions

Hours. About half of all employees work regular 40-hour weeks, but pressure to develop new products ahead of competitors may result in some R&D personnel working extensive overtime to meet deadlines. The competitive nature of the industry makes for an exciting, but sometimes stressful, work environment—especially for those in technical and managerial occupations.

Work environment. In general, those working in computer and electronic manufacturing—even production workers—enjoy relatively good working conditions. In contrast to those in many other manufacturing industries, production workers in this industry usually work in clean and relatively noise-free environments.

In 2006, the rate of work-related injuries and illnesses per 100 full-time workers was 2.0 in the computer and electronic parts manufacturing industry, lower than the average of 4.4 for the private sector. However, some jobs in the industry may present risks. For example, some workers who fabricate integrated circuits and other components may be exposed to hazardous chemicals, and working with small parts may cause eyestrain.

Employment

The computer and electronic product manufacturing industry employed 1.3 million wage and salary workers in 2006. Few workers were self-employed.

The industry comprised about 19,000 establishments in 2006, many of which were small, employing only one or a few workers. Large establishments of 100 or more workers employed the majority—78 percent—of the industry's workforce.

Companies in this industry also may employ many additional workers in establishments that are part of other industries. Some workers who perform R&D work at separate research establishments that are not actually part of a manufacturing facility in this industry, although owned by the companies in this industry, and so are included in a different industry—scientific research and development services (described in chapter 7).

Outlook

Employment in the computer and electronic product manufacturing industry is expected to decline over the next decade, but there should still be favorable employment opportunities in certain segments of the industry.

Employment change. Wage and salary employment in the computer and electronic product manufacturing industry is expected to decline by 12.0 percent between 2006 and 2016, compared with a projected increase of 11 percent in all industries. Although the output of this industry is projected to increase more rapidly than that of any other industry, employment will decline as a result of continued rapid productivity growth—the ability of the industry to produce more and better products with fewer employees. Employment also will be adversely affected by continued increases in imports of electronic and computer products, including intermediate products such as components and microchips. Although a great deal of the design work in this industry takes place in the U.S., much of the manufacturing process has been moved overseas.

The projected change in employment over the 2006–2016 period varies by industry segment. Although demand for computers should remain relatively strong worldwide, employment is expected to decline 33.5 percent in computers and peripheral equipment and 13.7 percent in semiconductor and other electronic component manufacturing. Declines in both will be due to the introduction of new technology and automated manufacturing processes, as well as a slowdown in the growth of output in these segments from previously high levels. Further, these segments will continue to face strong foreign competition.

Employment in navigational, measuring, electromedical, and control instruments manufacturing is expected to decline relatively slowly at 4.5 percent because of heavy spending on military and health-care electronics. Employment in audio and video equipment manufacturing is expected to decrease by 21.1 percent, due largely to continued import competition as well as improvements in productivity. Employment in communications equipment manufacturing is expected to increase by 0.4 percent despite automation and consolidation among firms in the industry. Employment in the manufacturing and reproduction of magnetic and optical media is expected to decrease by 3.7 percent because of higher productivity and more efficient production processes.

There should be a smaller decrease in employment among professional and related occupations than among most other occupations in the computer and electronic product manufacturing industry. Despite large numbers of engineering graduates in many foreign countries, many American manufacturers prefer U.S.-based engineering teams because they are believed to have a better knowledge of the domestic market. However, the use of the Internet and other new forms of communication make it possible for engineers to collaborate over great distances. At the same time, wages have been increasing rapidly among qualified engineers in developing countries. While offshore outsourcing of engineers will probably continue, there should be little danger to American workers, who report very low unemployment.

The computer and electronic product manufacturing industry is characterized by rapid technological advances and has grown faster than most other industries over the past several decades, although rising costs, imports, and the rapid pace of innovation continue to pose challenges. Certain segments of the industry and individual companies often experience problems. For example, the industry occasionally undergoes severe downturns, and individual companies—even those in segments of the industry doing well—can run into trouble because they have not kept up with the latest technological developments or because they have erred in deciding which products to manufacture. Such uncertainties can be expected to continue. In addition, the intensity of foreign competition and the future role of imports remain difficult to project. Import competition has wiped out major parts of the domestic consumer electronics industry, and future effects of such competition depend on trade policies and market forces. The industry is likely to continue to encounter strong competition from imported electronic goods and components from countries throughout Asia and Europe.

Because defense expenditures are expected to increase, sales of military electronics, an important segment of the industry, will likely pick up. Furthermore, firms producing electromedical equipment will continue to expand as new health-care breakthroughs are made. Smaller, more powerful computer chips are constantly being developed and incorporated into an even wider array of products, and the semiconductor content of all electronic products will continue to increase. New opportunities will continue to be created by the growth of digital technology, artificial intelligence, and nanotechnology, as well as the expansion of the Internet and the increasing demand for global information networking.

Job prospects. Despite the overall projected decrease in employment, many employment opportunities should continue to arise in the industry because of the technological revolutions taking place in computers, semiconductors, and telecommunications, as well as the need to replace the many workers who leave the industry due to retirement or other reasons. Opportunities should be best in research and development. The products of this industry—especially powerful computer chips—will continue to enhance productivity in all areas of the economy.

Prospects are especially good for professional workers such as engineers. Despite competition from abroad, U.S. companies prefer workers in research and development who have a strong understanding of the domestic marketplace. Although employment in the industry continues to decline, the relatively small number of engineers in the U.S. makes it very difficult for companies to find qualified workers when openings arise. Computer software engineers are also in high demand in this industry because many complicated hardware products will require software. This includes both drivers that help devices interface with computers and software that runs directly on complex devices.

Despite the rapid decline of production jobs, prospects should still be good for qualified workers, especially those with formal training in high-tech manufacturing. Although fewer positions are now available, changes in the nature of the work have meant that workers need to have a higher skill level than before. Many positions require a certificate or associate degree from a technical school.

Some Manufacturing Jobs That Are Likely to Benefit from the Stimulus Package

Aircraft Structure, Surfaces, Rigging, and Systems Assemblers

❀ Level of Education/Training: Long-term on-the-job training
❀ Annual Earnings: $45,420
❀ Growth: 12.8%
❀ Annual Job Openings: 6,550
❀ Personality Type: Realistic

> Because much of the assembly in the aerospace industry is done in hard-to-reach locations—inside airplane fuselages or gear boxes, for example—which are unsuited to robots, aircraft assemblers will not be easily replaced by automated processes.

Assemble, fit, fasten, and install parts of airplanes, space vehicles, or missiles, such as tails, wings, fuselage, bulkheads, stabilizers, landing gear, rigging and control equipment, or heating and ventilating systems. Form loops or splices in cables, using clamps and fittings, or reweave cable strands. Align and fit structural assemblies manually or signal crane operators to position assemblies for joining. Align, fit, assemble, connect, and install system components, using jigs, fixtures, measuring instruments, hand tools, and power tools. Assemble and fit prefabricated parts to form subassemblies. Assemble, install, and connect parts, fittings, and assemblies on aircraft, using layout tools; hand tools; power tools; and fasteners such as bolts, screws, rivets, and clamps. Attach brackets, hinges, or clips to secure or support components and subassemblies, using bolts, screws, rivets, chemical bonding, or welding. Select and install accessories in swaging machines, using hand tools. Fit and fasten sheet metal coverings to surface areas and other sections of aircraft prior to welding or riveting. Lay out and mark reference points and locations for installation of parts and components, using jigs, templates, and measuring and marking instruments. Inspect and test installed units, parts, systems, and assemblies for fit, alignment, performance, defects, and compliance with standards, using measuring instruments and test equipment. Install mechanical linkages and actuators and verify tension of cables, using tensiometers. Join structural assemblies such as wings, tails, and fuselage. Measure and cut cables and tubing, using master templates, measuring instruments, and cable cutters or saws. Read and interpret blueprints, illustrations, and specifications to determine layouts, sequences of operations, or identities and relationships of parts. Prepare and load live ammunition, missiles, and bombs onto aircraft according to established procedures. Adjust, repair, rework, or replace parts and assemblies to eliminate malfunctions and to ensure proper operation. Cut, trim, file, bend, and smooth parts and verify sizes and fitting tolerances in order to ensure proper fit and clearance of parts. Install and connect control cables to electronically controlled units, using hand tools, ring locks, cotter keys, threaded connectors, turnbuckles, and related devices.

Work Conditions—Noisy; contaminants; hazardous conditions; hazardous equipment; standing; using hands on objects, tools, or controls.

Computer Hardware Engineers

* Level of Education/Training: Bachelor's degree
* Annual Earnings: $91,860
* Growth: 4.6%
* Annual Job Openings: 3,572
* Personality Type: Investigative

> As computer and chip manufacturers contract out more of their engineering needs to both domestic and foreign design firms, much of the growth in employment of hardware engineers is expected in the computer systems design and related services industry.

Research, design, develop, and test computer or computer-related equipment for commercial, industrial, military, or scientific use. May supervise the manufacturing and installation of computer or computer-related equipment and components. Update knowledge and skills to keep up with rapid advancements in computer technology. Provide technical support to designers, marketing and sales departments, suppliers, engineers, and other team members throughout the product development and implementation process. Test and verify hardware and support peripherals to ensure that they meet specifications and requirements, analyzing and recording test data. Monitor functioning of equipment and make necessary modifications to ensure system operates in conformance with specifications. Analyze information to determine, recommend, and plan layout, including type of computers and peripheral equipment modifications. Build, test, and modify product prototypes, using working models or theoretical models constructed using computer simulation. Analyze user needs and recommend appropriate hardware. Direct technicians, engineering designers, or other technical support personnel as needed. Confer with engineering staff and consult specifications to evaluate interface between hardware and software and operational and performance requirements of overall system. Select hardware and material, assuring compliance with specifications and product requirements. Store, retrieve, and manipulate data for analysis of system capabilities and requirements. Write detailed functional specifications that document the hardware development process and support hardware introduction. Specify power supply requirements and configuration, drawing on system performance expectations and design specifications. Provide training and support to system designers and users. Assemble and modify existing pieces of equipment to meet special needs. Evaluate factors such as reporting formats required, cost constraints, and need for security restrictions to determine hardware configuration. Design and develop computer hardware and support peripherals, including central processing units (CPUs), support logic, microprocessors, custom integrated circuits, and printers and disk drives. Recommend purchase of equipment to control dust, temperature, and humidity in area of system installation.

Work Conditions—Indoors; sitting.

Computer-Controlled Machine Tool Operators, Metal and Plastic

❀ Level of Education/Training: Moderate-term on-the-job training
❀ Annual Earnings: $32,550
❀ Growth: –3.0%
❀ Annual Job Openings: 12,997
❀ Personality Type: Realistic

> Despite the projected slow decline in employment, job opportunities should be excellent, as employers are expected to continue to have difficulty finding qualified workers.

Operate computer-controlled machines or robots to perform one or more machine functions on metal or plastic workpieces. Measure dimensions of finished workpieces to ensure conformance to specifications, using precision measuring instruments, templates, and fixtures. Remove and replace dull cutting tools. Mount, install, align, and secure tools, attachments, fixtures, and workpieces on machines, using hand tools and precision measuring instruments. Listen to machines during operation to detect sounds such as those made by dull cutting tools or excessive vibration and adjust machines to compensate for problems. Adjust machine feed and speed, change cutting tools, or adjust machine controls when automatic programming is faulty or if machines malfunction. Stop machines to remove finished workpieces or to change tooling, setup, or workpiece placement according to required machining sequences. Lift workpieces to machines manually or with hoists or cranes. Modify cutting programs to account for problems encountered during operation and save modified programs. Calculate machine speed and feed ratios and the size and position of cuts. Insert control instructions into machine control units to start operation. Check to ensure that workpieces are properly lubricated and cooled during machine operation. Input initial part dimensions into machine control panels. Set up and operate computer-controlled machines or robots to perform one or more machine functions on metal or plastic workpieces. Confer with supervisors or programmers to resolve machine malfunctions and production errors and to obtain approval to continue production. Review program specifications or blueprints to determine and set machine operations and sequencing, finished workpiece dimensions, or numerical control sequences. Monitor machine operation and control panel displays and compare readings to specifications to detect malfunctions. Control coolant systems. Maintain machines and remove and replace broken or worn machine tools, using hand tools. Stack or load finished items or place items on conveyor systems. Clean machines, tooling, and parts, using solvents or solutions and rags. Enter commands or load control media such as tapes, cards, or disks into machine controllers to retrieve programmed instructions.

Work Conditions—Noisy; contaminants; hazardous equipment; standing; using hands on objects, tools, or controls; repetitive motions.

Electrical and Electronic Equipment Assemblers

* Level of Education/Training: Short-term on-the-job training
* Annual Earnings: $26,540
* Growth: –26.8%
* Annual Job Openings: 26,595
* Personality Type: Realistic

> Temporary workers are gaining in importance in the manufacturing sector and elsewhere as companies strive for a more flexible workforce to meet the fluctuations in the market.

Assemble or modify electrical or electronic equipment, such as computers, test equipment telemetering systems, electric motors, and batteries. Inspect and test wiring installations, assemblies, and circuits for resistance factors and for operation and record results. Assemble electrical or electronic systems and support structures and install components, units, subassemblies, wiring, and assembly casings, using rivets, bolts, and soldering and micro-welding equipment. Adjust, repair, or replace electrical or electronic component parts to correct defects and to ensure conformance to specifications. Clean parts, using cleaning solutions, air hoses, and cloths. Read and interpret schematic drawings, diagrams, blueprints, specifications, work orders, and reports to determine materials requirements and assembly instructions. Mark and tag components so that stock inventory can be tracked and identified. Position, align, and adjust workpieces and electrical parts to facilitate wiring and assembly. Pack finished assemblies for shipment and transport them to storage areas, using hoists or handtrucks. Confer with supervisors or engineers to plan and review work activities and to resolve production problems. Explain assembly procedures or techniques to other workers. Measure and adjust voltages to specified values to determine operational accuracy of instruments. Fabricate and form parts, coils, and structures according to specifications, using drills, calipers, cutters, and saws. Drill and tap holes in specified equipment locations to mount control units and to provide openings for elements, wiring, and instruments. Complete, review, and maintain production, time, and component waste reports. Paint structures as specified, using paint sprayers. Instruct customers in the installation, repair, and maintenance of products. Distribute materials, supplies, and subassemblies to work areas.

Work Conditions—Indoors; contaminants; hazardous equipment; sitting; using hands on objects, tools, or controls; repetitive motions.

Engineering Managers
- ❀ Level of Education/Training: Work experience plus degree
- ❀ Annual Earnings: $111,020
- ❀ Growth: 7.3%
- ❀ Annual Job Openings: 7,404
- ❀ Personality Type: Enterprising

> Opportunities will be best for workers with strong communication and business management skills.

Plan, direct, or coordinate activities or research and development in such fields as architecture and engineering. Coordinate and direct projects, making detailed plans to accomplish goals and directing the integration of technical activities. Consult or negotiate with clients to prepare project specifications. Present and explain proposals, reports, and findings to clients.

Direct, review, and approve product design and changes. Recruit employees; assign, direct, and evaluate their work; and oversee the development and maintenance of staff competence. Perform administrative functions such as reviewing and writing reports, approving expenditures, enforcing rules, and making decisions about the purchase of materials or services. Prepare budgets, bids, and contracts and direct the negotiation of research contracts. Analyze technology, resource needs, and market demand to plan and assess the feasibility of projects. Confer with management, production, and marketing staff to discuss project specifications and procedures. Review and recommend or approve contracts and cost estimates. Develop and implement policies, standards, and procedures for the engineering and technical work performed in the department, service, laboratory, or firm. Plan and direct the installation, testing, operation, maintenance, and repair of facilities and equipment. Administer highway planning, construction, and maintenance. Confer with and report to officials and the public to provide information and solicit support for projects. Set scientific and technical goals within broad outlines provided by top management. Direct the engineering of water control, treatment, and distribution projects. Plan, direct, and coordinate survey work with other staff activities, certifying survey work, and writing land legal descriptions.

Work Conditions—Indoors; noisy; sitting.

Heat Treating Equipment Setters, Operators, and Tenders, Metal and Plastic

❈ Level of Education/Training: Moderate-term on-the-job training
❈ Annual Earnings: $31,270
❈ Growth: −14.8%
❈ Annual Job Openings: 2,973
❈ Personality Type: Realistic

Those who can operate multiple machines will have the best opportunities for advancement and for gaining jobs with more long-term potential.

Set up, operate, or tend heating equipment such as heat-treating furnaces, flame-hardening machines, induction machines, soaking pits, or vacuum equipment to temper, harden, anneal, or heat-treat metal or plastic objects. Read production schedules and work orders to determine processing sequences, furnace temperatures, and heat cycle requirements for objects to be heat-treated. Record times that parts are removed from furnaces to document that objects have attained specified temperatures for specified times. Set up and operate or tend machines, such as furnaces, baths, flame-hardening machines, and electronic induction machines, that harden, anneal, and heat-treat metal. Determine types and temperatures of baths and quenching media needed to attain specified part hardness, toughness, and ductility, using heat-treating charts and knowledge of methods, equipment, and metals. Remove parts from furnaces after specified times and air dry parts or cool them in water, oil brine, or other baths. Position stock in furnaces, using tongs, chain hoists, or pry bars. Instruct new workers in machine operation. Adjust controls to maintain temperatures and heating times, using thermal instruments and charts, dials and gauges of furnaces, and color of stock in furnaces to make setting determinations. Determine flame temperatures, current frequencies, heating cycles, and induction heating coils needed, based on degree of hardness required and properties of stock to be treated. Load parts into containers and place containers on conveyors to be inserted into furnaces or insert parts into furnaces. Mount workpieces in fixtures, on arbors, or between centers of machines. Set up and operate die-quenching machines to prevent parts from warping. Move controls to light gas burners and to adjust gas and water flow and flame temperature. Reduce heat when processing is complete to allow parts to cool in furnaces or machinery. Signal forklift operators to deposit or extract containers of parts into and from furnaces and quenching rinse tanks. Test parts for hardness by using hardness-testing equipment or by examining and feeling samples. Position plastic sheets and molds in plastic bags, heat material under lamps, and force confrontation of sheets to molds by vacuum pressure. Examine parts to ensure metal shades and colors conform to specifications, utilizing knowledge of metal heat-treating.

Work Conditions—Noisy; very hot or cold; contaminants; minor burns, cuts, bites, or stings; standing; using hands on objects, tools, or controls.

Industrial Engineers

- ❀ Level of Education/Training: Bachelor's degree
- ❀ Annual Earnings: $71,430
- ❀ Growth: 20.3%
- ❀ Annual Job Openings: 11,272
- ❀ Personality Type: Enterprising

> Because their work is similar to that done in management occupations, many industrial engineers leave the occupation to become managers. Many openings will be created by the need to replace industrial engineers who transfer to other occupations or leave the labor force.

Design, develop, test, and evaluate integrated systems for managing industrial production processes, including human work factors, quality control, inventory control, logistics and material flow, cost analysis, and production coordination. Analyze statistical data and product specifications to determine standards and establish quality and reliability objectives of finished product. Develop manufacturing methods, labor utilization standards, and cost analysis systems to promote efficient staff and facility utilization. Recommend methods for improving utilization of personnel, material, and utilities. Plan and establish sequence of operations to fabricate and assemble parts or products and to promote efficient utilization. Apply statistical methods and perform mathematical calculations to determine manufacturing processes, staff requirements, and production standards. Coordinate quality control objectives and activities to resolve production problems, maximize product reliability, and minimize cost. Confer with vendors, staff, and management personnel regarding purchases, procedures, product specifications, manufacturing capabilities, and project status. Draft and design layout of equipment, materials, and workspace to illustrate maximum efficiency, using drafting tools and computer. Review production schedules, engineering specifications, orders, and related information to obtain knowledge of manufacturing methods, procedures, and activities. Communicate with management and user personnel to develop production and design standards. Estimate production cost and effect of product design changes for management review, action, and control. Formulate sampling procedures and designs and develop forms and instructions for recording, evaluating, and reporting quality and reliability data. Record or oversee recording of information to ensure currency of engineering drawings and documentation of production problems. Study operations sequence, material flow, functional statements, organization charts, and project information to determine worker functions and responsibilities. Direct workers engaged in product measurement, inspection, and testing activities to ensure quality control and reliability. Implement methods and procedures for disposition of discrepant material and defective or damaged parts and assess cost and responsibility.

Work Conditions—Indoors; noisy; contaminants; hazardous equipment; more often sitting than standing.

Industrial Machinery Mechanics
- ❋ Level of Education/Training: Long-term on-the-job training
- ❋ Annual Earnings: $42,350
- ❋ Growth: 9.0%
- ❋ Annual Job Openings: 23,361
- ❋ Personality Type: Realistic

Job candidates usually need some education after high school plus experience working on specific machines. Applicants with broad skills in machine repair and maintenance should have favorable job prospects.

Repair, install, adjust, or maintain industrial production and processing machinery or refinery and pipeline distribution systems. Disassemble machinery and equipment to remove parts and make repairs. Repair and replace broken or malfunctioning components of machinery and equipment. Repair and maintain the operating condition of industrial production and processing machinery and equipment. Examine parts for defects such as breakage and excessive wear. Reassemble equipment after completion of inspections, testing, or repairs. Observe and test the operation of machinery and equipment to diagnose malfunctions, using voltmeters and other testing devices. Operate newly repaired machinery and equipment to verify the adequacy of repairs. Clean, lubricate, and adjust parts, equipment, and machinery. Analyze test results, machine error messages, and information obtained from operators to diagnose equipment problems. Record repairs and maintenance performed. Study blueprints and manufacturers' manuals to determine correct installation and operation of machinery. Record parts and materials used, ordering or requisitioning new parts and materials as necessary. Cut and weld metal to repair broken metal parts, fabricate new parts, and assemble new equipment. Demonstrate equipment functions and features to machine operators. Enter codes and instructions to program computer-controlled machinery.

Work Conditions—Noisy; contaminants; hazardous conditions; hazardous equipment; standing; using hands on objects, tools, or controls.

Industrial Production Managers
* Level of Education/Training: Work experience in a related occupation
* Annual Earnings: $80,560
* Growth: –5.9%
* Annual Job Openings: 14,889
* Personality Type: Enterprising

Employers are likely to seek candidates who have excellent communication skills and related work experience and who are personable, flexible, and eager to enhance their knowledge and skills through ongoing training.

Plan, direct, or coordinate the work activities and resources necessary for manufacturing products in accordance with specifications for cost, quality, and quantity. Direct and coordinate production, processing, distribution, and marketing activities of industrial organization. Review processing schedules and production orders to make decisions concerning inventory requirements, staffing requirements, work procedures, and duty assignments, considering budgetary limitations and time constraints. Review operations and confer with technical or administrative staff to resolve production or processing problems. Develop and implement production tracking and quality control systems, analyzing reports on production, quality control, maintenance, and other aspects of operations to detect problems. Hire, train, evaluate, and discharge staff, and resolve personnel grievances. Set and monitor product standards, examining samples of raw products or directing testing during processing, to ensure finished products are of prescribed quality. Prepare and maintain production reports and personnel records. Coordinate and recommend procedures for maintenance or modification of facilities and equipment, including the replacement of machines. Initiate and coordinate inventory and cost control programs. Institute employee suggestion or involvement programs. Maintain current knowledge of the quality control field, relying on current literature pertaining to materials use, technological advances, and statistical studies. Review plans and confer with research and support staff to develop new products and processes. Develop budgets and approve expenditures for supplies, materials, and human resources, ensuring that materials, labor, and equipment are used efficiently to meet production targets. Negotiate prices of materials with suppliers.

Work Conditions—Indoors; noisy; contaminants; hazardous equipment; minor burns, cuts, bites, or stings; standing.

Industrial Truck and Tractor Operators

- ❋ Level of Education/Training: Short-term on-the-job training
- ❋ Annual Earnings: $28,010
- ❋ Growth: −2.0%
- ❋ Annual Job Openings: 89,547
- ❋ Personality Type: Realistic

> Workers must receive specialized training in safety awareness and procedures and be evaluated at least once every three years.

Operate industrial trucks or tractors equipped to move materials around a warehouse, storage yard, factory, construction site, or similar

location. Inspect product load for accuracy and safely move it around the warehouse or facility to ensure timely and complete delivery. Move controls to drive gasoline- or electric-powered trucks, cars, or tractors and transport materials between loading, processing, and storage areas. Move levers and controls that operate lifting devices such as forklifts, lift beams and swivel-hooks, hoists, and elevating platforms to load, unload, transport, and stack material. Position lifting devices under, over, or around loaded pallets, skids, and boxes and secure material or products for transport to designated areas. Manually or mechanically load and unload materials from pallets, skids, platforms, cars, lifting devices, or other transport vehicles. Perform routine maintenance on vehicles and auxiliary equipment, such as cleaning, lubricating, recharging batteries, fueling, or replacing liquefied-gas tank. Weigh materials or products and record weight and other production data on tags or labels. Operate or tend automatic stacking, loading, packaging, or cutting machines. Turn valves and open chutes to dump, spray, or release materials from dump cars or storage bins into hoppers. Signal workers to discharge, dump, or level materials. Hook tow trucks to trailer hitches and fasten attachments such as graders, plows, rollers, and winch cables to tractors, using hitchpins.

Work Conditions—Very hot or cold; contaminants; sitting; using hands on objects, tools, or controls; bending or twisting the body; repetitive motions.

Machinists

* ❋ Level of Education/Training: Long-term on-the-job training
* ❋ Annual Earnings: $35,230
* ❋ Growth: –3.1%
* ❋ Annual Job Openings: 39,505
* ❋ Personality Type: Realistic

> Although employment is projected to decline, job opportunities are expected to be good. The number of workers learning to be machinists is expected to be less than the number of job openings arising each year from the need to replace experienced machinists who retire or transfer to other occupations.

Set up and operate a variety of machine tools to produce precision parts and instruments. Includes precision instrument makers who fabricate, modify, or repair mechanical instruments. May also fabricate and modify parts to make or repair machine tools or maintain industrial machines, applying knowledge of mechanics, shop mathematics, metal properties, layout, and machining procedures. Calculate dimensions and tolerances, using knowledge of mathematics and instruments such as micrometers and vernier calipers. Align and secure holding fixtures, cutting tools, attachments, accessories, and materials onto machines. Select the appropriate tools, machines, and materials to be used in preparation of machinery work. Monitor the feed and speed of machines during the machining process. Machine parts to specifications, using machine tools such as lathes, milling machines, shapers, or grinders. Set up, adjust, and operate all of the basic machine tools and many specialized or advanced variation tools to perform precision machining operations. Measure, examine, and test completed units to detect defects and ensure conformance to specifications, using precision instruments such as micrometers. Set controls to regulate machining or enter commands to retrieve, input, or edit computerized machine control media. Position and fasten work pieces. Maintain industrial machines, applying knowledge of mechanics, shop mathematics, metal properties, layout, and machining procedures. Observe and listen to operating machines or equipment to diagnose machine malfunctions and to determine need for adjustments or repairs. Check work pieces to ensure that they are properly lubricated and cooled. Lay out, measure, and mark metal stock to display placement of cuts. Study sample parts, blueprints, drawings, and engineering information to determine methods and sequences of operations needed to fabricate products and determine product dimensions and tolerances. Confer with engineering, supervisory, and manufacturing personnel to exchange technical information. Program computers and electronic instruments such as numerically controlled machine tools. Operate equipment to verify operational efficiency. Clean and lubricate machines, tools, and equipment to remove grease, rust, stains, and foreign matter. Design fixtures, tooling, and experimental parts to meet special engineering needs. Evaluate experimental procedures and recommend changes or modifications for improved efficiency and adaptability to setup and production.

Work Conditions—Noisy; contaminants; hazardous equipment; minor burns, cuts, bites, or stings; standing; using hands on objects, tools, or controls.

Mechanical Engineering Technicians

❀ Level of Education/Training: Associate degree
❀ Annual Earnings: $47,280
❀ Growth: 6.4%
❀ Annual Job Openings: 3,710
❀ Personality Type: Realistic

Growth is expected to be limited by foreign competition in both design services and manufacturing.

Apply theory and principles of mechanical engineering to modify, develop, and test machinery and equipment under direction of engineering staff or physical scientists. Prepare parts sketches and write work orders and purchase requests to be furnished by outside contractors. Draft detail drawing or sketch for drafting room completion or to request parts fabrication by machine, sheet, or wood shops. Review project instructions and blueprints to ascertain test specifications, procedures, and objectives and test nature of technical problems such as redesign. Review project instructions and specifications to identify, modify, and plan requirements fabrication, assembly, and testing. Devise, fabricate, and assemble new or modified mechanical components for products such as industrial machinery or equipment and measuring instruments. Discuss changes in design, method of manufacture and assembly, and drafting techniques and procedures with staff and coordinate corrections. Set up and conduct tests of complete units and components under operational conditions to investigate proposals for improving equipment performance. Inspect lines and figures for clarity and return erroneous drawings to designer for correction. Analyze test results in relation to design or rated specifications and test objectives and modify or adjust equipment to meet specifications. Evaluate tool drawing designs by measuring drawing dimensions and comparing with original specifications for form and function, using engineering skills. Confer with technicians and submit reports of test results to engineering department and recommend design or material changes. Calculate required capacities for equipment of proposed system to obtain specified performance and submit data to engineering personnel for approval. Record test procedures and results, numerical and graphical data, and recommendations for changes in product or test methods. Read dials and meters to determine amperage, voltage, and electrical output and input at specific operating temperature to analyze parts performance. Estimate cost factors, including labor and material, for purchased and fabricated parts and costs for assembly, testing, or installing. Set up prototype and test apparatus and operate test-controlling equipment to observe and record prototype test results.

Work Conditions—Indoors; noisy; contaminants; hazardous equipment; sitting.

Production, Planning, and Expediting Clerks

❀ Level of Education/Training: Short-term on-the-job training
❀ Annual Earnings: $39,690
❀ Growth: 4.2%
❀ Annual Job Openings: 52,735
❀ Personality Type: Conventional

Manufacturing firms and wholesale and retail trade establishments are the primary employers.

Coordinate and expedite the flow of work and materials within or between departments of an establishment according to production schedules, inventory levels, costs, and production problems. Examine documents, materials, and products, and monitor work processes to assess completeness, accuracy, and conformance to standards and specifications. Review documents such as production schedules, work orders, and staffing tables to determine personnel and materials requirements, and material priorities. Revise production schedules when required due to design changes, labor or material shortages, backlogs, or other interruptions, collaborating with management, marketing, sales, production, and engineering. Confer with department supervisors and other personnel to assess progress and discuss needed changes. Confer with establishment personnel, vendors, and customers to coordinate production and shipping activities, and to resolve complaints or eliminate delays. Record production data, including volume produced, consumption of raw materials, and quality control measures. Requisition and maintain inventories of materials and supplies necessary to meet production demands. Calculate figures such as required amounts of labor and materials, manufacturing costs, and wages, using pricing schedules, adding machines, calculators, or computers. Distribute production schedules and work orders to departments. Compile information, such as production rates and progress, materials inventories, materials used, and customer information, so that status reports can be completed. Arrange for delivery, assembly, and distribution of supplies and parts to expedite flow of materials and meet production schedules. Contact suppliers to verify shipment details. Maintain files such as maintenance records, bills of lading, and cost reports. Plan production commitments and timetables for business units, specific programs, and/or jobs, using sales forecasts. Establish and prepare product construction directions and locations; information on required tools, materials, and equipment; numbers of workers needed; and cost projections. Compile and prepare documentation related to production sequences, transportation, personnel schedules, and purchase, maintenance, and repair orders. Provide documentation and information to account for delays, difficulties, and changes to cost estimates.

Work Conditions—Indoors; noisy; contaminants; sitting.

Semiconductor Processors

❋ Level of Education/Training: Associate degree
❋ Annual Earnings: $31,870
❋ Growth: –12.9%
❋ Annual Job Openings: 5,709
❋ Personality Type: Realistic

> Employment is expected to decline over the next 10 years because of increasing automation and the building of many new plants abroad. Opportunities will be best for applicants who have an associate degree in a relevant subject.

Perform any or all of these functions as part of manufacturing electronic semiconductors: Load semiconductor material into furnace; saw formed ingots into segments; load individual segment into crystal-growing chamber and monitor controls; locate crystal axis in ingot, using X-ray equipment, and saw ingots into wafers; and clean, polish, and load wafers into series of special-purpose furnaces, chemical baths, and equipment used to form circuitry and change conductive properties. Manipulate valves, switches, and buttons or key commands into control panels to start semiconductor processing cycles. Inspect materials, components, or products for surface defects and then measure circuitry by using electronic test equipment, precision measuring instruments, microscope, and standard procedures. Maintain processing, production, and inspection information and reports. Clean semiconductor wafers with cleaning equipment such as chemical baths, automatic wafer cleaners, or blow-off wands. Study work orders, instructions, formulas, and processing charts to determine specifications and sequence of operations. Load and unload equipment chambers and transport finished product to storage or to area for further processing. Clean and maintain equipment, including replacing etching and rinsing solutions and cleaning bath containers and work area. Place semiconductor wafers in processing containers or equipment holders, using vacuum wand or tweezers. Set, adjust, and readjust computerized or mechanical equipment controls to regulate power level, temperature, vacuum, and rotation speed of furnace according to crystal-growing specifications. Etch, lap, polish, or grind wafers or ingots to form circuitry and change conductive properties by using etching, lapping, polishing, or grinding equipment. Load semiconductor material into furnace. Monitor operation and adjust controls of processing machines and equipment to produce compositions with specific electronic properties, using computer terminals. Count, sort, and weigh processed items. Calculate etching time based on thickness of material to be removed from wafers or crystals. Inspect equipment for leaks, diagnose malfunctions, and request repairs. Align photo mask pattern on photoresist layer, expose pattern to ultraviolet light, and develop pattern via specialized equipment. Stamp, etch, or scribe identifying information on finished component according to specifications. Operate saw to cut remelt into sections of specified size or to cut ingots into wafers. Scribe or separate wafers into dice. Connect reactor to computer with hand tools and power tools.

Work Conditions—Indoors; noisy; contaminants; hazardous conditions; standing; using hands on objects, tools, or controls.

Team Assemblers

- ❋ Level of Education/Training: Moderate-term on-the-job training
- ❋ Annual Earnings: $24,630
- ❋ Growth: 0.1%
- ❋ Annual Job Openings: 264,135
- ❋ Personality Type: No data available

Job opportunities are expected to be good for qualified applicants in the manufacturing sector, particularly in jobs needing more training.

Work as part of a team having responsibility for assembling an entire product or component of a product. Team assemblers can perform all tasks conducted by the team in the assembly process and rotate through all or most of them rather than being assigned to a specific task on a permanent basis. May participate in making management decisions affecting the work. Team leaders who work as part of the team should be included. Rotate through all the tasks required in a particular production process. Determine work assignments and procedures. Shovel and sweep work areas. Operate heavy equipment such as forklifts. Provide assistance in the production of wiring assemblies.

Work Conditions—Indoors; noisy; contaminants; standing; using hands on objects, tools, or controls; repetitive motions.

Other Manufacturing Jobs

These jobs play supporting roles in the manufacturing industries, are not expected to have a good outlook (even with help from the recovery plan), or were omitted from the descriptions in this chapter for lack of room.

Chief Executives

Computer Programmers

Computer Software Engineers, Applications (see Computer Systems Design and Related Services, chapter 7)

Computer Support Specialists (see Computer Systems Design and Related Services, chapter 7)

Computer Systems Analysts (see Computer Systems Design and Related Services, chapter 7)

Electricians (see Infrastructure, chapter 3)

Electro-Mechanical Technicians (see Scientific Research and Development Services, chapter 7)

Engine and Other Machine Assemblers

First-Line Supervisors/Managers of Production and Operating Workers

Inspectors, Testers, Sorters, Samplers, and Weighers

Laborers and Freight, Stock, and Material Movers, Hand

Maintenance and Repair Workers, General

Multiple Machine Tool Setters, Operators, and Tenders, Metal and Plastic

Network and Computer Systems Administrators (see Computer Systems Design and Related Services, chapter 7)

Painters, Transportation Equipment

Purchasing Agents, Except Wholesale, Retail, and Farm Products (see Wholesale Trade, chapter 7)

Secretaries, Except Legal, Medical, and Executive

Shipping, Receiving, and Traffic Clerks (see Wholesale Trade, chapter 7)

Structural Metal Fabricators and Fitters

Tool and Die Makers

Welders, Cutters, and Welder Fitters (see Infrastructure, chapter 3)

Welding, Soldering, and Brazing Machine Setters, Operators, and Tenders

JOBS IN OTHER INDUSTRIES TARGETED BY THE OBAMA INITIATIVES

The initiatives in Obama's recovery plan do not have a one-to-one relationship with industries. For each of the four industries described in this chapter, there is no single initiative that is an obvious match. Nevertheless, all four industries are mentioned among those that will benefit by gaining or preserving jobs. The **management, scientific, and technical consulting services; scientific research and development services;** and **computer systems design and related services** industries are components of the professional and business services industry family, which the transition team expects to add or maintain 345,000 jobs by the fourth quarter of 2010. The other industry described in this chapter, **wholesale trade,** is projected to benefit from 158,000 jobs.

Even more jobs, 604,000, are projected for the **retail trade** industry, but that industry is so diverse that there isn't room to describe it in this book. The same lack of space means that it was necessary to omit descriptions of some other diverse industries that the Obama plan expects to boost substantially: for example, **leisure and hospitality** (499,000 jobs); **financial activities** (214,000 jobs); and **government** (244,000 jobs).

All of the industries described in this chapter prosper whenever the economy does well, and several of Obama's policies and programs are particularly targeted to stimulate them. For example, the energy initiative will include scientific research to develop practical uses of renewable-energy resources, and the infrastructure improvements planned for education and health care will involve many computer applications.

This chapter describes four industries and some important related jobs.

Management, Scientific, and Technical Consulting Services

Nature of the Industry

Management, scientific, and technical consulting firms influence how businesses, governments, and institutions make decisions. Often working behind the scenes, these firms offer technical expertise, information, contacts, and tools that clients cannot provide themselves. They then work with their clients to provide a service or solve a problem.

The industry has grown rapidly over the past several decades, with businesses increasingly using consulting services. Hiring consultants is advantageous because these experts are experienced; are well trained; and keep abreast of the latest technologies, government regulations, and management and production techniques. In addition, consultants are cost effective because they can be hired temporarily and can perform their duties objectively, free of the influence of company politics.

Working Conditions

Hours. In 2006, production workers in the industry averaged 35.9 hours per week, slightly higher than the national average of 33.9. However, many consultants must meet hurried deadlines, which frequently requires working long hours in stressful environments. Consultants whose services are billed hourly often are under pressure to manage their time very carefully. Occasionally, weekend work also is necessary, depending upon the job that is being performed.

Work environment. Working conditions in management, scientific, and technical consulting services are generally similar to those of most office workers operating in a team environment. The work is rarely hazardous, with a few exceptions—for example, environmental or safety consultants who inspect sites for contamination from hazardous materials. In 2006, the industry had only 0.6 injuries and illnesses per 100 full-time workers, compared with an average of 4.4 throughout private industry.

In addition, some projects might require many executives and consultants to travel extensively or to live away from home for extended periods of time. However, new technology—such as laptop computers with remote access to the firm's computer server and videoconferencing machines—allow some consultants to work from home or conduct meetings with clients in different locations, reducing some of the need for business travel.

Most firms encourage employees to attend employer-paid time-management classes. The classes·teach participants to reduce the stress sometimes associated with working under strict time constraints. Also, with today's hectic lifestyle, many firms in this industry offer or provide health facilities or clubs that employees may use to maintain good health.

Employment

The management, scientific, and technical consulting services industry had about 921,000 wage and salary workers in 2006; an additional 250,000 workers were self-employed and unpaid family workers, comprising 21 percent of all jobs in this industry.

The vast majority of establishments in the industry were fairly small, employing fewer than five workers. Self-employed individuals operated many of these small firms. Despite the prevalence of small firms and self-employed workers, large firms tend to dominate the industry. Approximately 58 percent of jobs are found in the 4 percent of establishments with 20 or more employees, and some of the largest firms in the industry employ several thousand people.

Many individuals move into consulting after gaining experience in their field by working in another industry. As a result, the average age in the consulting industry is higher than in all industries. The consulting industry has higher proportions of older workers and lower proportions of younger workers than are present across all industries.

Although employees in this industry work in all parts of the country, many workers are concentrated near large urban centers.

Outlook

Management, scientific, and technical consulting services is projected to be one of the fastest-growing industries over the next decade. However, because of the number of people looking to work in this industry, competition for jobs is expected to be keen.

Employment change. Between 2006 and 2016, wage and salary employment in the management, scientific, and technical consulting services industry is expected to grow by 78 percent, much faster than the 11 percent growth projected for all industries, ranking the industry as the fastest-growing industry in the economy. All areas of consulting should experience strong growth.

Projected job growth can be attributed primarily to economic growth and to the continuing complexity of business. A growing number of businesses means increased demand for advice in all areas of business planning. Firms will look to management consultants to draft business plans and budgets, develop strategy, and determine appropriate salaries and benefits for employees. The expansion of franchised restaurants and retail stores will spur demand for marketing consultants to determine the best locations and develop marketing plans. The expansion of business also will create opportunities for logistics consulting firms in order to link new suppliers with producers and to get the finished goods to consumers. Finally, businesses will continue to need advice on compliance with government workplace safety and environmental laws. Clients need consultants to keep them up to date on the latest changes in legislation affecting their businesses, including changes to tax laws, environmental regulations, and policies affecting employee benefits and health care and workplace safety. As a result, firms specializing in human resources, environmental, and safety consulting should be in strong demand.

The increasing use of new technology and computer software is another major factor contributing to growth in all areas of consulting. Management consulting firms help clients implement new accounting and payroll software, whereas environmental and safety consulting firms advise clients on the use of computer technology in monitoring harmful substances in the environment or workplace. Consulting firms also might help design new computer systems or online distribution systems. One of the biggest areas upon which technology has had an impact is logistics consulting. The Internet has greatly increased the ability of businesses to link to and communicate with their suppliers and customers, increasing productivity and decreasing costs. Technology-related consulting projects have become so important that many traditional consulting firms are now merging with or setting up joint ventures with technology companies so that each firm has access to the other's resources in order to better serve clients.

The trend toward outsourcing and mergers also will create opportunities for consulting firms. In order to cut costs, many firms are outsourcing administrative and human resources functions to consultants specializing in these services. This should provide opportunities in human resources consulting for firms that manage their clients' payroll systems and benefits programs. At the same time, increasing competition has led to more business mergers, providing opportunities for consulting firms to assist in the process. Also, as increasing numbers of older business owners retire, consultants will be used to assist in liquidation, acquisition, or restructuring of those businesses.

Globalization, too, will continue to provide numerous opportunities for consulting firms wishing to expand their services, or help their clients expand, into foreign markets. Consulting firms can advise clients on strategy, as well as foreign laws, regarding taxes, employment, worker safety, and the environment. The growth of international businesses will create numerous opportunities for logistics consulting firms as businesses seek to improve coordination in the expanding network of suppliers and consumers.

An increasing emphasis on protecting a firm's employees, facilities, and information against deliberate acts of sabotage will continue to create numerous opportunities for security consultants. These consultants provide assistance on every aspect of security, from protecting against computer viruses to reinforcing buildings against bomb blasts. Logistics consulting firms also are finding opportunities helping clients secure their supply chain against interruptions that might arise from terrorist acts, such as the disruption of shipping or railroad facilities. Growing security concerns, rising insurance costs, and the increasing threat of lawsuits provide added incentives for businesses to protect the welfare of their employees.

Growth in management, scientific, and technical consulting services might be hampered by increasing competition from nontraditional consulting firms such as investment banks, accounting firms, technology firms, and law firms. As consulting firms continue to expand their services, they will be forced to compete with a more diverse group of firms that provide similar services.

Economic downturns also can have an adverse effect on employment growth in consulting. As businesses are forced to cut costs, consultants may be among the first expenses that businesses eliminate. Furthermore, growth in some consulting specialties, such as executive search consulting, is directly tied to the health of the industries in which they operate. However, some consulting firms might experience growth during recessions; as firms look to cut costs and remain competitive, they might seek the advice of consultants on the best way to do so.

Job prospects. Despite the projected growth in the industry, there will be keen competition for jobs because the prestigious and independent nature of the work and the generous salary and benefits generally attract more job seekers than openings every year. Individuals with the most education and job experience will likely have the best job prospects.

Scientific Research and Development Services

Nature of the Industry

From carbon nanotubes to vaccines, workers in the scientific research and development services industry create today the technologies that will change the way people live and work in the future. The importance of this industry is demonstrated by the considerable attention paid to it by the press, business associations, politicians, and financial markets. Major discoveries are heralded in both the technical and the popular media, and many studies monitor the pace of research and development. New technologies can quickly revolutionize business and leisure, as the Internet has.

Because the scientific research and development services industry is continuously on the cutting edge of knowledge, it is constantly evolving. New technologies and research methods, such as nanotechnology and biotechnology in recent years, have opened new avenues of research. Similarly, recent advances in fundamental understanding of genetics, chemistry, and physics have led to the development of new technologies.

Working Conditions

Hours. In 2006, workers in scientific research and development services averaged 38.5 hours per week, compared with 33.9 for workers in all industries. The average for research and development in the physical, engineering, and life sciences was 39.0, while the average for research and development in the social sciences and humanities was only 34.6.

Work environment. Most workers in this industry work in offices or laboratories; the location and hours of work vary greatly, however, depending on the requirements of each project. Experiments may run at odd hours, require constant observation, or depend on external conditions such as the weather. In some fields, research or testing must be done in harsh environments to ensure the usefulness of the final product in a wide range of environments. Other research, particularly biomedical research, is conducted in hospitals. Workers in product development may spend much time building prototypes in workshops or laboratories, while research design typically takes place in offices.

Although there generally is little risk of injury or illness due to the working conditions, certain fields require working with potentially dangerous materials. In such cases, comprehensive safety procedures are strictly enforced.

Employment

Scientific research and development services provided 593,000 jobs in 2006. Research and development in the physical, engineering, and life sciences accounted for about 89 percent of the jobs; the rest were in research and development in the social sciences and humanities.

Workers in this industry conduct much, but not all, of the scientific research and development (R&D) in the economy. Under the North American

Industrial Classification System (NAICS), each establishment is categorized by the activity in which it is primarily engaged; an establishment is defined as a single physical location where business is conducted or services are performed. This means that much of the R&D conducted by companies in a wide range of industries—such as pharmaceuticals, chemicals, motor vehicles, and aerospace products—is conducted within the scientific research and development services industry because many companies maintain laboratories and other R&D facilities that are located apart from production plants and other establishments characteristic of these industries. While workers in separate R&D establishments are classified in the scientific research and development services industry, some R&D occurs in establishments that mainly engage in other activities, such as manufacturing (described in chapter 6) or educational services (described in chapter 5). The latter type of R&D is not included within the scientific research and development services industry.

Although scientific research and development services can be found in many places, the industry is concentrated in a few areas. Just seven states—California, New York, Massachusetts, Illinois, Maryland, Pennsylvania, and New Jersey—account for over half of all employment in the industry. Michigan also has a sizable amount of R&D, particularly in the automotive field. Although 92 percent of establishments have fewer than 50 workers, 53 percent of employment in the industry is in establishments with more than 250 workers.

Outlook

Employment change. Wage and salary employment in scientific research and development services is projected to increase 9 percent between 2006 and 2016, compared with 11 percent employment growth for the economy as a whole. Biotechnology and nanotechnology will continue to attract research funding and generate employment growth. Increased demand for medical and pharmaceutical advances also will lead to growth in these areas as the population ages. While demand for new R&D is expected to continue to grow across all major fields, this industry will continue to experience rapid productivity growth as a result of advances in computer and communications systems, reducing employment opportunities. Increasing international competition should also dampen employment growth.

Some of this slower job growth rate is attributable to the stagnation of the office and administrative support occupations, which are expected to see only modest employment growth as technology leads to greater efficiency in general office functions. Similarly slow growth is expected in other major occupational groups within the industry, but many new jobs will be created in professional occupations.

Significant job growth is expected among computer specialists, scientists, and engineers—particularly those in the life and medical sciences. With the aging of the population, the demand for lifesaving new drugs and procedures to cure and prevent disease will drive this demand. Biological scientists, for example, may be employed in biotechnology or pharmaceuticals, both growing areas. Many other scientists and engineers will be employed in defense and security R&D, also a growing field. As information technology continues to be an integral component of R&D, employment of computer specialists is expected to grow rapidly, particularly for those with some biological science background working in bioinformatics.

Job prospects. Opportunities for both scientists and engineers are expected to be best for those who have doctoral degrees, which prepare graduates for research. However, competition for basic and applied research funding is expected to be keen in all fields. Creativity is crucial, because scientists and engineers engaged in R&D are expected to propose new research or designs. For experienced scientists and engineers, it also is important to remain current and adapt to changes in technologies that may shift interest—and employment—from one area of research to another.

Most R&D programs have long project cycles that continue during economic downturns. However, funding of R&D, particularly by private industry, is closely scrutinized during these periods. Since the federal government provides a significant portion of all R&D funding, shifts in policy such as the Obama stimulus package also can have a marked impact on employment opportunities, particularly in basic research and aerospace.

Computer Systems Design and Related Services

Nature of the Industry

All organizations today rely on computer and information technology to conduct business and operate more efficiently. Often, however, these institutions do not have the internal resources to effectively implement new technologies or satisfy their changing needs. When faced with such limitations, organizations turn to the computer systems design and related services industry to meet their specialized needs.

The widespread use of the Internet and intranets has resulted in an increased focus on security. Security threats range from damaging computer viruses to online credit card fraud and identity theft. The robust growth of e-commerce highlights this concern as firms use the Internet to exchange sensitive information with an increasing number of clients. In order to mitigate this threat, many organizations are employing the services of security consulting firms, which specialize in all aspects of information technology (IT) security. These firms assess computer systems for areas of vulnerability, manage firewalls, and provide protection against intrusion and software "viruses." They also play a vital role in homeland security by keeping track of people and information.

Working Conditions

Hours. In 2006, workers in the computer systems design and related services industry averaged 38.3 hours per week, compared with 33.9 for all industries combined. Many workers in this industry worked more than the standard 40-hour workweek—about 19 percent worked 50 or more hours a week. For many professionals and technical specialists, evening or weekend work is commonly necessary to meet deadlines or solve problems. Professionals working for large establishments may have less freedom in planning their schedule than do consultants for very small firms, whose work may be more varied. Only about 7 percent of the workers in the computer systems design and related services industry work part time, compared with 15 percent of workers throughout all industries.

Work environment. Most workers in the computer systems design and related services industry work in clean, quiet offices. Those in facilities management and maintenance may work in computer operations centers. Given the technology available today, however, more work can be done from remote locations using fax machines, e-mail, and especially the Internet. For example, systems analysts may work from home with their computers linked directly to computers at the location of their employer or a client. Computer support specialists, likewise, can tap into a customer's computer remotely in order to identify and fix problems. Even programmers and consultants, who often relocate to a customer's place of business while working on a project, may perform work from offsite locations.

Those who work with personal computers for extended periods may experience musculoskeletal strain, eye problems, stress, or repetitive motion illnesses, such as carpal tunnel syndrome.

Employment

In 2006, there were about 1.3 million wage and salary jobs in the computer systems design and related services industry. While the industry has both large and small firms, the average establishment in computer systems design and related services is relatively small; about 78 percent of establishments employed fewer than 5 workers in 2006. Many of these small establishments are startup firms that hope to capitalize on a market niche. The majority of jobs, however, are found in establishments that employ 50 or more workers.

Compared with the rest of the economy, there are significantly fewer workers 45 years of age and older in the computer systems design and related services industry. This industry's workforce remains younger than most, with large proportions of workers in the 25-to-44 age range. This reflects the industry's explosive growth in employment in the 1980s and 1990s that provided opportunities to thousands of young workers who possessed the latest technological skills.

Outlook

The computer systems design and related services industry grew dramatically throughout the 1990s, as employment more than doubled. And despite recent job losses in certain sectors, this remains one of the 20 fastest-growing industries in the nation. However, due to increasing productivity and the offshore outsourcing of some services to lower-wage foreign countries, employment growth will not be as robust as it was during the last decade. Job opportunities should be favorable for most workers, but the best opportunities will be in professional and related occupations.

Employment change. Wage-and-salary employment is expected to grow 38 percent by the year 2016, compared with only 11 percent growth projected for the entire economy. In addition, this industry will add more than 489,000 jobs over the decade, placing it among the 10 industries with the largest job growth. An increasing reliance on information technology, combined with the falling prices of computers and related hardware, will spur demand for computer systems design and related services. Individuals and organizations will continue to turn to firms in this industry to maximize their return on investments in equipment and to help them satisfy their growing computing needs. Such needs include a growing reliance on the Internet, faster and more efficient internal and external communication, and the implementation of new technologies and applications.

The computer systems design and related services industry also has seen an increase in the offshore outsourcing of some of the more routine services to lower-wage foreign countries as companies strive to remain competitive. For example, firms have been able to cut costs by shifting some support services operations to countries with highly educated workers who have strong technical skills. This trend, however, will adversely affect employment of only certain types of workers, such as programmers and computer support specialists. Other tasks, such as integrating and designing systems, will be insulated from the effects of offshoring.

Given the overall rate of growth expected for the entire industry, most occupations should continue to grow rapidly, although some will grow faster than others. The most rapid growth will occur among network systems and data communications analysts. The growing use of sophisticated computer networks and Internet and intranet sites will increase the demand for their services. Other rapidly growing occupations include computer software engineers, computer systems analysts, and network and computer systems administrators. Employment of programmers should continue to expand, but more slowly than that of other occupations, as more routine programming functions are automated and as more programming services are offshored.

The demand for networking and the need to integrate new hardware, software, and communications technologies will drive demand for consulting and integration. A need for more customized applications development, and for support and services to assist users, will drive demand for applications development and facilities support services.

Recent events have made society more conscious of the vulnerability of technology and the Internet, and the increasing need for security will spur employment growth in cyberspace security services. Security specialists will be employed more often to assess system vulnerability, and custom programmers and designers will be needed to develop new antivirus software, programs, and procedures. Therefore, employment of analysts and of consultants in areas such as disaster recovery services, custom security programming, and security software installation services should rise rapidly.

The expansion of the Internet and the proliferation of "mobile" technologies have also created demand for a wide variety of new products and services. For example, the expansion of the wireless Internet, known as WiFi, brings a new aspect of mobility to information technology by allowing people to stay connected to the Internet anywhere, anytime. As businesses and individuals become more dependent on this new technology, there will be an increased need for "mobility consultants," or service firms that can design and integrate computer systems so that they will be compatible with mobile technologies.

The ways in which the Internet is used are constantly changing, along with the products, services, and personnel required to support new applications, including the medical-records software that will be encouraged by the Obama stimulus package. E-commerce changed the nature of business transactions, enabling markets to expand and an increasing array of services to be provided. And, as the amount of computer-stored information grows, organizations will continue to look for ways to tap the full potential of their vast stores of data. Demand for an even wider array of services should increase as companies continue to expand their capabilities, integrate new technologies, and develop new applications.

Job prospects. Given the rate at which the computer systems design and related services industry is expected to grow and the increasing complexity of technology, job opportunities should be favorable for most workers. The best opportunities will be in professional and related occupations, reflecting their growth and the continuing demand for higher-level skills to keep up with changes in technology. In addition, as individuals and organizations continue to conduct business electronically, the importance of maintaining system and network security will increase. Employment opportunities should be excellent for individuals involved in cyberspace security services such as disaster recovery services, custom security programming, and security software installation services.

Wholesale Trade

Nature of the Industry

When consumers purchase goods, they usually buy them from a retail establishment such as a supermarket, department store, gas station, or Internet site. When businesses, government agencies, or institutions, such as universities or hospitals, need to purchase goods, they normally buy them from wholesale trade establishments. Retail establishments purchase goods for resale to consumers, but other establishments purchase equipment, motor vehicles, office supplies, or any other items for their own use.

Recent consolidation of smaller wholesale distributors has led to more companies serving their customers regionally, nationally, and internationally. This has resulted in companies offering more lines of related products from a larger variety of manufacturers.

Additionally, radio frequency identification (RFID) technology is becoming used more frequently by larger wholesale distributors with warehouses. RFID tags coupled with a satellite and receiver system allow wholesalers to keep track of the goods they have in stock and through transit to ensure delivery. Although this technology is highly promising, many smaller companies do not use it because it has not yet become cost effective in those situations.

Many larger independent wholesale distribution companies have also started "private-labeling" their goods—contracting with the manufacturer to put their name on the label instead of the manufacturer's name.

Working Conditions

Hours. Most workers in wholesale trade worked at least 40 hours a week in 2006, and about 21 percent worked 50 or more hours a week. Many put in long shifts, particularly during peak times. Other workers, such as produce wholesalers, work unusual hours. Produce wholesalers must be on the job before dawn to receive shipments of vegetables and fruits, and they must be ready to begin delivering goods to local grocers in the early morning.

Work environment. Working conditions and physical demands of wholesale trade jobs vary greatly. Moving stock and heavy equipment can be strenuous, but freight, stock, and material movers may make use of forklifts in large warehouses. Workers in some automated warehouses use computer-controlled storage and retrieval systems that further reduce labor requirements. Employees in refrigerated meat warehouses work in a cold environment, and those in chemical warehouses often wear protective clothing to avoid harm from toxic chemicals. Outside sales workers are away from the office for much of the workday and may spend a considerable amount of time traveling. On the other hand, most management, administrative support, and marketing staff work in offices.

Overall, work in wholesale trade is relatively safe. In 2006 there were 4.1 work-related injuries or illnesses per 100 full-time workers, comparable with the rate of 4.4 per 100 for the entire private sector. Not all parts of wholesale trade are equally safe, however. Occupational injury and illness rates were considerably higher than the national average for wholesale trade workers who dealt with lumber and construction materials (6.3 per 100 workers); groceries (7.0 per 100 workers); and beer, wine, and distilled beverages (8.4 per 100 workers).

Employment

Wholesale trade had about 5.9 million wage and salary jobs in 2006. About 90 percent of the establishments in the industry are small, employing fewer than 20 workers, and they have about 35 percent of the industry's jobs. Although some large firms employ many workers, wholesale trade is characterized by a large number of relatively small establishments when compared with other industries. Wholesale trade jobs are spread throughout the country. Few workers in wholesale trade are members of unions.

Outlook

Employment in wholesale trade will increase slowly as consolidation into fewer and larger firms occurs, eliminating the jobs of redundant workers while new technology allows operations to become more efficient. Employment will decline in some occupations, but new jobs will be created in others.

Employment change. Over the 2006–2016 period, wage and salary employment in wholesale trade is projected to grow by 7 percent, compared to 11 percent growth for all industries combined. Consolidation and the spread of new technology are the main reasons for slow employment growth. Employment in the industry still depends primarily on overall levels of consumption of goods, which should grow with the economy. Growth will vary, however, depending on the products and sectors of the economy with which individual wholesale trade firms are involved. For example, because of the nation's aging population, growth is expected to be higher than average for wholesale trade firms that distribute pharmaceuticals and medical devices.

Consolidation of wholesale trade firms into fewer and larger companies is a trend that is likely to continue. There is strong competition among wholesale distribution companies, manufacturers' representative companies, and logistics companies for business from manufacturers. Globalization and cost pressures are likely to continue to force wholesale distributors to merge with other firms or to acquire smaller firms. As retail firms operate growing numbers of stores across the country, demand will increase for large, national wholesale distributors to supply them. The differences between large and small firms will become more pronounced as they compete less for the same customers and instead emphasize their area of expertise. The consolidation of wholesale trade into fewer, larger firms will make some staff redundant and reduce demand for some workers, especially office and administrative support workers.

New technologies are constantly changing the shape and scope of the workforce in wholesale trade. The internet, e-commerce, and Electronic Data Interchange (EDI) have allowed wholesalers and their customers to better gather price data, track deliveries, obtain product information, and market products. This technology will increasingly allow customers of wholesale firms to purchase goods and track deliveries electronically, limiting the growth of sales and customer service workers who would normally perform these functions. Further automation of recordkeeping, ordering, and processing will result in slower growth for office and administrative support occupations. Customers frequently order and pay for goods electronically, so fewer billing and posting clerks will be needed to process fewer paper transactions.

New radio frequency identification (RFID) technology has the potential to streamline the inventory and ordering process further, replace the need for manual barcode scans, and eliminate most counting and packing errors. As RFID spreads, it may lessen demand for administrative workers, particularly order clerks, file clerks, and stock clerks and order fillers. Not all wholesalers will implement this technology because specially trained workers will be needed to maintain the new systems and it may not be cost effective for some firms.

With these new technologies making it easier for firms to bypass the wholesaler and order directly from the manufacturer or supplier, wholesale firms are putting greater emphasis on customer service to differentiate themselves from these other suppliers. Wholesale firms are offering more services such as installation, maintenance, assembly, and repair work and creating many jobs for workers to perform these functions. Sales workers will also be in demand to more aggressively develop prospective clients, including demonstrating new products and offering improved customer service to clients. Additionally, the passing of the Sarbanes-Oxley Act in 2002, officially implemented in 2004, may also stimulate some growth in sales and other business occupations because of the new requirements for full transparency and accountability when dealing with public companies.

Job prospects. Job growth in wholesale trade will be slow, but a large number of job openings will arise as people retire or leave the occupation for other reasons. Job prospects are still expected to be good for some occupations.

This 21st-century supply chain will create favorable job prospects for computer specialists in the wholesale trade industry. Wholesalers' presence in e-commerce and the uses of electronic data interchanges (EDI) will require more computer specialists to develop, maintain, and update these systems. Computer specialists will also be needed to install and develop RFID systems for those firms that adopt them and to troubleshoot any problems these systems encounter.

There will also be some opportunities for self-employment, with some managers and sales workers starting their own manufacturers' representative company. For example, brokers match buyers with sellers and never actually own goods, so individuals with the proper connections can establish their own agency with only a small investment—perhaps even working out of their home.

Some Jobs in the Management, Scientific, and Technical Consulting Services Industry That Are Likely to Benefit from the Stimulus Package

Accountants

- ❋ Level of Education/Training: Bachelor's degree
- ❋ Annual Earnings: $57,060
- ❋ Growth: 17.7%
- ❋ Annual Job Openings: 134,463
- ❋ Personality Type: Conventional

The job openings listed here are shared with Auditors.

> Overall job opportunities should be favorable; job seekers who obtain professional recognition through certification or licensure, a master's degree, proficiency in accounting and auditing computer software, or specialized expertise will have the best opportunities.

Analyze financial information and prepare financial reports to determine or maintain record of assets, liabilities, profit and loss, tax liability, or other financial activities within an organization. Prepare, examine, or analyze accounting records, financial statements, or other financial reports to assess accuracy, completeness, and conformance to reporting and procedural standards. Compute taxes owed and prepare tax returns, ensuring compliance with payment, reporting, or other tax requirements. Analyze business operations, trends, costs, revenues, financial commitments, and obligations to project future revenues and expenses or to provide advice. Report to management regarding the finances of establishment. Establish tables of accounts and assign entries to proper accounts. Develop, maintain, and analyze budgets, preparing periodic reports that compare budgeted costs to actual costs. Develop, implement, modify, and document recordkeeping and accounting systems, making use of current computer technology. Prepare forms and manuals for accounting and bookkeeping personnel and direct their work activities. Survey operations to ascertain accounting needs and to recommend, develop, or maintain solutions to business and financial problems. Work as Internal Revenue Service (IRS) agents. Advise management about issues such as resource utilization, tax strategies, and the assumptions underlying budget forecasts. Provide internal and external auditing services for businesses or individuals. Advise clients in areas such as compensation, employee health-care benefits, the design of accounting or data processing systems, or long-range tax or estate plans. Investigate bankruptcies and other complex financial transactions and prepare reports summarizing the findings. Represent clients before taxing authorities and provide support during litigation involving financial issues. Appraise, evaluate, and inventory real property and equipment, recording information such as the description, value, and location of property. Maintain or examine the records of government agencies. Serve as bankruptcy trustees or business valuators.

Work Conditions—Indoors; sitting.

Bookkeeping, Accounting, and Auditing Clerks

❀ Level of Education/Training: Moderate-term on-the-job training

❀ Annual Earnings: $31,560

❀ Growth: 12.5%

❀ Annual Job Openings: 286,854

❀ Personality Type: Conventional

> Those who can carry out a wider range of bookkeeping and accounting activities will be in greater demand than specialized clerks.

Compute, classify, and record numerical data to keep financial records complete. Perform any combination of routine calculating, posting, and verifying duties to obtain primary financial data for use in maintaining accounting records. May also check the accuracy of figures, calculations, and postings pertaining to business transactions recorded by other workers. Operate computers programmed with accounting software to record, store, and analyze information. Check figures, postings, and documents for correct entry, mathematical accuracy, and proper codes. Comply with federal, state, and company policies, procedures, and regulations. Debit, credit, and total accounts on computer spreadsheets and databases, using specialized accounting software. Classify, record, and summarize numerical and financial data to compile and keep financial records, using journals and ledgers or computers. Calculate, prepare, and issue bills, invoices, account statements, and other financial statements according to established procedures. Code documents according to company procedures. Compile statistical, financial, accounting, or auditing reports and tables pertaining to such matters as cash receipts, expenditures, accounts payable and receivable, and profits and losses. Operate 10-key calculators, typewriters, and copy machines to perform calculations and produce documents. Access computerized financial information to answer general questions as well as those related to specific accounts. Reconcile or note and report discrepancies found in records. Perform financial calculations such as amounts due, interest charges, balances, discounts, equity, and principal. Perform general office duties such as filing, answering telephones, and handling routine correspondence. Prepare bank deposits by compiling data from cashiers; verifying and balancing receipts; and sending cash, checks, or other forms of payment to banks. Receive, record, and bank cash, checks, and vouchers. Calculate and prepare checks for utilities, taxes, and other payments. Compare computer printouts to manually maintained journals to determine if they match. Reconcile records of bank transactions. Prepare trial balances of books. Monitor status of loans and accounts to ensure that payments are up to date. Transfer details from separate journals to general ledgers or data-processing sheets. Compile budget data and documents based on estimated revenues and expenses and previous budgets. Calculate costs of materials, overhead, and other expenses, based on estimates, quotations, and price lists.

Work Conditions—Indoors; sitting; repetitive motions.

Electrical Engineering Technicians

❋ Level of Education/Training: Associate degree
❋ Annual Earnings: $52,140
❋ Growth: 3.6%
❋ Annual Job Openings: 12,583
❋ Personality Type: Realistic

The job openings listed here are shared with Electronics Engineering Technicians.

Although rising demand for electronic goods—including communications equipment, defense-related equipment, medical electronics, and consumer products—should continue to drive demand, foreign competition in design and manufacturing will limit employment growth.

Apply electrical theory and related knowledge to test and modify developmental or operational electrical machinery and electrical control equipment and circuitry in industrial or commercial plants and laboratories. Usually work under direction of engineering staff. Assemble electrical and electronic systems and prototypes according to engineering data and knowledge of electrical principles, using hand tools and measuring instruments. Provide technical assistance and resolution when electrical or engineering problems are encountered before, during, and after construction. Install and maintain electrical control systems and solid state equipment. Modify electrical prototypes, parts, assemblies, and systems to correct functional deviations. Set up and operate test equipment to evaluate performance of developmental parts, assemblies, or systems under simulated operating conditions and record results. Collaborate with electrical engineers and other personnel to identify, define, and solve developmental problems. Build, calibrate, maintain, troubleshoot, and repair electrical instruments or testing equipment. Analyze and interpret test information to resolve design-related problems. Write commissioning procedures for electrical installations. Prepare project cost and work-time estimates. Evaluate engineering proposals, shop drawings, and design comments for sound electrical engineering practice and conformance with established safety and design criteria and recommend approval or disapproval. Draw or modify diagrams and write engineering specifications to clarify design details and functional criteria of experimental electronics units. Conduct inspections for quality control and assurance programs, reporting findings and recommendations. Prepare contracts and initiate, review, and coordinate modifications to contract specifications and plans throughout the construction process. Plan, schedule, and monitor work of support personnel to assist supervisor. Review existing electrical engineering criteria to identify necessary revisions, deletions, or amendments to outdated material. Perform supervisory duties such as recommending work assignments, approving leaves, and completing performance evaluations. Plan method and sequence of operations for developing and testing experimental electronic and electrical equipment. Visit construction sites to observe conditions impacting design and to identify solutions to technical design problems involving electrical systems equipment that arise during construction.

Work Conditions—Indoors; noisy; sitting; using hands on objects, tools, or controls.

Electrical Engineers
* Level of Education/Training: Bachelor's degree
* Annual Earnings: $79,240
* Growth: 6.3%
* Annual Job Openings: 6,806
* Personality Type: Investigative

Electrical engineers working in firms providing engineering expertise and design services to manufacturers should have the best job prospects.

Design, develop, test, or supervise the manufacturing and installation of electrical equipment, components, or systems for commercial, industrial, military, or scientific use. Confer with engineers, customers, and others to discuss existing or potential engineering projects and products. Design, implement, maintain, and improve electrical instruments, equipment, facilities, components, products, and systems for commercial, industrial, and domestic purposes. Operate computer-assisted engineering and design software and equipment to perform engineering tasks. Direct and coordinate manufacturing, construction, installation, maintenance, support, documentation, and testing activities to ensure compliance with specifications, codes, and customer requirements. Perform detailed calculations to compute and establish manufacturing, construction, and installation standards and specifications. Inspect completed installations and observe operations to ensure conformance to design and equipment specifications and compliance with operational and safety standards. Plan and implement research methodology and procedures to apply principles of electrical theory to engineering projects. Prepare specifications for purchase of materials and equipment. Supervise and train project team members as necessary. Investigate and test vendors' and competitors' products. Oversee project production efforts to assure projects are completed satisfactorily, on time, and within budget. Prepare and study technical drawings, specifications of electrical systems, and topographical maps to ensure that installation and operations conform to standards and customer requirements. Investigate customer or public complaints, determine nature and extent of problem, and recommend remedial measures. Plan layout of electric-power-generating plants and distribution lines and stations. Assist in developing capital project programs for new equipment and major repairs. Develop budgets, estimating labor, material, and construction costs. Compile data and write reports regarding existing and potential engineering studies and projects. Collect data relating to commercial and residential development, population, and power system interconnection to determine operating efficiency of electrical systems. Conduct field surveys and study maps, graphs, diagrams, and other data to identify and correct power system problems.

Work Conditions—Indoors; sitting.

Graphic Designers

- ✺ Level of Education/Training: Bachelor's degree
- ✺ Annual Earnings: $41,280
- ✺ Growth: 9.8%
- ✺ Annual Job Openings: 26,968
- ✺ Personality Type: Artistic

Job seekers are expected to face keen competition; individuals with a bachelor's degree and knowledge of computer design software, particularly those with Web site design and animation experience, will have the best opportunities.

Design or create graphics to meet specific commercial or promotional needs such as packaging, displays, or logos. May use a variety of media to achieve artistic or decorative effects. Create designs, concepts, and sample layouts based on knowledge of layout principles and esthetic design concepts. Determine size and arrangement of illustrative material and copy; and select style and size of type. Confer with clients to discuss and determine layout designs. Develop graphics and layouts for product illustrations, company logos, and Internet Web sites. Review final layouts and suggest improvements as needed. Prepare illustrations or rough sketches of material, discussing them with clients or supervisors and making necessary changes. Use computer software to generate new images. Key information into computer equipment to create layouts for client or supervisor. Maintain archive of images, photos, or previous work products. Prepare notes and instructions for workers who assemble and prepare final layouts for printing. Draw and print charts, graphs, illustrations, and other artwork, using computer. Study illustrations and photographs to plan presentations of materials, products, or services. Research new software or design concepts. Mark up, paste, and assemble final layouts to prepare layouts for printer. Produce still and animated graphics for on-air and taped portions of television news broadcasts, using electronic video equipment. Photograph layouts, using cameras, to make layout prints for supervisors or clients. Develop negatives and prints to produce layout photographs, using negative and print developing equipment and tools.

Work Conditions—Indoors; sitting; using hands on objects, tools, or controls; repetitive motions.

Management Analysts

- ❋ Level of Education/Training: Work experience plus degree
- ❋ Annual Earnings: $71,150
- ❋ Growth: 21.9%
- ❋ Annual Job Openings: 125,669
- ❋ Personality Type: Enterprising

> Despite much-faster-than-average employment growth, keen competition is expected for jobs; opportunities should be best for those with a graduate degree, specialized expertise, and a talent for selling and public relations.

Conduct organizational studies and evaluations, design systems and procedures, conduct work simplifications and measurement studies, and prepare operations and procedures manuals to assist management in operating more efficiently and effectively. Includes program analysts and management consultants. Gather and organize information on problems or procedures. Analyze data gathered and develop solutions or alternative methods of proceeding. Confer with personnel concerned to ensure successful functioning of newly implemented systems or procedures. Develop and implement records management program for filing, protection, and retrieval of records and assure compliance with program. Review forms and reports and confer with management and users about format, distribution, and purpose and to identify problems and improvements. Document findings of study and prepare recommendations for implementation of new systems, procedures, or organizational changes. Interview personnel and conduct on-site observation to ascertain unit functions; work performed; and methods, equipment, and personnel used. Prepare manuals and train workers in use of new forms, reports, procedures, or equipment according to organizational policy. Design, evaluate, recommend, and approve changes of forms and reports. Plan study of work problems and procedures, such as organizational change, communications, information flow, integrated production methods, inventory control, or cost analysis. Recommend purchase of storage equipment and design area layout to locate equipment in space available.

Work Conditions—Indoors; sitting.

Market Research Analysts

❀ Level of Education/Training: Bachelor's degree
❀ Annual Earnings: $60,300
❀ Growth: 20.1%
❀ Annual Job Openings: 45,015
❀ Personality Type: Investigative

Job opportunities should be best for job seekers with a master's or Ph.D. degree in marketing or a related field and with strong quantitative skills. Ph.D. holders in marketing and related fields should have a range of opportunities in many industries, especially in consulting firms.

Research market conditions in local, regional, or national areas to determine potential sales of a product or service. May gather information on competitors, prices, sales, and methods of marketing and distribution. May use survey results to create a marketing campaign based on regional preferences and buying habits. Collect and analyze data on customer demographics, preferences, needs, and buying habits to identify potential markets and factors affecting product demand. Prepare reports of findings, illustrating data graphically and translating complex findings into written text. Measure and assess customer and employee satisfaction. Forecast and track marketing and sales trends, analyzing collected data. Seek and provide information to help companies determine their position in the marketplace. Measure the effectiveness of marketing, advertising, and communications programs and strategies. Conduct research on consumer opinions and marketing strategies, collaborating with marketing professionals, statisticians, pollsters, and other professionals. Attend staff conferences to provide management with information and proposals concerning the promotion, distribution, design, and pricing of company products or services. Gather data on competitors and analyze their prices, sales, and method of marketing and distribution. Monitor industry statistics and follow trends in trade literature. Devise and evaluate methods and procedures for collecting data, such as surveys, opinion polls, or questionnaires, or arrange to obtain existing data. Develop and implement procedures for identifying advertising needs. Direct trained survey interviewers.

Work Conditions—Indoors; sitting.

Marketing Managers
* Level of Education/Training: Work experience plus degree
* Annual Earnings: $104,400
* Growth: 14.4%
* Annual Job Openings: 20,189
* Personality Type: Enterprising

College graduates with related experience, a high level of creativity, and strong communication skills should have the best job opportunities. In particular, employers will seek those who have the computer skills to conduct marketing on the Internet.

Determine the demand for products and services offered by firms and their competitors and identify potential customers. Develop pricing strategies with the goal of maximizing firms' profits or shares of the market while ensuring that firms' customers are satisfied. Oversee product development or monitor trends that indicate the need for new products and services. Formulate, direct, and coordinate marketing activities and policies to promote products and services, working with advertising and promotion managers. Identify, develop, and evaluate marketing strategies, based on knowledge of establishment objectives, market characteristics, and cost and markup factors. Direct the hiring, training, and performance evaluations of marketing and sales staff and oversee their daily activities. Evaluate the financial aspects of product development, such as budgets, expenditures, research and development appropriations, and return-on-investment and profit-loss projections. Develop pricing strategies, balancing firm objectives and customer satisfaction. Compile lists describing product or service offerings. Initiate market research studies and analyze their findings. Use sales forecasting and strategic planning to ensure the sale and profitability of products, lines, or services, analyzing business developments and monitoring market trends. Coordinate and participate in promotional activities and trade shows, working with developers, advertisers, and production managers to market products and services. Consult with buying personnel to gain advice regarding the types of products or services expected to be in demand. Conduct economic and commercial surveys to identify potential markets for products and services. Select products and accessories to be displayed at trade or special production shows. Negotiate contracts with vendors and distributors to manage product distribution, establishing distribution networks and developing distribution strategies. Consult with product development personnel on product specifications such as design, color, and packaging. Advise businesses and other groups on local, national, and international factors affecting the buying and selling of products and services. Confer with legal staff to resolve problems such as copyright infringement and royalty sharing with outside producers and distributors.

Work Conditions—Indoors; sitting.

Training and Development Managers

❀ Level of Education/Training: Work experience plus degree

❀ Annual Earnings: $84,340

❀ Growth: 15.6%

❀ Annual Job Openings: 3,759

❀ Personality Type: Enterprising

> Demand may be particularly strong for certain specialists as employers respond to the increasing complexity of many jobs and technological advances that can leave employees with obsolete skills.

Plan, direct, or coordinate the training and development activities and staff of organizations. Prepare training budgets for departments or organizations. Evaluate instructor performances and the effectiveness of training programs, providing recommendations for improvements. Analyze training needs to develop new training programs or modify and improve existing programs. Conduct or arrange for ongoing technical training and personal development classes for staff members. Plan, develop, and provide training and staff development programs, using knowledge of the effectiveness of methods such as classroom training, demonstrations, on-the-job training, meetings, conferences, and workshops. Conduct orientation sessions and arrange on-the-job training for new hires. Confer with management and conduct surveys to identify training needs based on projected production processes, changes, and other factors. Train instructors and supervisors in techniques and skills for training and dealing with employees. Develop and organize training manuals, multimedia visual aids, and other educational materials. Develop testing and evaluation procedures. Review and evaluate training and apprenticeship programs for compliance with government standards. Coordinate established courses with technical and professional courses provided by community schools and designate training procedures.

Work Conditions—Indoors; sitting.

Some Jobs in the Scientific Research and Development Services Industry That Are Likely to Benefit from the Stimulus Package

Aerospace Engineering and Operations Technicians

※ Level of Education/Training: Associate degree
※ Annual Earnings: $54,930
※ Growth: 10.4%
※ Annual Job Openings: 707
※ Personality Type: Investigative

> Increases in the number and scope of military aerospace projects likely will generate new jobs. New technologies to be used on commercial aircraft produced during the next decade should also spur demand for these workers.

Operate, install, calibrate, and maintain integrated computer/ communications systems consoles; simulators; and other data acquisition, test, and measurement instruments and equipment to launch, track, position, and evaluate air and space vehicles. May record and interpret test data. Inspect, diagnose, maintain, and operate test setups and equipment to detect malfunctions. Record and interpret test data on parts, assemblies, and mechanisms. Confer with engineering personnel regarding details and implications of test procedures and results. Adjust, repair, or replace faulty components of test setups and equipment. Identify required data, data acquisition plans, and test parameters, setting up equipment to conform to these specifications. Construct and maintain test facilities for aircraft parts and systems according to specifications. Operate and calibrate computer systems and devices to comply with test requirements and to perform data acquisition and analysis. Test aircraft systems under simulated operational conditions, performing systems readiness tests and pre- and post-operational checkouts, to establish design or fabrication parameters. Fabricate and install parts and systems to be tested in test equipment, using hand tools, power tools, and test instruments. Finish vehicle instrumentation and deinstrumentation. Exchange cooling system components in various vehicles.

Work Conditions—Indoors; noisy; sitting; using hands on objects, tools, or controls; repetitive motions.

Biological Technicians

- ❋ Level of Education/Training: Associate degree
- ❋ Annual Earnings: $37,810
- ❋ Growth: 16.0%
- ❋ Annual Job Openings: 15,374
- ❋ Personality Type: Realistic

Job opportunities are expected to be best for graduates of applied science technology programs who are well trained on equipment used in laboratories or production facilities.

Assist biological and medical scientists in laboratories. Set up, operate, and maintain laboratory instruments and equipment; monitor experiments; make observations; and calculate and record results. May analyze organic substances, such as blood, food, and drugs. Keep detailed logs of all work-related activities. Monitor laboratory work to ensure compliance with set standards. Isolate, identify, and prepare specimens for examination. Use computers, computer-interfaced equipment, robotics, or high-technology industrial applications to perform work duties. Conduct research or assist in the conduct of research, including the collection of information and samples such as blood, water, soil, plants, and animals. Set up, adjust, calibrate, clean, maintain, and troubleshoot laboratory and field equipment. Provide technical support and services for scientists and engineers working in fields such as agriculture, environmental science, resource management, biology, and health sciences. Clean, maintain, and prepare supplies and work areas. Participate in the research, development, or manufacturing of medicinal and pharmaceutical preparations. Conduct standardized biological, microbiological, or biochemical tests and laboratory analyses to evaluate the quantity or quality of physical or chemical substances in food or other products. Analyze experimental data and interpret results to write reports and summaries of findings. Measure or weigh compounds and solutions for use in testing or animal feed. Monitor and observe experiments, recording production and test data for evaluation by research personnel. Examine animals and specimens to detect the presence of disease or other problems. Conduct or supervise operational programs such as fish hatcheries, greenhouses, and livestock production programs. Feed livestock or laboratory animals.

Work Conditions—Indoors; standing; using hands on objects, tools, or controls; repetitive motions.

Chemists

❋ Level of Education/Training: Bachelor's degree
❋ Annual Earnings: $63,490
❋ Growth: 9.1%
❋ Annual Job Openings: 9,024
❋ Personality Type: Investigative

> New chemists at all levels may experience competition for jobs, particularly in declining chemical manufacturing industries; graduates with a master's degree, and particularly those with a Ph.D., will enjoy better opportunities at larger pharmaceutical and biotechnology firms.

Conduct qualitative and quantitative chemical analyses or chemical experiments in laboratories for quality or process control or to develop new products or knowledge. Analyze organic and inorganic compounds to determine chemical and physical properties, composition, structure, relationships, and reactions, utilizing chromatography, spectroscopy, and spectrophotometry techniques. Develop, improve, and customize products, equipment, formulas, processes, and analytical methods. Compile and analyze test information to determine process or equipment operating efficiency and to diagnose malfunctions. Confer with scientists and engineers to conduct analyses of research projects, interpret test results, or develop nonstandard tests. Direct, coordinate, and advise personnel in test procedures for analyzing components and physical properties of materials. Induce changes in composition of substances by introducing heat, light, energy, and chemical catalysts for quantitative and qualitative analysis. Write technical papers and reports and prepare standards and specifications for processes, facilities, products, or tests. Study effects of various methods of processing, preserving, and packaging on composition and properties of foods. Prepare test solutions, compounds, and reagents for laboratory personnel to conduct test.

Work Conditions—Indoors; contaminants; hazardous conditions; standing.

Civil Engineers

❋ Level of Education/Training: Bachelor's degree
❋ Annual Earnings: $71,710
❋ Growth: 18.0%
❋ Annual Job Openings: 15,979
❋ Personality Type: Realistic

> Because construction industries and architectural, engineering, and related services employ many civil engineers, employment opportunities will vary by geographic area and may decrease during economic slow-downs, when construction is often curtailed.

Perform engineering duties in planning, designing, and overseeing construction and maintenance of building structures and facilities such as roads, railroads, airports, bridges, harbors, channels, dams, irrigation projects, pipelines, power plants, water and sewage systems, and waste disposal units. Includes architectural, structural, traffic, ocean, and geo-technical engineers. Manage and direct staff members and construction, operations, or maintenance activities at project site. Provide technical advice regarding design, construction, or program modifications and structural repairs to industrial and managerial personnel. Inspect project sites to monitor progress and ensure conformance to design specifications and safety or sanitation standards. Estimate quantities and cost of materials, equipment, or labor to determine project feasibility. Test soils and materials to determine the adequacy and strength of foundations, concrete, asphalt, or steel. Compute load and grade requirements, water flow rates, and material stress factors to determine design specifications. Plan and design transportation or hydraulic systems and structures, following construction and government standards and using design software and drawing tools. Analyze survey reports, maps, drawings, blueprints, aerial photography, and other topographical or geologic data to plan projects. Prepare or present public reports on topics such as bid proposals, deeds, environmental impact statements, or property and right-of-way descriptions. Direct or participate in surveying to lay out installations and establish reference points, grades, and elevations to guide construction. Conduct studies of traffic patterns or environmental conditions to identify engineering problems and assess the potential impact of projects.

Work Conditions—Indoors; sitting.

Electro-Mechanical Technicians

- ✸ Level of Education/Training: Associate degree
- ✸ Annual Earnings: $46,610
- ✸ Growth: 2.6%
- ✸ Annual Job Openings: 1,142
- ✸ Personality Type: Realistic

Job growth should be driven by increasing demand for electro-mechanical products such as pilotless aircraft and robotic equipment. However, growth will be tempered by advances in productivity and strong foreign competition.

Operate, test, and maintain unmanned, automated, servo-mechanical, or electro-mechanical equipment. May operate unmanned submarines, aircraft, or other equipment at worksites, such as oil rigs, deep ocean exploration, or hazardous waste removal. May assist engineers in testing and designing robotics equipment. Test performance of electro-mechanical assemblies, using test instruments such as oscilloscopes, electronic voltmeters, and bridges. Read blueprints, schematics, diagrams, and technical orders to determine methods and sequences of assembly. Install electrical and electronic parts and hardware in housings or assemblies, using soldering equipment and hand tools. Align, fit, and assemble component parts, using hand tools, power tools, fixtures, templates, and microscopes. Inspect parts for surface defects. Analyze and record test results and prepare written testing documentation. Verify dimensions and clearances of parts to ensure conformance to specifications, using precision measuring instruments. Operate metalworking machines to fabricate housings, jigs, fittings, and fixtures. Repair, rework, and calibrate hydraulic and pneumatic assemblies and systems to meet operational specifications and tolerances. Train others to install, use, and maintain robots. Develop, test, and program new robots.

Work Conditions—Indoors; noisy; contaminants; hazardous equipment; standing; using hands on objects, tools, or controls.

Environmental Engineers
* Level of Education/Training: Bachelor's degree
* Annual Earnings: $72,350
* Growth: 25.4%
* Annual Job Openings: 5,003
* Personality Type: No data available

More environmental engineers will be needed to comply with environmental regulations and to develop methods of cleaning up existing hazards. Job opportunities should be good even as more students earn degrees.

Design, plan, or perform engineering duties in the prevention, control, and remediation of environmental health hazards, using various engineering disciplines. Work may include waste treatment, site remediation, or pollution control technology. Collaborate with environmental scientists, planners, hazardous waste technicians, engineers, and other specialists and experts in law and business to address environmental problems. Inspect industrial and municipal facilities and programs to evaluate operational effectiveness and ensure compliance with environmental regulations. Prepare, review, and update environmental investigation and recommendation reports. Design and supervise the development of systems processes or equipment for control, management, or remediation of water, air, or soil quality. Provide environmental engineering assistance in network analysis, regulatory analysis, and planning or reviewing database development. Obtain, update, and maintain plans, permits, and standard operating procedures. Provide technical-level support for environmental remediation and litigation projects, including remediation system design and determination of regulatory applicability. Monitor progress of environmental improvement programs. Inform company employees and other interested parties of environmental issues. Advise corporations and government agencies of procedures to follow in cleaning up contaminated sites to protect people and the environment. Develop proposed project objectives and targets and report to management on progress in attaining them. Request bids from suppliers or consultants. Advise industries and government agencies about environmental policies and standards. Assess the existing or potential environmental impact of land use projects on air, water, and land. Assist in budget implementation, forecasts, and administration. Serve on teams conducting multimedia inspections at complex facilities, providing assistance with planning, quality assurance, safety inspection protocols, and sampling. Coordinate and manage environmental protection programs and projects, assigning and evaluating work. Maintain, write, and revise quality assurance documentation and procedures. Provide administrative support for projects by collecting data, providing project documentation, training staff, and performing other general administrative duties.

Work Conditions—More often indoors than outdoors; noisy; contaminants; sitting; using hands on objects, tools, or controls.

Physicists

- ❊ Level of Education/Training: Doctoral degree
- ❊ Annual Earnings: $96,850
- ❊ Growth: 6.8%
- ❊ Annual Job Openings: 1,302
- ❊ Personality Type: Investigative

> Job applicants may face competition for basic research positions because of limited funding; however, those with a background in physics may have good opportunities in related occupations.

Conduct research into phases of physical phenomena, develop theories and laws on basis of observation and experiments, and devise methods to apply laws and theories to industry and other fields. Perform complex calculations as part of the analysis and evaluation of data, using computers. Describe and express observations and conclusions in mathematical terms. Analyze data from research conducted to detect and measure physical phenomena. Report experimental results by writing papers for scientific journals or by presenting information at scientific conferences. Design computer simulations to model physical data so that it can be better understood. Collaborate with other scientists in the design, development, and testing of experimental, industrial, or medical equipment, instrumentation, and procedures. Direct testing and monitoring of contamination of radioactive equipment and recording of personnel and plant area radiation exposure data. Observe the structure and properties of matter and the transformation and propagation of energy, using equipment such as masers, lasers, and telescopes, in order to explore and identify the basic principles governing these phenomena. Develop theories and laws on the basis of observation and experiments and apply these theories and laws to problems in areas such as nuclear energy, optics, and aerospace technology. Teach physics to students. Develop manufacturing, assembly, and fabrication processes of lasers, masers, and infrared and other light-emitting and light-sensitive devices. Conduct application evaluations and analyze results in order to determine commercial, industrial, scientific, medical, military, or other uses for electro-optical devices. Develop standards of permissible concentrations of radioisotopes in liquids and gases. Conduct research pertaining to potential environmental impacts of atomic energy–related industrial development in order to determine licensing qualifications. Advise authorities of procedures to be followed in radiation incidents or hazards and assist in civil defense planning.

Work Conditions—Indoors; sitting.

Statisticians

- Level of Education/Training: Master's degree
- Annual Earnings: $69,900
- Growth: 8.5%
- Annual Job Openings: 3,433
- Personality Type: Investigative

> Individuals with a degree in statistics should have opportunities in a variety of fields. About 30 percent of statisticians work for federal, state, and local governments; other employers include scientific research and development services and finance and insurance firms.

Engage in the development of mathematical theory or apply statistical theory and methods to collect, organize, interpret, and summarize numerical data to provide usable information. May specialize in fields such as bio-statistics, agricultural statistics, business statistics, economic statistics, or other fields. Report results of statistical analyses, including information in the form of graphs, charts, and tables. Process large amounts of data for statistical modeling and graphic analysis, using computers. Identify relationships and trends in data, as well as any factors that could affect the results of research. Analyze and interpret statistical data in order to identify significant differences in relationships among sources of information. Prepare data for processing by organizing information, checking for any inaccuracies, and adjusting and weighting the raw data. Evaluate the statistical methods and procedures used to obtain data in order to ensure validity, applicability, efficiency, and accuracy. Evaluate sources of information in order to determine any limitations in terms of reliability or usability. Plan data collection methods for specific projects and determine the types and sizes of sample groups to be used. Design research projects that apply valid scientific techniques and utilize information obtained from baselines or historical data in order to structure uncompromised and efficient analyses. Develop an understanding of fields to which statistical methods are to be applied in order to determine whether methods and results are appropriate. Supervise and provide instructions for workers collecting and tabulating data. Apply sampling techniques or utilize complete enumeration bases in order to determine and define groups to be surveyed. Adapt statistical methods in order to solve specific problems in many fields such as economics, biology, and engineering. Develop and test experimental designs, sampling techniques, and analytical methods. Examine theories, such as those of probability and inference, in order to discover mathematical bases for new or improved methods of obtaining and evaluating numerical data.

Work Conditions—Indoors; sitting; using hands on objects, tools, or controls; repetitive motions.

Some Jobs in the Computer Systems Design and Related Services Industry That Are Likely to Benefit from the Stimulus Package

Computer Security Specialists

❀ Level of Education/Training: Bachelor's degree
❀ Annual Earnings: $64,690
❀ Growth: 27.0%
❀ Annual Job Openings: 37,010
❀ Personality Type: Investigative

The job openings listed here are shared with Network and Computer Systems Administrators.

> Job prospects should be best for college graduates who are up to date with the latest skills and technologies; certifications and practical experience are essential for persons without degrees.

Plan, coordinate, and implement security measures for information systems to regulate access to computer data files and prevent unauthorized modification, destruction, or disclosure of information. Train users and promote security awareness to ensure system security and to improve server and network efficiency. Develop plans to safeguard computer files against accidental or unauthorized modification, destruction, or disclosure and to meet emergency data processing needs. Confer with users to discuss issues such as computer data access needs, security violations, and programming changes. Monitor current reports of computer viruses to determine when to update virus protection systems. Modify computer security files to incorporate new software, correct errors, or change individual access status. Coordinate implementation of computer system plan with establishment personnel and outside vendors. Monitor use of data files and regulate access to safeguard information in computer files. Perform risk assessments and execute tests of data-processing system to ensure functioning of data-processing activities and security measures. Encrypt data transmissions and erect firewalls to conceal confidential information as it is being transmitted and to keep out tainted digital transfers. Document computer security and emergency measures policies, procedures, and tests. Review violations of computer security procedures and discuss procedures with violators to ensure violations are not repeated. Maintain permanent fleet cryptologic and carry-on direct support systems required in special land, sea surface, and subsurface operations.

Work Conditions—Indoors; sitting.

Computer Software Engineers, Applications

- ❀ Level of Education/Training: Bachelor's degree
- ❀ Annual Earnings: $83,130
- ❀ Growth: 44.6%
- ❀ Annual Job Openings: 58,690
- ❀ Personality Type: Investigative

> Very good opportunities are expected for college graduates with at least a bachelor's degree in computer engineering or computer science and with practical work experience.

Develop, create, and modify general computer applications software or specialized utility programs. Analyze user needs and develop software solutions. Design software or customize software for client use with the aim of optimizing operational efficiency. May analyze and design databases within an application area, working individually or coordinating database development as part of a team. Confer with systems analysts, engineers, programmers, and others to design system and to obtain information on project limitations and capabilities, performance requirements, and interfaces. Modify existing software to correct errors, allow it to adapt to new hardware, or improve its performance. Analyze user needs and software requirements to determine feasibility of design within time and cost constraints. Consult with customers about software system design and maintenance. Coordinate software system installation and monitor equipment functioning to ensure specifications are met. Design, develop, and modify software systems, using scientific analysis and mathematical models to predict and measure outcome and consequences of design. Develop and direct software system testing and validation procedures, programming, and documentation. Analyze information to determine, recommend, and plan computer specifications and layouts and peripheral equipment modifications. Supervise the work of programmers, technologists, and technicians and other engineering and scientific personnel. Obtain and evaluate information on factors such as reporting formats required, costs, and security needs to determine hardware configuration. Determine system performance standards. Train users to use new or modified equipment. Store, retrieve, and manipulate data for analysis of system capabilities and requirements. Specify power supply requirements and configuration. Recommend purchase of equipment to control dust, temperature, and humidity in area of system installation.

Work Conditions—Indoors; sitting; using hands on objects, tools, or controls; repetitive motions.

Computer Software Engineers, Systems Software

* ❀ Level of Education/Training: Bachelor's degree
* ❀ Annual Earnings: $89,070
* ❀ Growth: 28.2%
* ❀ Annual Job Openings: 33,139
* ❀ Personality Type: Investigative

> Computer software engineers must continually strive to acquire new skills in conjunction with the rapid changes that are occurring in computer technology.

Research, design, develop, and test operating systems-level software, compilers, and network distribution software for medical, industrial, military, communications, aerospace, business, scientific, and general computing applications. Set operational specifications and formulate and analyze software requirements. Apply principles and techniques of computer science, engineering, and mathematical analysis. Modify existing software to correct errors, to adapt it to new hardware, or to upgrade interfaces and improve performance. Design and develop software systems, using scientific analysis and mathematical models to predict and measure outcome and consequences of design. Consult with engineering staff to evaluate interface between hardware and software, develop specifications and performance requirements, and resolve customer problems. Analyze information to determine, recommend, and plan installation of a new system or modification of an existing system. Develop and direct software system testing and validation procedures. Direct software programming and development of documentation. Consult with customers or other departments on project status, proposals, and technical issues such as software system design and maintenance. Advise customer about, or perform, maintenance of software system. Coordinate installation of software system. Monitor functioning of equipment to ensure system operates in conformance with specifications. Store, retrieve, and manipulate data for analysis of system capabilities and requirements. Confer with data processing and project managers to obtain information on limitations and capabilities for data-processing projects. Prepare reports and correspondence concerning project specifications, activities, and status. Evaluate factors such as reporting formats required, cost constraints, and need for security restrictions to determine hardware configuration. Supervise and assign work to programmers, designers, technologists and technicians, and other engineering and scientific personnel. Train users to use new or modified equipment. Utilize microcontrollers to develop control signals; implement control algorithms; and measure process variables such as temperatures, pressures, and positions. Recommend purchase of equipment to control dust, temperature, and humidity in area of system installation. Specify power supply requirements and configuration.

Work Conditions—Indoors; sitting; using hands on objects, tools, or controls; repetitive motions.

Computer Support Specialists

- ❈ Level of Education/Training: Associate degree
- ❈ Annual Earnings: $42,400
- ❈ Growth: 12.9%
- ❈ Annual Job Openings: 97,334
- ❈ Personality Type: Investigative

> Job prospects should be best for college graduates who are up to date with the latest skills and technologies; certifications and practical experience are essential for persons without degrees.

Provide technical assistance to computer system users. Answer questions or resolve computer problems for clients in person, via telephone, or from remote locations. May provide assistance concerning the use of computer hardware and software, including printing, installation, word processing, e-mail, and operating systems. Oversee the daily performance of computer systems. Answer user inquiries regarding computer software or hardware operation to resolve problems. Enter commands and observe system functioning to verify correct operations and detect errors. Set up equipment for employee use, performing or ensuring proper installation of cables, operating systems, or appropriate software. Install and perform minor repairs to hardware, software, or peripheral equipment, following design or installation specifications. Maintain records of daily data communication transactions, problems and remedial actions taken, or installation activities. Read technical manuals, confer with users, or conduct computer diagnostics to investigate and resolve problems or to provide technical assistance and support. Refer major hardware or software problems or defective products to vendors or technicians for service. Develop training materials and procedures or train users in the proper use of hardware or software. Confer with staff, users, and management to establish requirements for new systems or modifications. Prepare evaluations of software or hardware and recommend improvements or upgrades. Read trade magazines and technical manuals or attend conferences and seminars to maintain knowledge of hardware and software. Hire, supervise, and direct workers engaged in special project work, problem solving, monitoring, and installing data communication equipment and software. Inspect equipment and read order sheets to prepare for delivery to users. Modify and customize commercial programs for internal needs. Conduct office automation feasibility studies, including workflow analysis, space design, or cost comparison analysis.

Work Conditions—Indoors; sitting; using hands on objects, tools, or controls.

Computer Systems Analysts

* Level of Education/Training: Bachelor's degree
* Annual Earnings: $73,090
* Growth: 29.0%
* Annual Job Openings: 63,166
* Personality Type: Investigative

> While there is no universally accepted way to prepare for this job, most employers place a premium on some formal college education.

Analyze science, engineering, business, and all other data-processing problems for application to electronic data processing systems. Analyze user requirements, procedures, and problems to automate or improve existing systems and review computer system capabilities, workflow, and scheduling limitations. May analyze or recommend commercially available software. May supervise computer programmers. Provide staff and users with assistance solving computer-related problems, such as malfunctions and program problems. Test, maintain, and monitor computer programs and systems, including coordinating the installation of computer programs and systems. Use object-oriented programming languages as well as client and server applications development processes and multimedia and Internet technology. Confer with clients regarding the nature of the information processing or computation needs a computer program is to address.

Coordinate and link the computer systems within an organization to increase compatibility and so information can be shared. Consult with management to ensure agreement on system principles. Expand or modify system to serve new purposes or improve workflow. Interview or survey workers, observe job performance, or perform the job to determine what information is processed and how it is processed. Determine computer software or hardware needed to set up or alter system. Train staff and users to work with computer systems and programs. Analyze information processing or computation needs and plan and design computer systems, using techniques such as structured analysis, data modeling, and information engineering. Assess the usefulness of pre-developed application packages and adapt them to a user environment. Define the goals of the system and devise flow charts and diagrams describing logical operational steps of programs. Develop, document, and revise system design procedures, test procedures, and quality standards. Review and analyze computer printouts and performance indicators to locate code problems; correct errors by correcting codes. Recommend new equipment or software packages. Read manuals, periodicals, and technical reports to learn how to develop programs that meet staff and user requirements. Supervise computer programmers or other systems analysts or serve as project leaders for particular systems projects. Utilize the computer in the analysis and solution of business problems such as development of integrated production and inventory control and cost analysis systems.

Work Conditions—Indoors; sitting.

Database Administrators

❋ Level of Education/Training: Bachelor's degree
❋ Annual Earnings: $67,250
❋ Growth: 28.6%
❋ Annual Job Openings: 8,258
❋ Personality Type: Investigative

> A bachelor's degree is a prerequisite for many jobs; however, some jobs may require only a two-year degree. Relevant work experience also is very important.

Coordinate changes to computer databases. Test and implement the databases, applying knowledge of database management systems. May plan, coordinate, and implement security measures to safeguard computer databases. Test programs or databases, correct errors, and make necessary modifications. Modify existing databases and database management systems or direct programmers and analysts to make changes. Plan, coordinate, and implement security measures to safeguard information in computer files against accidental or unauthorized damage, modification, or disclosure. Work as part of project teams to coordinate database development and determine project scope and limitations. Write and code logical and physical database descriptions and specify identifiers of database to management system or direct others in coding descriptions. Train users and answer questions. Specify users and user access levels for each segment of databases. Approve, schedule, plan, and supervise the installation and testing of new products and improvements to computer systems such as the installation of new databases. Review project requests describing database user needs to estimate time and cost required to accomplish project. Develop standards and guidelines to guide the use and acquisition of software and to protect vulnerable information. Review procedures in database management system manuals for making changes to database. Develop methods for integrating different products so they work properly together such as customizing commercial databases to fit specific needs. Develop data models describing data elements and how they are used, following procedures and using pen, template, or computer software. Select and enter codes to monitor database performances and to create production databases. Establish and calculate optimum values for database parameters, using manuals and calculators. Revise company definition of data as defined in data dictionary. Review workflow charts developed by programmer analysts to understand tasks computer will perform, such as updating records. Identify and evaluate industry trends in database systems to serve as a source of information and advice for upper management.

Work Conditions—Indoors; noisy; sitting; using hands on objects, tools, or controls; repetitive motions.

Network and Computer Systems Administrators

- ❋ Level of Education/Training: Bachelor's degree
- ❋ Annual Earnings: $64,690
- ❋ Growth: 27.0%
- ❋ Annual Job Openings: 37,010
- ❋ Personality Type: Investigative

The job openings listed here are shared with Computer Security Specialists.

Computer networks have become an integral part of business, and demand for these workers will increase as firms continue to invest in new technologies. The wide use of electronic commerce and the increasing adoption of mobile technologies mean that more establishments will use the Internet to conduct business online.

Install, configure, and support organizations' local area networks (LANs), wide area networks (WANs), and Internet systems or segments of network systems. Maintain network hardware and software. Monitor networks to ensure network availability to all system users and perform necessary maintenance to support network availability. May supervise other network support and client server specialists and plan, coordinate, and implement network security measures. Maintain and administer computer networks and related computing environments, including computer hardware, systems software, applications software, and all configurations. Perform data backups and disaster recovery operations. Diagnose, troubleshoot, and resolve hardware, software, or other network and system problems and replace defective components when necessary. Plan, coordinate, and implement network security measures to protect data, software, and hardware. Configure, monitor, and maintain e-mail applications or virus protection software. Operate master consoles to monitor the performance of computer systems and networks and to coordinate computer network access and use. Load computer tapes and disks and install software and printer paper or forms. Design, configure, and test computer hardware, networking software, and operating system software. Monitor network performance to determine whether adjustments need to be made and to determine where changes will need to be made in the future. Confer with network users about how to solve existing system problems. Research new technologies by attending seminars, reading trade articles, or taking classes and implement or recommend the implementation of new technologies. Analyze equipment performance records to determine the need for repair or replacement. Implement and provide technical support for voice services and equipment such as private branch exchanges, voice mail systems, and telecom systems. Maintain inventories of parts for emergency repairs. Recommend changes to improve systems and network configurations and determine hardware or software requirements related to such changes. Gather data pertaining to customer needs and use the information to identify, predict, interpret, and evaluate system and network requirements. Train people in computer system use. Coordinate with vendors and with company personnel to facilitate purchases. Perform routine network startup and shutdown procedures and maintain control records. Maintain logs related to network functions, as well as maintenance and repair records.

Work Conditions—Indoors; noisy; sitting; using hands on objects, tools, or controls; repetitive motions.

Network Systems and Data Communications Analysts

- ❊ Level of Education/Training: Bachelor's degree
- ❊ Annual Earnings: $68,220
- ❊ Growth: 53.4%
- ❊ Annual Job Openings: 35,086
- ❊ Personality Type: Investigative

> Evening or weekend work may be necessary to meet deadlines or solve specific problems. With the technology available today, telecommuting is common for computer professionals.

Analyze, design, test, and evaluate network systems such as local area networks (LAN); wide area networks (WAN); and Internet, intranet, and other data communications systems. Perform network modeling, analysis, and planning. Research and recommend network and data communications hardware and software. Includes telecommunications specialists who deal with the interfacing of computer and communications equipment. May supervise computer programmers. Maintain needed files by adding and deleting files on the network server and backing up files to guarantee their safety in the event of problems with the network. Monitor system performance and provide security measures, troubleshooting, and maintenance as needed. Assist users to diagnose and solve data communication problems. Set up user accounts, regulating and monitoring file access to ensure confidentiality and proper use. Design and implement systems, network configurations, and network architecture, including hardware and software technology, site locations, and integration of technologies. Maintain the peripherals, such as printers, that are connected to the network. Identify areas of operation that need upgraded equipment such as modems, fiber-optic cables, and telephone wires. Train users in use of equipment. Develop and write procedures for installation, use, and troubleshooting of communications hardware and software. Adapt and modify existing software to meet specific needs. Work with other engineers, systems analysts, programmers, technicians, scientists, and top-level managers in the design, testing, and evaluation of systems. Test and evaluate hardware and software to determine efficiency, reliability, and compatibility with existing system and make purchase recommendations. Read technical manuals and brochures to determine which equipment meets establishment requirements. Consult customers, visit workplaces, or conduct surveys to determine present and future user needs. Visit vendors, attend conferences or training, and study technical journals to keep up with changes in technology.

Work Conditions—Indoors; sitting.

Some Jobs in the Wholesale Trade Industry That Are Likely to Benefit from the Stimulus Package

Customer Service Representatives

※ Level of Education/Training: Moderate-term on-the-job training

※ Annual Earnings: $29,040

※ Growth: 24.8%

※ Annual Job Openings: 600,937

※ Personality Type: Conventional

> Most jobs require only a high school diploma, but educational requirements are rising.

Interact with customers to provide information in response to inquiries about products and services and to handle and resolve complaints. Confer with customers by telephone or in person to provide information about products and services, to take orders or cancel accounts, or to obtain details of complaints. Keep records of customer interactions and transactions, recording details of inquiries, complaints, and comments, as well as actions taken. Resolve customers' service or billing complaints by performing activities such as exchanging merchandise, refunding money, and adjusting bills. Check to ensure that appropriate changes were made to resolve customers' problems. Contact customers to respond to inquiries or to notify them of claim investigation results and any planned adjustments. Refer unresolved customer grievances to designated departments for further investigation. Determine charges for services requested, collect deposits or payments, or arrange for billing. Complete contract forms, prepare change of address records, and issue service discontinuance orders, using computers. Obtain and examine all relevant information to assess validity of complaints and to determine possible causes, such as extreme weather conditions, that could increase utility bills. Solicit sale of new or additional services or products. Review insurance policy terms to determine whether a particular loss is covered by insurance. Review claims adjustments with dealers, examining parts claimed to be defective and approving or disapproving dealers' claims. Compare disputed merchandise with original requisitions and information from invoices and prepare invoices for returned goods. Order tests that could determine the causes of product malfunctions. Recommend improvements in products, packaging, shipping, service, or billing methods and procedures to prevent future problems.

Work Conditions—Indoors; sitting; using hands on objects, tools, or controls; repetitive motions.

First-Line Supervisors/Managers of Non-Retail Sales Workers

- ❀ Level of Education/Training: Work experience in a related occupation
- ❀ Annual Earnings: $67,020
- ❀ Growth: 3.7%
- ❀ Annual Job Openings: 48,883
- ❀ Personality Type: Enterprising

> Long, irregular hours, including evenings and weekends, are common.

Directly supervise and coordinate activities of sales workers other than retail sales workers. May perform duties such as budgeting, accounting, and personnel work in addition to supervisory duties. Listen to and resolve customer complaints regarding services, products, or personnel. Monitor sales staff performance to ensure that goals are met. Hire, train, and evaluate personnel. Confer with company officials to develop methods and procedures to increase sales, expand markets, and promote business. Direct and supervise employees engaged in sales, inventory-taking, reconciling cash receipts, or performing specific services such as pumping gasoline for customers. Provide staff with assistance in performing difficult or complicated duties. Plan and prepare work schedules and assign employees to specific duties. Attend company meetings to exchange product information and coordinate work activities with other departments. Prepare sales and inventory reports for management and budget departments. Formulate pricing policies on merchandise according to profitability requirements. Examine merchandise to ensure correct pricing and display and ensure that it functions as advertised. Analyze details of sales territories to assess their growth potential and to set quotas. Visit retailers and sales representatives to promote products and gather information. Keep records pertaining to purchases, sales, and requisitions. Coordinate sales promotion activities and prepare merchandise displays and advertising copy. Prepare rental or lease agreements, specifying charges and payment procedures for use of machinery, tools, or other items. Inventory stock and reorder when inventories drop to specified levels. Examine products purchased for resale or received for storage to determine product condition.

Work Conditions—Indoors; noisy.

Purchasing Agents, Except Wholesale, Retail, and Farm Products

❀ Level of Education/Training: Work experience in a related occupation
❀ Annual Earnings: $52,460
❀ Growth: 0.1%
❀ Annual Job Openings: 22,349
❀ Personality Type: Enterprising

> Some firms prefer to promote existing employees to these positions, while others recruit and train college graduates. Opportunities should be best for those with a college degree.

Purchase machinery, equipment, tools, parts, supplies, or services necessary for the operation of an establishment. Purchase raw or semi-finished materials for manufacturing. Purchase the highest-quality merchandise at the lowest possible price and in correct amounts. Prepare purchase orders, solicit bid proposals, and review requisitions for goods and services. Research and evaluate suppliers based on price, quality, selection, service, support, availability, reliability, production and distribution capabilities, and the supplier's reputation and history. Analyze price proposals, financial reports, and other data and information to determine reasonable prices. Monitor and follow applicable laws and regulations. Negotiate, or renegotiate, and administer contracts with suppliers, vendors, and other representatives. Monitor shipments to ensure that goods come in on time and trace shipments and follow up undelivered goods in the event of problems. Confer with staff, users, and vendors to discuss defective or unacceptable goods or services and determine corrective action. Evaluate and monitor contract performance to ensure compliance with contractual obligations and to determine need for changes. Maintain and review computerized or manual records of items purchased, costs, delivery, product performance, and inventories. Review catalogs, industry periodicals, directories, trade journals, and Internet sites and consult with other department personnel to locate necessary goods and services. Study sales records and inventory levels of current stock to develop strategic purchasing programs that facilitate employee access to supplies. Interview vendors and visit suppliers' plants and distribution centers to examine and learn about products, services, and prices. Arrange the payment of duty and freight charges. Hire, train, and/or supervise purchasing clerks, buyers, and expediters. Write and review product specifications, maintaining a working technical knowledge of the goods or services to be purchased. Monitor changes affecting supply and demand, tracking market conditions, price trends, or futures markets. Formulate policies and procedures for bid proposals and procurement of goods and services. Attend meetings, trade shows, conferences, conventions, and seminars to network with people in other purchasing departments.

Work Conditions—Indoors; sitting; using hands on objects, tools, or controls; repetitive motions.

Sales Managers

* ❋ Level of Education/Training: Work experience plus degree
* ❋ Annual Earnings: $94,910
* ❋ Growth: 10.2%
* ❋ Annual Job Openings: 36,392
* ❋ Personality Type: Enterprising

> Keen competition is expected for these highly coveted jobs. Because of the importance and high visibility of their jobs, these managers often are prime candidates for advancement to the highest ranks.

Direct the actual distribution or movement of products or services to customers. Coordinate sales distribution by establishing sales territories, quotas, and goals and establish training programs for sales representatives. Analyze sales statistics gathered by staff to determine sales potential and inventory requirements and monitor the preferences of customers. Resolve customer complaints regarding sales and service. Oversee regional and local sales managers and their staffs. Plan and direct staffing, training, and performance evaluations to develop and control sales and service programs. Determine price schedules and discount rates. Review operational records and reports to project sales and determine profitability. Monitor customer preferences to determine focus of sales efforts. Prepare budgets and approve budget expenditures. Confer or consult with department heads to plan advertising services and to secure information on equipment and customer specifications. Direct and coordinate activities involving sales of manufactured products, services, commodities, real estate, or other subjects of sale. Confer with potential customers regarding equipment needs and advise customers on types of equipment to purchase. Direct foreign sales and service outlets of an organization. Advise dealers and distributors on policies and operating procedures to ensure functional effectiveness of businesses. Visit franchised dealers to stimulate interest in establishment or expansion of leasing programs. Direct clerical staff to keep records of export correspondence, bid requests, and credit collections and to maintain current information on tariffs, licenses, and restrictions. Direct, coordinate, and review activities in sales and service accounting and recordkeeping and in receiving and shipping operations. Assess marketing potential of new and existing store locations, considering statistics and expenditures. Represent company at trade association meetings to promote products.

Work Conditions—Indoors; sitting.

Sales Representatives, Wholesale and Manufacturing, Except Technical and Scientific Products

❀ Level of Education/Training: Moderate-term on-the-job training

❀ Annual Earnings: $50,750

❀ Growth: 8.4%

❀ Annual Job Openings: 156,215

❀ Personality Type: Enterprising

Job prospects for sales representatives will be better for those working with essential goods, as the demand for these products do not fluctuate with the economy.

Sell goods for wholesalers or manufacturers to businesses or groups of individuals. Work requires substantial knowledge of items sold. Answer customers' questions about products, prices, availability, product uses, and credit terms. Recommend products to customers based on customers' needs and interests. Contact regular and prospective customers to demonstrate products, explain product features, and solicit orders. Estimate or quote prices, credit or contract terms, warranties, and delivery dates. Consult with clients after sales or contract signings to resolve problems and to provide ongoing support. Prepare drawings, estimates, and bids that meet specific customer needs. Provide customers with product samples and catalogs. Identify prospective customers by using business directories, following leads from existing clients, participating in organizations and clubs, and attending trade shows and conferences. Arrange and direct delivery and installation of products and equipment. Monitor market conditions; product innovations; and competitors' products, prices, and sales. Negotiate details of contracts and payments and prepare sales contracts and order forms. Perform administrative duties such as preparing sales budgets and reports, keeping sales records, and filing expense account reports. Obtain credit information about prospective customers. Forward orders to manufacturers. Check stock levels and reorder merchandise as necessary. Plan, assemble, and stock product displays in retail stores or make recommendations to retailers regarding product displays, promotional programs, and advertising. Negotiate with retail merchants to improve product exposure such as shelf positioning and advertising. Train customers' employees to operate and maintain new equipment. Buy products from manufacturers or brokerage firms and distribute them to wholesale and retail clients.

Work Conditions—Outdoors; noisy; contaminants; more often standing than sitting; walking and running.

Sales Representatives, Wholesale and Manufacturing, Technical and Scientific Products

- ✽ Level of Education/Training: Moderate-term on-the-job training
- ✽ Annual Earnings: $68,270
- ✽ Growth: 12.4%
- ✽ Annual Job Openings: 43,469
- ✽ Personality Type: Enterprising

> Employment opportunities will be best for those with a college degree, the appropriate knowledge or technical expertise, and the personal traits necessary for successful selling.

Sell goods for wholesalers or manufacturers where technical or scientific knowledge is required in such areas as biology, engineering, chemistry, and electronics that is normally obtained from at least two years of postsecondary education. Contact new and existing customers to discuss their needs and to explain how these needs could be met by specific products and services. Answer customers' questions about products, prices, availability, product uses, and credit terms. Quote prices, credit terms, and other bid specifications. Emphasize product features based on analyses of customers' needs and on technical knowledge of product capabilities and limitations. Negotiate prices and terms of sales and service agreements. Maintain customer records, using automated systems. Identify prospective customers by using business directories, following leads from existing clients, participating in organizations and clubs, and attending trade shows and conferences. Prepare sales contracts for orders obtained and submit orders for processing. Select the correct products or assist customers in making product selections, based on customers' needs, product specifications, and applicable regulations. Collaborate with colleagues to exchange information such as selling strategies and marketing information. Prepare sales presentations and proposals that explain product specifications and applications. Provide customers with ongoing technical support. Demonstrate and explain the operation and use of products. Inform customers of estimated delivery schedules, service contracts, warranties, or other information pertaining to purchased products. Attend sales and trade meetings and read related publications in order to obtain information about market conditions, business trends, and industry developments. Visit establishments to evaluate needs and to promote product or service sales. Complete expense reports, sales reports, and other paperwork. Initiate sales campaigns and follow marketing plan guidelines in order to meet sales and production expectations. Recommend ways for customers to alter product usage in order to improve production. Complete product and development training as required. Provide feedback to company's product design teams so that products can be tailored to clients' needs. Arrange for installation and test-operation of machinery.

Work Conditions—Indoors; sitting.

Shipping, Receiving, and Traffic Clerks

* Level of Education/Training: Short-term on-the-job training
* Annual Earnings: $26,990
* Growth: 3.7%
* Annual Job Openings: 138,967
* Personality Type: Conventional

> Employers prefer to hire those familiar with computers and other electronic office and business equipment.

Verify and keep records on incoming and outgoing shipments. Prepare items for shipment. Examine contents and compare with records such as manifests, invoices, or orders to verify accuracy of incoming or outgoing shipment. Prepare documents such as work orders, bills of lading, and shipping orders to route materials. Determine shipping method for materials, using knowledge of shipping procedures, routes, and rates. Record shipment data such as weight, charges, space availability, and damages and discrepancies for reporting, accounting, and recordkeeping purposes. Contact carrier representative to make arrangements and to issue instructions for shipping and delivery of materials. Confer and correspond with establishment representatives to rectify problems such as damages, shortages, and nonconformance to specifications. Requisition and store shipping materials and supplies to maintain inventory of stock. Deliver or route materials to departments, using work devices such as handtruck, conveyor, or sorting bins. Compute amounts such as space available and shipping, storage, and demurrage charges, using calculator or price list. Pack, seal, label, and affix postage to prepare materials for shipping, using work devices such as hand tools, power tools, and postage meter.

Work Conditions—Indoors; noisy; contaminants; sitting; walking and running; using hands on objects, tools, or controls.

Truck Drivers, Heavy and Tractor-Trailer

- ❀ Level of Education/Training: Moderate-term on-the-job training
- ❀ Annual Earnings: $36,220
- ❀ Growth: 10.4%
- ❀ Annual Job Openings: 279,032
- ❀ Personality Type: Realistic

> A commercial driver's license is required to operate most larger trucks.

Drive a tractor-trailer combination or a truck with a capacity of at least 26,000 GVW to transport and deliver goods, livestock, or materials in liquid, loose, or packaged form. May be required to unload truck. May require use of automated routing equipment. Requires commercial drivers' license. Follow appropriate safety procedures when transporting dangerous goods. Check vehicles before driving them to ensure that mechanical, safety, and emergency equipment is in good working order. Maintain logs of working hours and of vehicle service and repair status, following applicable state and federal regulations. Obtain receipts or signatures when loads are delivered and collect payment for services when required. Check all load-related documentation to ensure that it is complete and accurate. Maneuver trucks into loading or unloading positions, following signals from loading crew as needed; check that vehicle position is correct and any special loading equipment is properly positioned. Drive trucks with capacities greater than 3 tons, including tractor-trailer combinations, to transport and deliver products, livestock, or other materials. Secure cargo for transport, using ropes, blocks, chain, binders, or covers. Read bills of lading to determine assignment details. Report vehicle defects, accidents, traffic violations, or damage to the vehicles. Read and interpret maps to determine vehicle routes. Couple and uncouple trailers by changing trailer jack positions, connecting or disconnecting air and electrical lines, and manipulating fifth-wheel locks. Collect delivery instructions from appropriate sources, verifying instructions and routes. Drive trucks to weigh stations before and after loading and along routes to document weights and to comply with state regulations. Operate equipment such as truck cab computers, CB radios, and telephones to exchange necessary information with bases, supervisors, or other drivers. Check conditions of trailers after contents have been unloaded to ensure that there has been no damage. Crank trailer landing gear up and down to safely secure vehicles. Wrap goods, using pads, packing paper, and containers, and secure loads to trailer walls, using straps. Perform basic vehicle maintenance tasks such as adding oil, fuel, and radiator fluid or performing minor repairs. Load and unload trucks or help others with loading and unloading, operating any special loading-related equipment on vehicles and using other equipment as necessary.

Work Conditions—Outdoors; very hot or cold; contaminants; sitting; using hands on objects, tools, or controls; repetitive motions.

Truck Drivers, Light or Delivery Services

- ❋ Level of Education/Training: Short-term on-the-job training
- ❋ Annual Earnings: $26,380
- ❋ Growth: 8.4%
- ❋ Annual Job Openings: 154,330
- ❋ Personality Type: Realistic

> Competition is expected for jobs offering the highest earnings or most favorable work schedules.

Drive a truck or van with a capacity of under 26,000 GVW primarily to deliver or pick up merchandise or to deliver packages within a specified area. May require use of automatic routing or location software. May load and unload truck. Obey traffic laws and follow established traffic and transportation procedures. Inspect and maintain vehicle supplies and equipment such as gas, oil, water, tires, lights, and brakes to ensure that vehicles are in proper working condition. Report any mechanical problems encountered with vehicles. Present bills and receipts and collect payments for goods delivered or loaded. Load and unload trucks, vans, or automobiles. Turn in receipts and money received from deliveries. Verify the contents of inventory loads against shipping papers. Maintain records such as vehicle logs, records of cargo, or billing statements in accordance with regulations. Read maps and follow written and verbal geographic directions. Report delays, accidents, or other traffic and transportation situations to bases or other vehicles, using telephones or mobile two-way radios. Sell and keep records of sales for products from truck inventory. Drive vehicles with capacities under three tons to transport materials to and from specified destinations such as railroad stations, plants, residences, and offices or within industrial yards. Drive trucks equipped with public address systems through city streets to broadcast announcements for advertising or publicity purposes. Use and maintain the tools and equipment found on commercial vehicles, such as weighing and measuring devices. Perform emergency repairs such as changing tires or installing light bulbs, fuses, tire chains, and spark plugs.

Work Conditions—Outdoors; very hot or cold; contaminants; cramped work space, awkward positions; minor burns, cuts, bites, or stings; using hands on objects, tools, or controls.

Other Jobs in the Industries Covered by This Chapter

These jobs play supporting roles in the industries covered by this chapter, are not expected to have a good outlook (even with help from the recovery plan), or were omitted from the descriptions in this chapter for lack of room.

Actuaries

Aerospace Engineers

Agricultural Engineers

Automotive Service Technicians and Mechanics

Billing and Posting Clerks and Machine Operators

Biomedical Engineers

Bus and Truck Mechanics and Diesel Engine Specialists

Chemical Engineers

Chief Executives

Civil Engineering Technicians

Computer and Information Systems Managers

Computer Hardware Engineers (see Manufacturing, chapter 6)

Computer Programmers

Computer, Automated Teller, and Office Machine Repairers

Data Entry Keyers

Demonstrators and Product Promoters

Editors

Electrical and Electronic Engineering Technicians

Electronics Engineering Technicians

Electronics Engineers, Except Computer

Environmental Engineering Technicians (see Infrastructure, chapter 3)

Environmental Science and Protection Technicians, Including Health

Environmental Scientists and Specialists, Including Health

Farm Equipment Mechanics

Financial Analysts

Financial Managers

First-Line Supervisors/Managers of Office and Administrative Support Workers

General and Operations Managers

Health and Safety Engineers, Except Mining Safety Engineers and Inspectors

Human Resources Managers

Industrial Engineering Technicians (see Manufacturing, chapter 6)

Industrial Engineers (see Manufacturing, chapter 6)

Industrial Machinery Mechanics (see Manufacturing, chapter 6)

Industrial Truck and Tractor Operators (see Manufacturing, chapter 6)

Interviewers, Except Eligibility and Loan

Laborers and Freight, Stock, and Material Movers, Hand

Logisticians

Marine Engineers and Naval Architects

Materials Engineers

Mechanical Engineering Technicians (see Manufacturing, chapter 6)

Mechanical Engineers (see Manufacturing, chapter 6)

Mining and Geological Engineers, Including Mining Safety Engineers (see Energy, chapter 2)

Mobile Heavy Equipment Mechanics, Except Engines (see Energy, chapter 2)

Nuclear Engineers

Office Clerks, General

Operations Research Analysts

Order Clerks

Packers and Packagers, Hand

Petroleum Engineers (see Energy, chapter 2)

Public Relations Specialists

Receptionists and Information Clerks

Retail Salespersons

Sales Engineers

Secretaries, Except Legal, Medical, and Executive

Team Assemblers (see Manufacturing, chapter 6)

Technical Writer

Telemarketers

CHAPTER 8

TAKING ACTION

You may be hearing that this is a terrible time to look for a job, and maybe you have made some attempts and have become discouraged. Furthermore, many occupations in this book will take several months or even a year or two to show the effects of the stimulus package by offering increased job openings.

Nevertheless, people are being hired, even during a bad recession. Think of the job situation as a collection of hits and misses: When someone gets hired, that's a hit; when someone loses a job, that's a miss. Since 2008 started, we have seen more misses than hits, but *there have been many hits* regardless.

This chapter is about strategies for getting hired, and the proven techniques you'll learn here are effective in both good times and bad times.

Focusing on Your Goal

Your first step is to become highly focused on your goal. Colin Frager, an executive recruiter and CEO of the Colin Phillips Group, says that the key to success is a combination of preparation and motivation. From his many years of experience in helping people find good jobs, he has learned that most people begin the job hunt without giving sufficient thought to *what they want* and *what they can bring to the table.*

Most employers, especially during economic downturns, want to hire workers who will hit the ground running and perform a very specific set of job tasks. If the job involves some on-the-job training so that workers can't perform the work tasks from day one, the employer still wants recruits who are highly committed, will learn quickly, and will apply their training to money-making work without much delay. That means these employers are not interested in job candidates who have only a general notion of the kind of work they are looking for.

Understanding your interests and preferences is a first cut. Maybe you have already done this and have chosen an occupation as your goal. Identifying and preparing for a suitable occupation narrows the field further. Maybe you already have a college degree or have completed an apprenticeship. If you have work experience in an industry, that can help you clarify your goal still more.

But your degree, apprenticeship, or work experience doesn't necessarily entitle you to a good job, especially during tough economic times. Before you are ready to compete successfully in the job market, you still need to make up your mind what *specialized work role* you want to play in the occupation and perhaps what industry you want to work in.

That means you need a good understanding of the occupation and of the industries and work roles in which workers are employed. Just reading about them in this book is not enough. You need to explore them further in other reference books about jobs—ideally, books and articles about the specific occupation. People who teach the relevant educational programs can provide many good insights. Informational interviewing (discussed later in this chapter) and worksite visits also can help.

The other part of preparing for the job hunt is being able to explain coherently what you have to offer employers and what qualifies you to hold this specific job in the context of their business. Some people have difficulty talking about their skills and experience out of fear of appearing boastful. As Colin Frager observes, it helps to think of yourself not as a person, but as a product or service that you're selling to the employer. This allows you to be objective about your strengths and also helps guide your research on employers' needs.

Ideally, you'll be able to think of yourself as a brand. Just as it's easy to summarize Volvo as the really safe car or Walmart as the store with the low prices, you should be able to think of yourself as having some special attribute or record of achievement that defines what you have to offer an employer. Okay, what's *your* brand? What is going to make the employer want to hire you instead of dozens of other people with impressive resumes?

This process of focusing on your goals and your brand can take hours or even months, but it is much more productive than sending off nontargeted resumes like a dandelion puff scattering its seeds. You wouldn't think of entering an athletic competition without months or years of preparation. What makes you think you can compete in the job market without preparing first?

Finding Jobs

You may have heard about the "hidden job market." Studies have revealed that most jobs are found not by answering an advertisement in a newspaper or by using a Web site to match you to an employer, but rather through personal contacts. This is true for all kinds of jobs at all times, but especially during recessions. If you were an employer, wouldn't you rather hire someone you learned about through a personal connection than dig through a mountain of resumes sent by desperate strangers? The personal connection does not have to be a strong one; if the boss had a friend who qualified for the job, the friend would already be hired for it. Weak personal connections turn up most job openings.

Understand that your goal is to connect with the person making the hiring decision, not with the human resources department. HR people specialize in reviewing hundreds of resumes, interviewing dozens of people, and screening out all but a few candidates by a methodical process. Many employers, perhaps most, would rather avoid working through HR and prefer to select candidates through personal contacts. Sometimes, after making a hiring decision the latter way, employers go through the motions of using HR to give the appearance of deciding methodically.

There are two basic strategies for finding unadvertised jobs: **cold-calling** employers who hire people like you and **networking** so that you hear about potential job openings. The two overlap to some extent: through a cold call to an employer, you may hear about a possible job elsewhere, and through your network, you may hear about employers who are most likely to be worth cold-calling. You can pursue both strategies simultaneously.

To pursue either strategy, you need to have your resume in good shape so you can send it off on short notice. The resume needs to show the tight focus you have achieved through the preparation process outlined in the previous section. Your focused thinking should be visible in what the resume says about your career goal as well as what it says about your qualifications for that goal. The cover letter also should be based on this focused thinking.

If you have a lot of work experience and your resume runs several pages, keep in mind that a long document can blur your focus and probably needs a one-page executive summary so readers can quickly identify what you seek and what you have to offer. Conversely, the resume may benefit from an additional detailed document, headed something like "Key Initiatives and Successes," that highlights your record of achievement for those readers who want more specifics. (Some even include graphs.)

This book does not have room for examples of these documents, but here are two JIST books about resume writing that should prove helpful:

- *Résumé Magic: Trade Secrets of a Professional Résumé Writer,* by Susan Britton Whitcomb

- *The Quick Resume & Cover Letter Book: Write and Use an Effective Resume in Only One Day,* by Michael Farr

For assistance with cover letters, these two best-selling JIST books can help:

- *Cover Letter Magic: Trade Secrets of Professional Resume Writers,* by Wendy S. Enelow and Louise M. Kursmark

- *Gallery of Best Cover Letters: A Collection of Quality Cover Letters by Professional Resume Writers,* by David F. Noble

Whether you use networking or cold-calling, you also need to have an "elevator speech" prepared and rehearsed. This is a brief statement of who you are, what kind of job you're seeking, and why you qualify for this kind of job. Like the resume, it distills what you learned in your goal-focusing process. No matter where you use this speech, it must be concise enough that you could say it to someone on an elevator and get all your points across before the elevator stops. You can practice using this speech, or at least parts of it, whenever anyone asks you what you do for a living (which is a very common question). Instead of giving merely a job title and letting the other person assume that you fit various stereotypes about that occupation, say things about your background and aspirations.

Both networking and cold-calling require you to move outside your comfort zone. Your problem is that you don't know about these hidden job openings. You won't learn about them by talking only to your friends, because your friends tend to know most of the same things you know. The principle behind networking is that by connecting to *the people your friends know,* you can learn information (in this case, about jobs) that ordinarily would not be available to you. The principle behind cold-calling is that by talking directly to *the people who make hiring decisions,* you can learn about jobs that may never be advertised.

Networking

Make a list of everyone you know. Include people you went to school with years ago, people you used to work with, relatives you don't see very often, the person who cuts your hair, people in your faith group, the real estate agent who sold you your house, and so forth. Join a professional association, go to meetings, make contact with people in your field, and join online networks like LinkedIn. All of these people have connections to people you don't know, people who may know about open jobs. Give them your elevator speech and make it clear to them what sort of work you're looking for. If your job goal is still not fully crystallized, you may find it useful to ask these people for advice and look on this as a final stage of career exploration. For example, you might ask them what industries or businesses need people like you, or you might ask whether they know anyone who does this kind of work and what that person's experiences have been. Conversations like this plant a seed: These people now think of you as a job seeker in this field and may later relay to you news of a job opening. More likely, they will be able to tell you the name of someone who is more knowledgeable about the field, and *that* person may be your actual lead for a job opening. Make a point of asking for the name of someone who knows lots of people in the field you're targeting. Studies of networks show that most contacts are made through a small number of very well-connected people.

Cold-Calling

Someone in your network may mention your name to a manager who is hiring, and that person may give you a call. But, in many situations, the person in your network will give you the name of someone who is hiring, and it will be up to you to make the call. In that case, you are shifting to the cold-calling strategy.

You don't have to wait for your network to turn up likely employers to call. The most effective way to conduct a cold-calling campaign is to research the businesses that hire people for the kind of position you seek. Business directories such as the yellow pages, either in print or online, can help. Or go to the Web site of the relevant professional association, find the membership directory, and note which companies employ a lot of members. Another clue is to observe which businesses sponsor the association or its activities.

When you have identified a likely business, bypass the human resources department and find the name and phone number of someone who has the power to make a hiring decision. In a small company, this may be the CEO or other top manager. In a large company, it may be a department head. Telephone this person. If you call between 8 and 9 in the morning or 5 and 6 in the evening, you may improve the odds that the phone will be answered by the person you seek rather than by a secretary. If you get the person's voice mailbox, hang up and try again at another time; cold calls are unlikely to be returned. E-mail takes less courage than the telephone, but it is too easily lost in the pile of messages cluttering your target's inbox and may automatically be flagged as spam. Still another way to make contact is to drop in on the business in person. This tends to work best at small businesses, where you can ask to speak to the person in charge. At a large organization, you are likely to be sent to the human resources department, where your job application and resume will be tucked into a file drawer and probably never be read again.

Once you are talking to a person who can make a hiring decision, you have two tactics open to you: direct and indirect. The direct method is to give your elevator speech, make it clear that you are interested in a job, and ask for an interview. Be prepared to ask several times, because this shows your interest and determination. Don't ask whether the business has job openings, but perhaps ask if the business is likely to have openings in the future. If the person on the other end says that the company is not hiring now, ask for a get-acquainted interview—maybe a coffee or lunch date. At the very least, ask for leads to people who might be hiring elsewhere, call those leads, and tell them who referred you. *Expect a lot of rejection,* but keep in mind that these calls take only a few minutes, so you can cover a large number of employers in one afternoon.

The indirect method is similar—it uses an elevator speech about your background and aims for an interview—but it stops short of asking for a *job* interview. Instead, you treat the person like a highly targeted networking contact; the goal is an interview that will focus on *learning more information* rather than on being hired. For example, you might say that you are thinking of specializing in the kind of work that goes on in that person's business and you want to learn more about the pros and cons of that specialization. If the person on the other end tries to cut you off by saying that the company is not hiring, make it clear that you are not asking for a job interview—you want information or perhaps advice. The informational interview may not, in fact, lead to a job at that company—at least not at present—but it may lead to a future job offer, and at least it has a good chance of taking your networking campaign to a higher level. This person is much more likely than your second cousin or your high school friend to know someone in another department or a similar business who has a job opening.

This book is not the place to learn about interview techniques, but JIST has several books that may help with this important hurdle:

- *Interview Magic: Job Interview Secrets from America's Career and Life Coach,* by Susan Britton Whitcomb

- *The Career Coward's Guide to Interviewing: Sensible Strategies for Overcoming Job Search Fears,* by Katy Piotrowski

Get Started Now

Maybe you're not quite ready to look for a job. You may still be in an educational or training program or be planning to enter one. In fact, that can be a very smart move at a time when jobs are hard to find. Instead of experiencing the frustration of being unemployed or underemployed, you'll be upgrading your skills and adding an impressive line to your resume—maybe more than one, if you do an internship or win an academic honor. A stint in the military or in a national service program such as the Peace Corps or AmeriCorps can also enhance your credentials and provide educational benefits.

If you have young children, maybe you're focusing now on raising them. But that can be an excellent time to reinvent yourself so you can re-enter the workforce later in a new role. Consider taking night classes to prepare for your re-entry.

Even if you're not in the job market now—and right now is a challenging time for finding employment—keep your future job hunt in mind. Work on clarifying your job goal and on building your network so you'll be closer to being able to look actively when the time is right.

Index